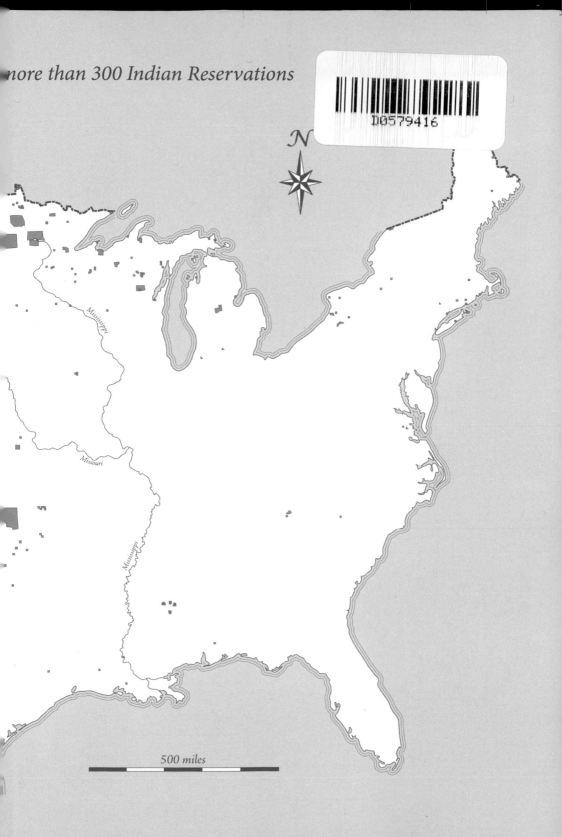

N

Mississippi

Missouri

Mississippi

500 miles

Indian Reservations in Minnesota & Wisconsin

Red Lake

Bois Forte

Grand Portage

White Earth

Leech Lake

Lake Superior

Red Cliff

Bad River

Lac Courte Oreilles

Lac du Flambeau

Forest County

Menominee

Fond Du Lac

Mille Lacs

Mole Lake

St. Croix

Mohican

Shakopee
Mdewakanton

Upper Sioux

Oneida

Lower Sioux

Prairie
Island

Lake Michigan

Minnesota

Ho Chunk

Potawatomi

Wisconsin

Indian reservations

100 miles

REZ LIFE

REZ LIFE

An Indian's Journey
Through Reservation Life

David Treuer

Atlantic Monthly Press
New York

Published simultaneously in Canada
Printed in the United States of America

FIRST EDITION

ISBN: 978-0-8021-1971-1

Atlantic Monthly Press
an imprint of Grove/Atlantic, Inc.
841 Broadway
New York, NY 10003

Distributed by Publishers Group West

www.groveatlantic.com

12 13 14   10 9 8 7 6 5 4 3 2 1

In memory

Ron LaFriniere, Eugene Seelye, Thomas Stillday Jr.,
and
Art Koch

for
Elsina, Noka, and Bine

Jesse Seelye at the United States Penitentiary, Florence, Colorado, 2010.

INTRODUCTION

In northern Minnesota, not far from the headwaters of the Mississippi River, you may see a sign. From a passing car it is easy to miss: in the summer the trees that march over fields and the ditch grass that crowds the road threaten to overwhelm it; in the winter, when the snow has been pushed from the road and has leveled off the ditches, the sign sometimes blends too well with the snow to be seen at all. Seen or not, the sign reads: WELCOME TO THE LEECH LAKE INDIAN RESERVATION HOME OF THE LEECH LAKE BAND OF OJIBWE PLEASE KEEP OUR ENVIRONMENT CLEAN, PROTECT OUR NATURAL RESOURCES NO SPECIAL LICENCES REQUIRED FOR HUNTING, FISHING, OR TRAPPING.

If you're driving—as since this is America is most likely the case—the sign is soon behind you and soon forgotten. However, something is different about life on one side of it and life on the other. It's just hard to say exactly what. The landscape is unchanged. The same pines, and the same swamps, hay fields, and jeweled lakes dropped here and there

1

among the trees, exist on both sides of the sign. The houses don't look all that different, perhaps a little smaller, a little more ramshackle. The children playing by the road do look different, though. Darker. The cars, most of them, seem older. And perhaps something else is different, too.

You can see these kinds of signs all over America. There are roughly 310 Indian reservations in the United States, though the Bureau of Indian Affairs (BIA) doesn't have a sure count of how many reservations there are (this might say something about the BIA, or it might say something about the nature of reservations). Not all of the 564 federally recognized tribes in the United States have reservations. Some Indians don't have reservations, but all reservations have Indians, and all reservations have signs. There are tribal areas in Brazil, Afghanistan, and Pakistan, among many other countries. But reservations as we know them are, with the exception of Canada, unique to America. You can see these signs in more than thirty of the states, but most of them are clustered in the last places to be permanently settled by Europeans: the Great Plains, the Southwest, the Northwest, and along the Canadian border stretching from Montana to New York. You can see them in the middle of the desert, among the strewn rocks of the Badlands, in the suburbs of Green Bay, and within the misty spray of Niagara Falls. Some of the reservations that these signs announce are huge. There are twelve reservations in the United States bigger than the state of Rhode Island. Nine reservations are larger than Delaware (named after a tribe that was pushed from the region). Some reservations are so small that the sign itself seems larger than the land it denotes. Most reservations are poor. A few have become wealthy. In 2007 the Seminole bought the Hard Rock Café franchise. The Oneida of Wisconsin helped renovate Lambeau Field in Green Bay. And whenever Brett Favre (who claims Chickasaw blood) scored a touchdown there as a Packer, a Jet, or a Minnesota Viking, he did it under Oneida lights cheered on by fans sitting on Oneida bleachers, not far from the Oneida Nation itself.

Indian reservations, and those of us who live on them, are as American as apple pie, baseball, and muscle cars. Unlike apple pie, however, Indians contributed to the birth of America itself. The Oneida were allies of the Revolutionary Army who fed U.S. troops at Valley Forge and helped defeat the British in New York, and the Iroquois Confederacy served as one of the many models for the American constitution. Marx and Engels also cribbed from the Iroquois as they developed their theories of communism. Indians have been disproportionally involved in every war America has fought since its first, including one we're fighting now: on July 27, 2007, the last soldiers of Able Company 2nd-136th Combined Arms battalion returned home to Bemidji, Minnesota, after serving twenty-two months of combat duty in Iraq. At the time Able Company was the most deployed company in the history of the Iraq War and was also deployed in Afghanistan and Bosnia. Some of the members of Able Company are Indians from reservations in northern Minnesota.

Despite how *involved* in America's business Indians have been, most people will go a lifetime without ever knowing an Indian or spending any time on an Indian reservation. Indian land makes up 2.3 percent of the land in the United States. We number slightly over 2 million (up significantly from not quite 240,000 in 1900). It is pretty easy to avoid us and our reservations. Yet Americans are captivated by Indians. Indians are part of the story that America tells itself, from the first Thanksgiving to the Boston Tea Party up through Crazy Horse, the Battle of the Little Bighorn, and Custer's Last Stand. Indian casinos have grown from small bingo halls lighting up the prairie states into an industry making $14 billion a year. No one in America today is untouched by our lives—from a schoolchild learning about the birth of his or her country to the millions of Americans who have lost (and sometimes won) money in an Indian casino.

Whites have not just been captivated by us; they've been captured. In 1790, when he was only ten years old, John Tanner was captured from his family's home in Kentucky by the Shawnee. Later, he was sold to an Ojibwe family as a slave and traveled with this family as far north and west as the Little Saskatchewan River. (My tribe, the Ojibwe, has been called Chippewa, Ojibway, and Chippeway—but Ojibwe is our name for ourselves). He spent his life among the Ojibwe and eventually married an Ojibwe woman. As an adult he was reunited with his birth family, but he was uncomfortable out East and went back to his Indian home as soon as he could. Then there is the story of Mary Jemison. She was also taken captive, along with a neighbor and her brothers, also by Shawnee, in 1758. Her brothers and another captive were scalped en route to Fort Duquesne (in modern-day Pittsburgh). Mary survived. She married a Delaware. But, afraid that she would be stolen back, the young couple moved to the Genesee Valley in what is now upstate New York. Mary's husband died and she remarried a Seneca and had many children with him. She never went back to "white society." Many captives didn't go back, preferring life with Indians.

That is exactly what many people whose lives are intertwined with Indians say today. My father, after escaping Austria and the Holocaust in 1938, fled to the United States with his parents. After much wandering and one marriage and three children he settled just off the Leech Lake Reservation in northern Minnesota. Here he felt safe for the first time in his life. More than that, he felt he had found, with his new friends and new family, something that had eluded him all the years before. He devoted his life (and still devotes it) to the community he has come to call his own, and is as passionate today about the rights and respect owed to Indians as he was when he moved to Indian country in the 1950s.

A lot of people (this includes Indians and non-Indians) don't think of the story of rez life as a story of beauty. Most often rez life is associated with tragedy. We are thought of in terms of what we have lost or what we have survived. Life on the rez is usually described as harsh, violent, drug-infested, criminal, poor, and short. White-on-Indian violence occurs at ten times the rate of white-on-white violence. Indian-on-Indian violence is close behind; in 2006, the police department on the Red Lake Reservation received more 911 calls than Beltrami County, which has ten times the population of Red Lake. The small village where my family comes from once had the highest ratio in the state of felons who had done hard time to people who had not been to jail: it has been said one in six residents of Bena (population 140) had done more than ten years in prison. The average life expectancy for Indian men is sixty-four. When white people turn sixty-five they, on average, retire. Indians are lucky to live long enough to see retirement. The average household income on my reservation is $21,000. On some reservations in the Dakotas the median income hovers just above $10,000; for the rest of America, median income is $52,029, as of 2008. Life is hard for many on the rez.

If the usual story we hear of life on the rez is one of hardship, the subplot is about conflict. More often than not, the story of "the Indian" is understood as a story of "Indians versus whites" or "Indians versus everyone." This notion is further sharpened by the cherished idea (cherished by Indians and whites alike) that the real story of Indian life is "how Indians, quietly going about their business in the New World, were abruptly and violently screwed by white people against whom the Indians had no defenses and gosh it's really a pity because Indians *were* a noble people." Most treatments of the history of Native America can be represented by a running balance sheet with positive Indian values and contributions on one side and white transgression and crimes on the other. Like this:

Native Americans	Anglo-Americans
Provided food and shelter to Pilgrims	Gave Indians blankets saturated with smallpox
Introduced Europeans to corn, squash, tomatoes, and chocolate	Introduced Indians to "firewater"
Love Mother Earth	Hurt Mother Earth
Promote community and togetherness	Promote capitalism
Were forced onto reservations	Were forced into the suburbs
Signed treaties in good faith	Broke treaties in bad faith

But this isn't the whole story. Reservations and the Indians on them are not simply victims of the white juggernaut. And what one finds on reservations is more than scars, tears, blood, and noble sentiment. There is beauty in Indian life, as well as meaning and a long history of interaction. We love our reservations.

My tribe, the Ojibwe, has it good compared with others. We are both vast and underrated. Originally a coastal tribe from the eastern seaboard belonging to the Algonquian language family—which includes Cree, Pequot, Passamaquody, and Delaware, among others—we began a slow migration west before the first white people set foot on this continent. Our language still bears traces of this coastal existence. We have words for "seal," "whale," and "bagel," though these aren't used very often where we now live. The migration, as it's called, lasted for many centuries, and according to tribal lore the tribe was following a vision of one member who dreamed that we should move west to where food grows on water. As far as prophecies or directives go, this has to be one of the weirdest. But here we are, in the land of wild rice, where food does grow on water. We occupy the land around the entire Great Lakes, stretching from just east of Toronto westward to Montana and from as far south as Chicago all the way up to the underbelly of Hudson Bay. We are the most populous tribe in North America, though not the most populous in the United States. That would be the Cherokee.

And even though we were ass-kickers and name-takers—having fought and defeated the Iroquois, the Sac and Fox, and the illustrious Sioux—we aren't really known as such. In fact, the Sioux (perhaps the most famous Indian warriors are Sioux) used to live where we now live—in the northern forests of Minnesota, Wisconsin, and northwestern Ontario. But we pushed them out to the plains, where they made a good living hunting buffalo. And maybe that's the problem. The Sioux hunt buffalo from horseback and we Ojibwe go out on snowshoes to snare rabbits. The Sioux have cornered the market on Indian cool. This is true for Indian names, too. They had chiefs named Crazy Horse, Sitting Bull, and Red Cloud. We had chiefs called Moose Dung, Little Frenchman, Flat Mouth, Bad Boy, Yellow Head, and Hole in the Day. But we did have a chief with the name White Cloud, which is almost as cool as Red Cloud. These were tough men, but a guy named Yellow Guts doesn't sound much like a death-dealer and doesn't make for good copy. We do have a lot of "wind" and "sky" names, which you might think would be cool. But Big Wind, Downwind, and Fineday (which are names I think of as being among the most beautiful Indian names) don't compare to Mankiller (Cherokee) or Destroytown (Seneca).

It's a blessing, I suppose. We have largely avoided being written about by others—who prefer to write about the Apache, Comanche, Blackfeet, Nez Perce, and Sioux. And we have avoided being overrun by wannabes and "culture vultures" because, after all, who wants to be an Indian who doesn't own horses and lives in a swamp and traps beavers and didn't evolve striking geometric beading patterns or cool war bonnets? But to the victors go the spoils, as they say, and also to the victors go naming rights. Many other tribes labor under names given to them by us. Sioux is short for "Naadwesiwag" (snakes, a euphemism for enemies). Winnebago comes from the Ojibwe word "Wiinibiigoog" (the "Ones by the Dirty Water"), and Eskimo comes from "Eshkimoog" ("Eaters of Raw Flesh").

We have reservations in Michigan, Wisconsin, Minnesota, North Dakota, and Montana. We have "reserves"—as they were called in Canada, though now they are called First Nations—in Quebec, Ontario, Manitoba, Saskatchewan, and Alberta. Some are tiny and can be walked across in less than an hour. Others, such as Red Lake, are large, larger than Rhode Island. The result is that there is more variation among our people than in most other tribes: from "bush Indians" in Canada living on reserves that are accessible only by floatplane in the summer and by roads across the ice in the winter to large corporate (and comparatively wealthy) entities such as the Mille Lacs Band of Ojibwe in central Minnesota. We have people who know and practice traditional Ojibwe lifeways—trapping, hunting, and fishing for sustenance—who are Catholics, and we have lawyers and lobbyists who follow Ojibwe ceremonial traditions. You can travel for days or weeks and still be in Ojibwe country—the woodlands around the Great Lakes, the boreal forests of central Canada, and the margins of the Great Plains and Canadian high country. We live, I think, in some of the most beautiful places on earth.

We are known for making beautiful things, too. We evolved the birch bark canoe, a true engineering feat: a 300-pound canoe that was thirty feet long could carry twelve men and 3,000 pounds of cargo. During the fur trade it did, all the way from the far end of Lake Superior to Montreal, loaded with bales of beaver furs. In addition to canoes we made and make snowshoes and porcupine quill designs on leather and birch bark. We even figured out how to cook over open fires without metal or ceramics.

Even though we haven't become as much a part of the public consciousness as, say, the Sioux or the Iroquois, our language has. Once listed in the *Guinness Book of World Records* as the most difficult language to learn, the Ojibwe language has given English the words "moccasin," "toboggan," "wigwam," "moose," "totem," and "muskeg." We've even met on middle ground. We provided "musk" from "mashkiig," or swamp, English provided "rat" and together we built the word for a swamp-dwelling rodent that looks an awful lot like a rat—muskrat. If that's not a fine example of cultural exchange I don't know what is. Through years of trade we imported only two words from the French—*couchon,* which became "kookoosh"; and *bonjour,* which was transformed into a greeting, "boozhoo." Hello.

And, on top of all of that, we're funny. We really are. I should state, however, that I am among some of the less funny Ojibwe people. John Buckanaga (which means "He Wins," another perplexing Ojibwe name), from White Earth Reservation, is funny. John Buck was at a seniors all-Indian golf tournament at Fond du Lac Reservation near Duluth and someone was trying to get him to mess up his tee shot by asking him, *Hey, John, so you're getting older—do you use Viagra?* And John Buck said, *Yeah. Sure I do. Well, does it work? I guess so. At least I don't piss all over my shoes anymore.* And then he drove his ball 220 yards down the fairway.

Which brings us to stoicism. Ojibwe are not usually described as stoic. We're not usually described at all. This is just fine with most of us. We have been called some choice names in the past, though. "These people are a wild, barbarous, and benighted race, and are, perhaps more than any other people under the influence of the chiefs, head men, and Prophets," suggested one writer. I would have to disagree.

On August 3, 2007, I drove past one of the signs on the southern edge of my reservation on my way back to Bena, our ancestral village. My grandfather had killed himself earlier that day. Eugene William Seelye, an eighty-three-year-old veteran of D-day and the Battle of the Bulge—a man who left the reservation only once in his life and made a promise never to leave again, an Indian man who dodged thousands of bullets—shot himself in the head and died alone on his bedroom floor.

My grandfather was not an easy man. He was not one of those sweet, somewhat bashful elderly Indians you see at powwows or feasts or at the clinic, willing to talk and tell dirty jokes; not the kind of traditional elder that a lot of younger people seek out for approval and advice; not the kind of woodsy Indian man who will take you hunting and explain, patiently, how to lead on ducks or where to find the best mushrooms. When we were kids and my cousins and I came into the house from playing, more often than not he would say, "Get the hell out." He was, and everyone will tell you this, a hard-ass.

His looks reinforced this impression. He was thin and rangy. He wasn't especially tall, but he *seemed* tall. He never changed his hairstyle. His full head of hair, black, then gray, and finally all white, was cut longish and combed back and held in an Elvis-type pompadour with Brylcreem. In many pictures he poses without a shirt on. He was tough. He was the only person I knew who had a sword hanging on his wall. The family story was that it was a Nazi officer's sword and that he took it off a German corpse. Once, when I was a teenager, I got up the nerve to ask him if he had gotten it from a German during the war. *Hell no*, he said. *That's a Knights of Columbus sword. It ain't a real sword*. I asked him where he got it. *I traded a Luger for it*. I asked him where he got that. *Where you think, boy? I shot a German and took it*.

We had never been close while I was growing up. He scared me. We didn't have much to say to each another. I wasn't the only one who felt small next to his anger, his rage, his perpetual dissatisfaction. He didn't have a lot to say to anyone. When, as a girl, my mother saw him working without a shirt on and saw the scar that circled his shoulder, she'd asked him what happened. *Got shot* was all he said. He didn't say that after surviving D-day and the Battle of the Bulge and many other battles in France and Belgium, he and his patrol had crossed into Germany near Aachen (not half a mile from where Charlemagne had reigned as emperor). He did not say that the man in front of him, a guy named Van Winkle from Arkansas, stepped on a land mine. The mine blew off Van Winkle's legs and blew apart my grandfather's shoulder. He told us nothing about any of this.

In the 1950s he was living with my grandmother and their four children in a small two-room shack in the small village of Bena on the Leech Lake Reservation. The shack had been built around the turn of the century and at that time it was the only house with walls and a ceiling in the village—the rest of the dwellings were wigwams made from bent poles and covered with bark. All six members of the family lived in this run-down thing. No running water, no bathroom, a woodstove on which to cook. The family was terribly poor. My mother remembers one winter when they had only thirty-five cents to their name. My grandfather took the thirty-five cents and bought a plaque that read: "The Lord Shall Provide." That night at dinner my grandmother served the four kids, but instead of serving him she put the plaque on his plate. *If he's going to provide and you're not, then eat that. See how good it tastes.*

He was offered a job eight miles away—still on the reservation, only eight miles down the highway—that included a good salary; a fully furnished house with plumbing, electricity, and heat; and a beautiful view of Leech Lake itself. My grandfather turned it down.

It's only eight miles away, Gene. Eight miles.

I made a promise to God that if I made it home I'd never leave again. This is home. I plan to keep my promise. I'm not fucking leaving. He never moved away from Bena and never traveled off the reservation if he could help it.

Our small ancestral town of Bena has a population of around 140 and a bad reputation. Even though it sits on a major highway and a lot of people drive through it, it is really known for only two things: a cool-looking gas station that's on the national register of historic places, and the number of outlaws who call it home. Gerald Vizenor once called Bena "Little Chicago" because of the rough handling outsiders sometimes get there. Vizenor has not been forgiven for that. He doesn't go to Bena much. It's got, in addition to the gas station, a bar and a post office. It used to have three gas stations, two hardware stores, two grocery stores, seven hotels, and two bars. My grandmother's father—known to everyone as Grandpa Harris—owned both bars during his life. A full-blooded Scot from Chicago, he had somehow ended up in Bena in the early part of the century. After spending most of his young life in logging camps, he eventually bought the Wigwam Bar, sold it, and then bought the Gitigan (Ojibwe for "garden") across the street. He married my great-grandmother, an Indian. An irony for you: at the time my grandmother's father, Harris, owned the Wigwam Bar, my grandfather's grandmother still lived in a real wigwam made of bent willow saplings and tar paper across the sandy street a hundred yards down the road. During the 1930s and 1940s, it was illegal to serve liquor to Indians. So Harris Matthews sold whisky and beer to his in-laws out the back door and they drank back there but came in the front to dance. Harris was, by all accounts, kind of an asshole. Once he was fixing the roof of the Gitigan and someone walked by and asked, *What are you building, Harris? A whorehouse?* He replied, *If I was building a whorehouse I'd have to put a roof over the whole fucking town.*

I got the news that my grandfather had shot himself on the morning of August 3. I was in Bena by early evening. I passed the "big house," which is what everyone calls (without irony) the house my grandfather lived in. It isn't actually big, just bigger than most of the other houses in Bena. His new Chevy Silverado was in the yard. I pulled to a stop at my grandmother's trailer, just down the hill.

Cars huddled around my grandmother's trailer and I heard voices coming from the porch, the deck, and inside. It was packed. Some people were already drinking beer; most were not. My favorite uncle was staggering around the living room without his shirt on and gave me a hug. My grandmother sat on the couch with my mother. My grandmother was the one who had found him. Other relatives—my uncle Diddy and aunts JoAnne and Kay, and friends Rocky Tibbets and his brother Buddy—milled around on the deck. Buddy had the sideways look in his eyes that he seems to get when he's been drinking all day. Some of my first cousins were already there—Nate, Josh, and Justin. Sam was driving in from South Dakota. Jesse was back in jail and wouldn't make it. The trailer was warm and well lit, and I felt folded into the soupy, complicated, and comforting trouble of family almost immediately.

The next day was beautiful. It was early August but it was sunny and crisp and clear. My cousin Sam had arrived in the night with his girlfriend and they were tangled up on the couch. He wasn't wearing a shirt; this is obviously a family trait (one I don't share). They woke up and we talked a bit and then they left for the café to get some breakfast. I talked my grieving mother into going down to the café, too. After breakfast we drove back up to my grandmother's trailer and I asked her if there was anything I could do. There's always something to do. That's one nice thing about Indian funerals whether Catholic, traditional, or a mixture of both. There's always something—gathering sage, cooking, digging the grave, getting tar paper to cover the mound of dirt until a gravehouse can be built, building the rough box, carving and shaping the clan marker, getting drunk. I actually like digging the grave. It's mindless and communal.

My grandmother asked me to do two things. Would I be willing to write a eulogy to read at the service? And would I go up to the big house and take care of the bedroom? Clean it up. *We want to make it look nice in there,* she said. She was shaky. Her eyes watered constantly. *We just want to make it look nice. And your uncles, well, you know; they just can't go in there.* She asked me to do this not because I had been close to my grandfather but because, compared with the rest of the family, I hadn't been.

It felt strange to be in the big house without my grandfather there. He had spent eighty of his eighty-three years in Bena. Sixty of those years had been spent in that house. Whenever I came over to visit him I'd find him sitting in his chair by the window, the police scanner on—with the scanner, he could often follow the progress the police were making tracking down our relatives. He'd smoke and drink coffee. If he was lucky he'd have peanut brittle or beans to eat.

A stack of books and the Bible rested to the left of the chair on the small end table laden with all sorts of other things: two broken watches, glasses, a screwdriver, long and unreadable information about his medication. The chair was empty now. But his cigarettes and lighter were on the table, as though he were about to smoke. Someone had written "Dads" on a Post-it and stuck it on the pack. Without the possessive it made me think of fathers. Dads. Parents and mothers and cousins and brothers and sisters and all of us and how we could have ended up like this. I sat at the table across from the chair and smoked one of my own cigarettes. When I was finished I walked back to his bedroom.

A narrow iron-frame bed. A dresser stuffed with socks, mostly the nonslip hospital kind, and T-shirts. A drawer full of medical supplies. A large oak table mounded with clothes and the weird effluvia that are a product of living in the same place for a long time; a broken printer, two dusty bedspreads, a boom box, and a portrait of my mother as a high school student, painted by his brother-in-law while he was in prison. A small safe served as his night table. When I opened it I found a few bundles of one-dollar bills, banded into stacks of 100, some rolls of quarters and silver dollars, and my cousin Vanessa's cheap gold necklace. This was the necklace she had been wearing when she got into an argument at a party and drove across two yards, up a ditch, and onto the highway, where she was struck by a passing motor home.

I looked down at my feet. A small throw rug was turned at a funny angle. What looked like grape juice had blotted through it in places. When I lifted it I found the blood.

And then I got to work.

I emptied the dresser, removed the drawers, and bagged the clothes on the oak table and the contents of the safe. I lifted the safe out of the room and lugged the mattress through the narrow door. I saw that, unbeknownst to anyone, my grandfather's dog had been waging war against him by shitting under his bed. That dog's turds, no bigger than those of a cat, were hard, preserved, nested in the humus of hair, dust, and dead skin that had collected there. I choked on the dust. The whole room smelled like my grandfather. Especially the blood—it didn't smell like "death." It smelled like him; sweet, smoky, thick.

I took a break and wandered through the house until my older brother Anton arrived. I was glad he was there. He has the right personality for such jobs—calm, seemingly unperturbed.

Anton and I lifted out the heavy furniture until all that was left was the small rectangle of a room and the smaller, more potent, more significant rectangle of the braided throw rug that covered what was left of my grandfather's brain. We weren't doing a great job and neither was the rug. It tugged at the feet, and carrying furniture while stepping over it was hard, and in short time the rug had been stepped on and flipped over and bunched up. Quite a lot of blood showed through. We tried not to notice.

We moved the bed frame out to the garage. Since my grandfather, in addition to being a hard-ass, was somewhat sentimental, he held on to a lot of junk. For instance, he had saved all of his father's logging equipment, and so one wall was covered with two-man Swede saws, crosscut saws, axes, peaveys, and the like. In the far corner hung a small hand drum. I remember hearing about this drum from my mother.

When she was a young girl, growing up in Bena in the 1940s, everyone was Catholic, or at least acted Catholic. Her parents made all the children get dressed and go to church on Sundays even though they themselves did not attend. The Catholic church in Bena is a small, very modest building with the footprint of a very small house. The usher was a man named George Martin, an old, quiet man, who lived across from the church with his wife. My mother said that everyone was scared of George because he was rumored to be a medicine man. Whenever a dog went missing everyone would say, *George must have got him. Watch your dogs or George will get them.* Every Saturday night you could hear him singing medicine songs on a water drum. The drum, whose sound can carry for miles, sounded throughout the village. But then, on Sunday morning, George would be standing by the front door of the church in a brown suit, showing the good people of Bena to their pews and helping to pass the plate and tend the grounds. He never took Communion or knelt or joined in the prayers. Before he died he gave my grandfather—a man, it should be said, who had absolutely no

interest in hand drums or traditional songs or anything of the sort—
the hand drum that he had used when he played the moccasin game
(a team gambling game involving singing and sleight of hand). George
was the last grand medicine man from Bena.

My brother couldn't stay long. He has seven children ranging in
age from six months to fifteen years. I told him I'd finish alone. I did.

The day had grown warm and as I cut the carpet and rolled it the
dust and dander rose into the air and choked me. It was not hard work
as far as tearing up carpet goes, but it wasn't fun. The carpet tore easily, and that was a blessing. Nonetheless, I took my time. I stopped
occasionally and wandered out into the main part of the house and
sat across from my grandfather's chair and smoked cigarettes, still a
little shocked that he wasn't there. When I went back to the bedroom
and was confronted by the patch of blood, brain, and lymph, I had
the strange feeling that my grandfather—all of him, his body and self
and words, his whole life—had somehow disappeared into the floor.
I began to resent the carpet. So cheap. So easily torn. So incapable of
holding my grandfather's blood, which had soaked through the carpet
and into the subfloor.

I began to curse. I cursed that carpet as I'd never cursed anyone in
my life. On I went. I hated that cheap, thin, blue, foam-backed, glue-
down carpet more than I have ever hated anyone or anything. That
carpet, that cheap cheap carpet, that carpet the same color as the reservation is colored on some maps of northern Minnesota. And just as
torn, dusty, and damaged. Just as durable. Just as inadequate. We all
struggle to do our jobs—the job of living, the job of dying, the job of
muddling the two—but that carpet didn't do its job. It didn't keep its
end of the bargain.

I left for home in the early evening to write the eulogy and it wasn't
until eleven o'clock that I finally crawled into bed. I couldn't sleep. I

wouldn't say I was traumatized by my grandfather's death or by cleaning up his blood and brain. But when I closed my eyes all I saw was
blood. I read for a while and then shut off the light. Again, blood. I
didn't "think" anything. I wasn't "sad." I didn't lie there in the dark
pondering the greater import of what had happened. I didn't dwell on
lost opportunities or missed chances. But every time I closed my eyes
I saw the blood and pink curd of my grandfather's brain. I couldn't
distract myself, and nothing turned into anything greater: no greater
catharsis, sadness, or realization. When I closed my eyes I began to
hate this, too: our Indian life. Our reservations. Is this what it's all
about? Is it just this? Our brains on the floor? Is it just this? Our blood
splattered all over the rug? The Native author Greg Sarris said recently
that reservations are just "red ghettos." I've always disagreed with that
way of thinking. There has to be something more. But when I closed
my eyes that night I couldn't imagine what else we might be up to, or
how better to describe our lives.

Eventually my thoughts turned to other thoughts—about my
cousins, siblings, aunts, and uncles and the place we call ours. I thought
about my cousin Jesse, the one who couldn't make it to the funeral
because he was back in jail. Earlier that summer Jesse had overdosed on
methadone. The year before he was hit by a train; his car was pushed
down the tracks for over a mile. Surprisingly, he lived, but not without
some damage. Jesse is a big likable guy. The methadone overdose put
him in the ICU. When my brother and I went to visit him he was still
sedated and he had a breathing tube down his throat so he could not
talk. His girlfriend, fresh out of treatment, was there.

He's drifting in and out. Can't talk because of the tube, she said.

The room smelled bad. His hospital gown was open to his waist.

*Yeah, he was awake this morning. He can write but it don't make a
lot of sense. They don't know. They don't know if it's from this or the train
wreck. He makes some sense though.*

We made small talk but it was hard. Every few minutes Jesse jerked in his sleep. His arms and legs flailed and then he quieted down again. When we ran out of things to talk about I looked around the room. I've grown to hate these places. I looked at Jesse. His chest was shallow. I noticed that he had a tattoo on his stomach. It was gang-style, large letters following the arc of his rib cage. REZ LIFE. We watched TV and then I picked up the loose typing paper from the side table. Some of the writing was that of my family and of Jesse's girlfriend. A lot of it was covered with Jesse's attempts at communication. She was right. A lot of it didn't make sense. Words and letters trailed off or drifted, rudderless, across the pages. WHAT HAPPENED? I DID? And then a few pages later: THEY GONNA THINK I DID IT ON PURPOSE FUCK. And then later: I GOT LOTA HEART AND STRENGTH MORE THAN THEY THINK.

I wondered then and I wonder now. Does he? Do we? And what is this place—this rez, these reservations? What are these places that kill us every day but that we'd die to protect and are like no place else on earth? And what can we find here behind the signs that announce us?

꙳

This book, then, is about what can be found behind that sign and others—planted in American soil. It is about how reservations began, what they are now, and where they are going. You can tell a lot about a place by its exceptions, by turning over and inspecting the frayed corners of its quilt. You can tell a lot about the whole by looking at the part. You can tell a lot about America, about its sins and its ideals, by looking at and behind the signs that advertise our existence, the existence of a kind of American who was supposed to have died out a long time ago.

I once heard a journalist state that to write a book of nonfiction, a book about the lives of others, the writer had to feel in his gut that his informants owed him something, that he owned a piece of their lives. But I don't think this is true. I think the opposite is true. I don't think my family or my people owe me anything. I feel that I owe my life to them and I set out to write a book that reflects this, reflects the debt I owe them, and does them honor. To understand American Indians is to understand America. This is the story of the paradoxically least and most American place in the twenty-first century. Welcome to the Rez.

Charley Grolla, Red Lake Nation Conservation Officer

1

It was a hot day in May 2006 when two Red Lake tribal conservation officers sped across the mirror-smooth waters of Upper Red Lake, uncased M4 assault rifles and shotguns leaning against the bow of the reservation conservation boat. Officers Nelson and Grolla never left the guns onshore—someone could break into their vehicle and take them. They had been on routine patrol when they saw two white men fishing on reservation waters. Grolla is a big man, an intimidating man if you don't know him, or, for some, even if you do. He laughs a lot. He weighs nearly 400 pounds. His Ojibwe name is Ogimaa-giizhig (literally "Head of the Sky" but, more figuratively, "Head Thunderbird") and he belongs to the Caribou Clan, just as his great-great-great-grandfather the famous Ojibwe war chief Waabojiig had. "When I was at the police academy in New Mexico," Grolla said, "it was like boot camp, you know, like that movie *Full Metal Jacket*. It was tough. You got yelled at a lot. I saw a few girls cry the first day. A lot of those guys had never been yelled at before, they didn't know how to do anything for themselves. I was glad I was raised the way I was. I grew up hauling wood, doing chores. At the academy all that work I did grow-ing up helped. A lot of guys didn't know how to do laundry or how to press their clothes. I knew all of that. When I got back from the academy I got my class number tattooed on my shoulder: IPA 71. I was half the size I am now. I was about 235 pounds. I could bench three hundred-something. Now I eat all the time. Because of the stress, I think." Grolla used to work for the Red Lake police force, but he switched over to conservation in 2000, largely because of the stress. "A lot of guys quit this job. They do it for a few years and get tired of it and become what's called being 'retired on duty.' They just don't care anymore. I was getting to that place. I just didn't care anymore and I didn't want to be like that. It got to be too much. So I switched to con-servation. I like being in the woods more." Grolla's partner, Corporal Tyson Nelson, is also imposing: dark, six feet tall, 235 pounds. Nelson is a boxer, one of the best from Red Lake, a place that has produced many good Golden Gloves.

Grolla's shoes and socks were on the floor of the boat. He raced across the water wearing only his pants and shirt. His gun belt was off. Later, during the trial in Red Lake Tribal Court, his manner of dress would become an issue. "You looked like you were ready to tango, like you wanted to fight," said Jerry Mueller, one of the fishermen. "No. You learn pretty quick not to go on the water wearing heavy boots. If you go over you could drown," says Charley.

Grolla and Tyson had been watching as the boat with the two white fishermen neared the reservation boundary, marked onshore with a sign and on the water with white plastic buoys. Sport fishermen often ripped down the signs and cut the buoys. Only a road remains as a reminder of where the reservation boundary lies. Even though Jerry Mueller and his son-in-law were close to shore and could see the sign, they did not turn around; they continued fishing on Red Lake waters until they were a mile inside the reservation. When Mueller saw the conservation officers approaching he started his boat, gunned it, and then stopped—clearly the officers had the faster boat. "He knew where he was," recalled Grolla. "We took him in and he was cooperative at first. He played stupid. 'We didn't know,' he said. 'We didn't know.' But we were really respectful, professional. Even though they saw the signs down everyone knows where the boundary is. You can see it on the shore. And it was totally calm. How could you drift a mile over the boundary when there's no wind at all?"

Grolla and Nelson powered up alongside Mueller and his son-in-law (the case is referred to as the Mueller case although the boat actually belonged to the son-in-law), took hold of the 1984 Forester seventeen-foot fiberglass boat, and said that they were fishing on Red Lake Reservation waters and that the boat, motor, and fishing gear were being confiscated.

"If I'm on the reservation, I'm real sorry for this," Mueller recalled saying. "I had no intention of fishing on your side of the lake."

Mueller claimed later that Grolla said, "Your apology don't hold no weight with me."

The officers moved their assault rifles to the stern and commanded Mueller and his son-in-law to get into the bow. With the boat in tow they proceeded back to the boat landing. The son-in-law was polite, even contrite. He paid his fine and got his boat and trailer back without complaint. Mueller was a different story. When he returned home he received a summons to appear in Red Lake Reservation tribal court or to pay a fine of $250 for fishing illegally in Red Lake waters. He said that he would not obey the summons, and that the fine was unfair. Many other whites agreed with him. He received pro bono legal representation to help him fight the fine in tribal court. A non-profit citizen action group called Citizens for Truth in Government, based in Bagley, Minnesota, was formed in part because of the issues of water rights and fishing rights stirred up by the Mueller case. The action group argued, among other things, that Red Lake Reservation shouldn't have sole jurisdiction over the waterways inside the reservation, that it had no right to fine non–band members or confiscate their property, and that the reservation shouldn't receive any money from the state for schools on its land. "The reservation is set up to fail," says Terry Maddy, the secretary-treasurer for Citizens for Truth in Government. "I want to be clear: I'm not anti-Indian. I'm pro-Indian. I've got a lot of Indian friends. And let me tell you—when they come visit me they don't want to park out front. They're scared to be seen with me because Buck Jourdain [the chairman of the Red Lake Tribe] has got spies. They're scared to death of him. He gets a cut of everything up there," contends Maddy. "Like a kingpin. If people speak out publicly, they'll die. We're not anti-Indian, we're anti-reservation, because reservations are keeping people down. No one's happy up there. And it's because people feel entitled. They get special treatment, special rights." A coalition of sport fishermen vowed to form a floating blockade of Red Lake waters with their fishing boats. What might have been an instance of willful trespass or simply a navigational blunder looked as if it would become a serious challenge to the sovereignty of Red Lake Reservation.

Doug Lindgren, a Republican candidate for the state legislature in 2006, made Red Lake his main campaign issue. "It's been upheld in the highest court in the nation," said Lindgren, "that Red Lake belongs— and this is from the U.S. Supreme Court—is that they are saying that the navigable waters belong to the state of Minnesota. If Minnesota has the right, through the laws, then yes, Minnesota should step in and have all control over what goes on on the Red Lakes." Michael Barrett, a Republican running for a seat in the U.S. House of Representatives, said, "This is not meant to be racist in any manner. In fact, the opposite is true. This is a statement that identifies that we're all Minnesotans, that we should all have the same opportunities and we should all live by the same rules. We have to have a state and a nation that embraces equal rights and equal access for all, not special privileges for a few."

It's the idea of "special privileges" that upsets people so much. But what Barrett, Lindgren, and Maddy don't realize is that tribes and tribal sovereignty allowed there to be a state of Minnesota in the first place. Without the concessions made by tribes during the treaty process there wouldn't be anyplace for white people to settle. Be that as it may, Terry Maddy, the treasurer for Citizens for Truth in Government, summed up Red Lake's position by saying they've "long had a tradition up there of having their cake and eating it, too."

Red Lake Reservation is mostly water. It is a beautiful place, unlike any other in America. For starters, Upper and Lower Red Lake are almost completely undeveloped. Elm, ash, and maple march down to the water's edge. In a time when lakeshore property on sandy lakes in Minnesota and Wisconsin with good fishing has been almost completely divided and developed, sand beaches stretch for miles on Red Lake without interruption. Red Lake is actually two lakes—Upper and Lower Red Lake—connected by a narrow channel. The southern Lower Red Lake is sandy and shallow, and its 152,000 acres sit completely inside the reservation. Upper Red Lake is divided more or less in half—the 48,000 acres of the northern portion of Upper Red Lake are off the reservation; 60,000 acres of the southern half are within the boundaries of Red Lake.

There aren't really any farms on Red Lake Reservation, and there are only a few backwoods businesses advertising welding, small-engine repair, or logging. There are only four convenience stores I know of on the rez—one each in Little Rock, Red Lake Village, Redby, and Ponemah. The village of Red Lake has a grocery store and a Laundromat. Other than these small convenience stores, there is no place to buy gas or food. There were no hotels until the spring of 2010, when

Red Lake opened a casino on the southern boundary, far from the lake. There are no hair salons, Starbucks, Einstein Brothers Bagels, cell phone stores, RadioShacks, Jiffy Lubes, McDonald's, Arby's, Rent-A-Centers, car dealerships, Gaps or Old Navy Stores. There aren't even any real billboards. What signs do exist are often small, hand-painted on plywood, and as often as not propped against a tree rather than planted in the ground. The first sign you see upon driving into the village of Red Lake on Highway 89 is nicely painted and reads "Don's West-End Video," in red block letters written freehand on whitewashed half-inch plywood. All of this . . . this nothing, on a reservation the same size as Rhode Island. Until the new casino was built in 2010, the biggest building on the rez (except for the hospital) was the BIA jail.

The reasons for this apparent nothing are varied. Red Lake suffers from some of the most crippling economic conditions of any community in the country. Unemployment stands at 60 percent. The *average* income at Red Lake is well below the poverty level. High school graduation rates are the lowest in the state.

The village of Red Lake, arguably the capital of the rez, since that's where the high school and government offices are, doesn't offer much to look at. There is the former Red Lake Trading Post, which is now called Red Lake Foods. It is a combination grocery store, gas station, convenience store, Laundromat, and check-cashing place. There are government buildings, a few houses, a small casino, the grade school, the high school, and the powwow grounds next to the old casino. All in all, the village has a meanly municipal feel to it.

All land is held in common by the Red Lake Band, so no non–band member can own or rent out any house on tribal land. Charley Grolla, the officer who arrested Jerry Mueller, is an enrolled member of a different reservation, the small backwoods community of Nett Lake in northeastern Minnesota. "When I was real little my ma was going to go to an AA meeting in the Cities. So she dropped me and my brother off with Dale and Sandy [Johns] at Red Lake. She didn't come back for a few weeks. When she did come back she was kind of drunk. Dale said, 'You can stay if you want. You got to do what you've been doing, work hard, work around the house, take care of yourselves.' So I went out and told my mom I was going to stay. She said OK, and I didn't see her again for three or four months, maybe." Grolla went back to his biological family at Nett Lake later, but life was much the same. More chaos. More drinking. "My mom had been drinking and stuff. I was fourteen. The uncle I was going to stay with, my favorite uncle Ike Leecy, he happened to do some time in jail. I was going to stay with him but I couldn't. So I hitchhiked back to Red Lake. A couple of weeks later the social workers came over. I told them I'm not going to go back. I gotta live my life, too. So I showed up at court and told them why I didn't want to live with her. It was a good life at Red Lake. A forest life. Set nets, did sugarbush, picked blueberries. And that's where my Ojibwe stuff started, with my grandmother Fannie Johns. When I first learned my trees I learned them in Ojibwe. I didn't even know the English words for the trees. Birds, too. There's that one, she called it 'manoominikenshiinh.' It runs on the water in the rice. I still don't know what it is in English." So Charley grew up with a prominent Red Lake family, living a Red Lake life. He got married to a member of the Red Lake Band and they lived there and raised their kids there. But when he and his wife divorced, he couldn't live at Red Lake anymore. He is engaged now to a Red Lake tribal member.

While non–band members can't, as a rule, live on the rez, there is an exception, which has led to perhaps the strangest sight in the village: the Compound. Situated alongside the main highway, number 1, the Compound houses the Indian Health Services Hospital, the Jourdain Perpich Extended Care Facility, and all the "foreign" workers—government officials, doctors, teachers, and so on—who have jobs on Red Lake but are not band members. Some of the houses, known as

"Walking Shield" houses, were moved here from an abandoned air force base in North Dakota. There are two batches of them, and after they were moved from North Dakota all of them had to be stripped and abated because they were insulated with asbestos. Some of the other houses were built on site. The HUD planners who designed the arrangement were smitten with the winding streets and culs-de-sac of American suburbia, and they let their love show: the Compound's ramblers and split-levels grace curving streets with curbs and streetlights, but no sidewalks. And until recently the whole thing was encased in an eight-foot-high Cyclone fence. Some people joke that the fence was there to keep Indians out. (And this is possible. When the old agency building and hospital were on the other side of the creek, they too were enclosed in a fence and referred to as "the compound"; but when the hospital and other facilities moved to where they are now, the old compound became known as "Pill Hill" because that's where everyone used to go to get medical care.) Clearly, outsiders have a complicated stake in Red Lake.

The high school sits just past the compound on the other side of the creek. It is a large, modern affair, built with bonded state and federal money in the early 1990s. Despite all the troubles that plague the reservation—crime, gangs, unemployment, suicide, and low graduation rates—the whole community is very proud, especially proud, of this school. It is the most important, most central, most conspicuous building on the reservation.

To an outsider Red Lake could look like a great nothing. But what appears as a great nothing, an economic disaster, is linked to a particular Red Lake phenomenon of independence. The "nothing" is the result of character and leadership stretching back over 150 years. Red Lake Reservation, unlike nearly every other reservation in the United States, is a closed reservation. No one can live, work, travel, or fish anywhere within the reservation boundaries without the tribe's blessing. Mueller and his son-in-law were fishing on the wrong side of the rez.

When Terry Maddy said that the Indians at Red Lake were used to having their cake and eating it, too, the "cake" he was referring to was sovereignty, and it had been baking for more than 400 years before Jerry Mueller's boat was confiscated by the sovereign nation of Red Lake. There is probably no aspect of Indian life more misunderstood by Indians and non-Indians alike than sovereignty.

Sovereignty in the Western sense—the supreme independent authority over a land or territory vested in a people or a government—predated the conquest of America. So when tribes began making treaties with colonial powers and later with the U.S. government, sovereignty, as a concept, was well in place. It was out of this concept that reservations were, in large part, born. There were ad hoc arrangements that resembled, to some extent, modern reservations, dating back to the early seventeenth century. The Delaware from New Jersey, for example, had one such arrangement. The Delaware were also the beneficiaries of what could be considered the first "reservations" in the United States, when, in the early 1700s, they were promised land that would exist under their authority in Chester County, Pennsylvania. The Province of Maryland created a 5,000-acre reservation for the Nanticoke Indians in 1698, and created another reservation of 3,000 acres in 1711. The first and last reservation in the state of New Jersey was created for 200 Brotherton Delaware on August 29, 1758, in Evesham Township, Burlington County, New Jersey. Despite the reservation created for them in New Jersey, the Brotherton Delaware became one of the most nomadic tribes of all time. The Brotherton Reservation fell into decline almost immediately after it was created, mostly because the community's benefactor, John Brainerd, became ill

and left in 1777. The Oneida of upstate New York invited the Brotherton Delaware to live with them in 1796. The Brotherton agreed.
They had no power or protection in New Jersey. Instead of growing,
their numbers had shrunk from 200 in 1758 to a mere 85 in 1796.
They sold the reservation to New Jersey and moved to New York in
1802. The stay with the Oneida in New York was short. Some of the
Oneida planned a move to Wisconsin—having lost land, rights, and
villages during and after the rampages of the Revolutionary War. The
Oneida, having sided with the Americans, returned to their villages
to find them burned and looted by the British, the Americans, and
even some of their own Indian allies. And this after the Oneida men
had carried 600 bushels of corn on their backs to relieve the famine
at Valley Forge during the winter of 1777–1778. An Oneida woman
named Polly Cooper accompanied the men and showed the soldiers
how to prepare the corn by soaking it in lye and rolling it into hominy. So grateful were Washington and his troops that Martha Washington personally presented Polly Cooper with a bonnet and shawl.
That gratitude was short-lived. After the war the Oneida suffered and
sought better conditions out west. The Brotherton Indians accompanied them. Other Delaware moved to Indian territories in present-day
Oklahoma. Still others fled to Canada.

During the seventeenth and eighteenth centuries up to the Revolutionary War, there were a series of arrangements, trade relationships,
and antiaggression treaties between many tribes and the many European colonial powers in North America, chief among them the Spanish, Dutch, French, and English. These relationships varied among
tribes and colonists, with some tribes playing both sides because they
could. In many instances, as late as the mid-eighteenth century, Indian
tribes controlled the natural resources, the routes of travel, and the
technology to effectively control large areas of North America. The
Indians in the Great Lakes region showed they were powerful enough

to make any colonial power in North America think long and hard about how to deal with Indians. Nowhere was this more clear than during the Seven Years' War. When that war began in Europe in 1756, it involved every major European and colonial power, making it what some call the first world war. Great Britain and its allies (including Prussia) fought against France, Austria, Saxony, and Sweden. When the war was done, between 900,000 and 1.4 million were dead. The major clashes between Great Britain and France had been far from their own homelands; these took place in America during the French and Indian War, which was really the North American theater of the Seven Years' War but was so vast, long, and bloody that many people have come to think of it as a separate conflict. The very name of the war can be confusing—the conflict was not between the French and the Indians but rather between the French and their Indian allies and the British in North America. At the outset of the war in 1754 the British maintained a strong presence on the eastern seaboard from North Carolina to Maine, whereas the French occupied the territories farther north and west. Mixed in with the French and British colonies were many Indian tribes—Seneca, Mohawk, Ottawa, Ojibwe, Hurons, Delaware, Shawnee, Winnebago, and others—whose territories often overlapped those of the French and the British. Most of the Indian tribes sided with the French, who were, by colonial standards, somewhat decent neighbors and trading partners. Some tribes, notably the majority of the Iroquois Confederacy (which comprised the Mohawk, Oneida, Onondaga, Cayuga, Seneca, and Tuscarora but in this case was minus the Seneca), joined the British. The war—brutal and total—lasted from 1754 until 1763, when France gave up most of its New World possessions at the Treaty of Paris, though it left its citizens and traders in their former holdings.

When, under the leadership of General Jeffrey Amherst, the British took possession of the French territories around the Great Lakes, they made a number of mistakes. They understaffed the forts and shortchanged their new Indian trading partners. Most of these errors resulted from Amherst's low opinion of Natives. He thought them disorganized, weak, and worthless. Whereas the French treated the Indians as allies and urged, through diplomacy and trade, the creation of mutually beneficial alliances, the British treated Indians as a defeated people. They did away with the symbolic and quasi-religious gifting ceremonies the French had observed, during which village chiefs were presented with blankets, guns, and trade goods. Amherst's general approach was desultory and his attitude derisive; he cut rations and instructed traders not to sell gunpowder to the Indians. Few French colonists made inroads into Indian territories, but the British came in waves. And finally, the great tribes of the East had enough.

An alliance was forged between three different tribal regions: the Great Lakes tribes, consisting of the Ottawa, Ojibwe, Huron, and Potawatomi; the tribes from Illinois country to the west, made up of Miamis, Kickapoos, Mascoutens, Weas, and Piankashaws; and the tribes from the Ohio country, including Mingos, Shawnee, Wyandots, and Delaware. These came together largely under the leadership of the Ottawa chief Pontiac and Kiywasuta, a Seneca leader. The Seneca, having long supported the British, were disaffected. They threw in their lot, and their many warriors, with the tribes allied against the British. When fighting started at Fort Detroit in the spring of 1763 and lasted until late 1764, the Indians used every strategy they had. They sneaked in concealed weapons, pretending to want to have a council. The leader of Fort Miami was lured out of the fort by his Indian mistress and killed by Miami warriors lying in wait. The most daring method of capture was used when the Ojibwe and Sac staged a lacrosse game outside the gates of Fort Mitchilimackinac. They threw the ball in past the open gates and chased after it (nothing was "out of bounds" in early lacrosse). Once inside the fort the lacrosse players grabbed weapons smuggled in earlier by their women and opened fire, killing fifteen of the fort's thirty-five soldiers; five solders were tortured to death later.

During the conflict many hundreds of British soldiers and civilians were burned, tortured, and scalped. One was ritually cannibalized. The British, for their part, weren't very nice either. During the siege of Fort Pitt General Amherst wrote to Colonel Bouquet, who commanded a force sent to relieve him, "Could it not be contrived to send the small pox among the disaffected tribes of Indians? We must on this occasion use every stratagem in our power to reduce them." Colonel Bouquet agreed heartily: "I will try to inoculate the bastards with some blankets that may fall into their hands, and take care not to get the disease myself." This was Amherst's response: "You will do well to inoculate the Indians by means of blankets, as well as every other method that can serve to extirpate this execrable race." Even in Pennsylvania, far from the fighting, fear and tempers ran high. Around Paxton, Pennsylvania, rumors circulated that a war party had been seen in Conestoga. A local militia, later known as Paxton's Boys, grabbed weapons and attacked a peaceful village of Christian Susquehannock farmers, killing six of them. The rest fled to Philadelphia with fifty Paxton Boys right behind them, but they were protected by the British and a local militia, led by Benjamin Franklin.

When it was all over, 500 British troops were dead and 2,000 British colonists had been captured or killed. The number of Indian dead is unknown and hard to estimate—smallpox claimed many, including many who weren't involved in the conflict at all. The war ended in a stalemate. The Indian alliance wasn't able to drive out the British, and the British weren't able to subdue the Indians. Such an outcome had long-lasting effects. British policy toward Natives was hastily reconfigured in the Royal Proclamation of 1763. In it, the British restructured their trade and social relations to mimic those of the French and drew a boundary between British and Indian lands that ran from the Appalachians to the Mississippi River and from Florida to Maine. The land to the west of the Appalachians was considered "Indian land" and British colonists were warned to leave it alone. Conciliation and compromise rather than all-out war became the method of dealing with Indian tribes. And Indians were understood to have individual and collective rights to their lands. Indian tribes also understood that pan-Indian alliances were the best way to deal with colonial outsiders. This was a major shift in policy and in thinking on both sides.

Then the Revolutionary War broke out. Indian tribes on the eastern seaboard and in the Ohio River valley were actively courted by the British and the colonists. Some tribes picked sides; others played both sides. By 1778 the Continental Army was in deep trouble and looking for help from every quarter—from the French and Germans, naturally, but also from the Indian tribes: the Tuscarora, Shawnee, Delaware, Seneca, Cayuga, Mohawk, Onondaga, Oneida, Wyandot, and Munsies. Some of these tribes sided with the British. Some, like the Delaware, threw in their lot with the Americans. None of the tribes fared well in the end.

As Pontiac's War of 1763–1764 proved, the Indians at the western edge of the colonies were a force to be reckoned with. As of 1778, the United States could not afford to fight the Indians of the eastern Great Lakes as it fought the British to the east. It desperately needed the Indians' neutrality, if not their help. The offer from the revolutionaries (and evidence that, though the outcome was not clear, they already thought of themselves and their Indian neighbors as nations) to the Delaware came in the form of a treaty. The Treaty of Fort Pitt, signed on September 17, 1778, was to set the tone for future formal treaties between Indian nations and the U.S. government. In it, the United States recognized that the Delaware were a sovereign nation, not beholden to any rule other than their own; the treaty guaranteed their rights to administer their own affairs and to protect their territories, and recognized the "usefructory" rights of the Delaware, that is, the right to hunt, fish, gather, log, build, and otherwise dispose of the resources within the limits of their territory mentioned in the treaty. The Continental Congress also promised to build a fort for the tribe, most likely to protect the Delaware against retaliation by the Wyandot—enemies of the Delaware who sided with the British. In return, the Delaware promised to allow Continental troops to pass through Delaware land, and to provide warriors to fight alongside the colonists. The United States was so keen to enlist the support of the Delaware that it made an unprecedented and never-repeated gesture: as a term of the treaty it offered the Delaware the opportunity to become the fourteenth state of the union. "It is further agreed on," reads the treaty, "between the contracting parties should it for the future be found conducive for the mutual interest of both parties to invite any other tribes who have been friends to the interest of the United States, to join the present confederation, and to form a state whereof the Delaware nation shall be the head, and have a representation in Congress." Sadly, it never happened. The promise was not made in good faith and the negotiations were not conducted with any faith at all. "There never was a conference with the Indians so improperly or villainously conducted," wrote Colonel Morgan, one participant in the proceedings. The Delaware were invited to an early version of an "open bar" and in the general inebriation the translators (in the pay of the Continental Congress) deliberately deceived the Indian delegates. The Delaware were betrayed almost immediately. White Eyes, one of the Delaware chiefs who signed the treaty and who was one of the staunchest supporters of the United States, was murdered by his allies within a month; his death was covered up and officially attributed to smallpox. So much for the first formal, written treaty between the United States and an Indian tribe.

Treaties were based on two suppositions that reflect a history of thought rather than fact: that tribes were nations (in the European sense of "nation") and that negotiation was preferable to all-out war. Treaties were not made between nations and lesser states, or between colonies and nations—they were made between sovereign nations. At the time—and later, during what has been called the "treaty period" between 1783 and 1889 (though the U.S. government officially stopped making treaties with tribes in 1871)—Indian tribes were considered nations, and though circumstances varied greatly, the U.S. government made treaties with Indians for two main reasons. First, the United States had to make treaties, because Indian tribes were powerful. They had command of routes of travel, many warriors, and plenty of resources when the United States had very little of any of these. The second reason was cynical: paper was cheaper than bullets. Despite the power of Indian tribes, it was often the case that the United States had no intention of honoring the treaties it made. Treaties were a way to reduce the power of tribes. Nonetheless, Indian tribes were so much on the mind of the revolutionaries that they included a special clause in the U.S. Constitution: only Congress had the power to regulate trade with Indian tribes and, furthermore, only the federal government (the president and the Senate) had the right to make treaties, as the "supreme law of the land," with Indian tribes. In the 1870s, the House of Representatives, which felt left out of the treaty-making process, effectively put a stop to the process unless the representatives could be involved.

Treaties—between tribes and European colonial powers, and between tribes and the newly formed U.S. government, had long been the "law of the land," but it wasn't until the Indian Appropriations Act of 1851 that the modern Indian reservation was born. At the time the U.S. government was in a quandary. It felt it needed room for the country to grow—and except for overseas colonial expansion, the only direction in which the country could grow was west—but Indians were in the way. All-out war with the tribes would be too costly, and the outcome—given the strength and position of many Indian tribes—would be far from certain. The U.S. government wanted to avoid the kind of conflict that had hurt the British so badly during the Seven Years' War and Pontiac's War. To repeat, then: frontier wars were costly and bloody, and their outcome (since they are fought against shifting tribal alliances of Indians who knew and controlled the terrain, with extended supply lines, and with so many unprotected settlers at risk) was unclear. Until 1851 the U.S. government had used two conflicting policies—assimilation and removal. But with the Appropriations Act, the policy became removal and containment. Instead of large tracts of land positioned in the way of western expansion, smaller, contained parcels of Indian land were seen as the answer. The Indian Appropriations Act, the first step in this process, empowered the U.S. government to enter into treaties with Indian tribes and to set aside land, money, and supplies for their establishment.

Following the passage of the Indian Appropriations Act of 1851 the United States embarked on an almost compulsive policy of making treaties with tribes, most of whom wanted some certainty of their continued existence and some autonomy in the face of increasing pressure from white settlers. From Texas to Minnesota and from Lake Michigan to the Pacific, tribes great and small found themselves at the negotiating table with the United States. The usual formula, if not the result, was quite simple: Indian tribes relinquished title to some of their lands and reserved the remainder for themselves. These remaining portions were called "reservations." In Ojibwe the word for "reservation" is "ishkonigan," which means, rather sardonically, "leftovers." In addition to the reserved land, where Indians were supposed to be able to live unmolested and on their own terms, the treaties usually had other provisions involving what are known as "treaty rights." These rights—to hunt, fish, gather, harvest timber—were many and usually extended to the territories outside the reservation that the tribe used to control, known as ceded territories.

Reservations sprang up from Oklahoma to Neah Bay, in the remote northwest corner of Washington state. Some of them were established in the ancestral homelands of the tribe in question. The Sioux of Pine Ridge, Rosebud, and Cheyenne River live, more or less, where they always did, in portions of their original homeland. The Pueblo still occupy the pueblos they have lived in for thousands of years. In fact, one of the oldest continuously occupied cities in North America is Acoma Pueblo; people have been living there nonstop since the twelfth century. But some reservations were established hundreds of miles away and the tribe, as part of the treaty, agreed to move to its new land.

This is what happened to some of the Ho-Chunk, formerly called the Winnebago. They were once the dominant force on the western shores of Lake Michigan, but their population plummeted from about 20,000 in 1620 to about 1,000 in 1820. Beginning in the nineteenth century many, but not all, Ho-Chunk were moved from Wisconsin to Minnesota, from there to South Dakota, then to Iowa, and finally to Nebraska. Many did not like their new reservation and, traveling at night, walked back to Wisconsin. In all, the Ho-Chunk were subjected to nine removal orders, and their survival and expansion in the twentieth century are a heartening story of toughness, tenacity, and courage. Likewise, some Seneca from upstate New York were removed to Oklahoma. Sac and Fox from Wisconsin wound up in Iowa, Oklahoma, and even Mexico. Apache were sent from the southwest to Florida. Seminole were removed from Florida and sent to Oklahoma. Connections to place and culture were compromised and sometimes totally destroyed.

The early to mid-nineteenth century was dark for Indian tribes. White encroachment continued. The newly formed reservations mostly were run under the auspices of an Indian agent, commissioned under the Department of War. The Indian agent hired tribal police, administered annuities and other treaty payments, and was responsible for economic development. More often than not Indian agents were drawn from unscrupulous people. Fraud, cronyism, nepotism, double-dealing, skimming, and outright murder were common.

By the early 1880s—just 100 years since the Treaty of Fort Pitt and three decades since the Indian Appropriations Act had ushered in the modern reservation period—almost everyone recognized that the reservation system was a failure. The policy of containment and control funded by the Indian Appropriations Act hadn't really done away with Indians as hoped—the Dakota Wars in the 1870s were costly proof of that. And as far as Indians were concerned, the reservation was not what they expected, either: a place to live unmolested and on their own terms. A new policy of "allotment" was put in place with the help of the Dawes Act of 1887. The act authorized the United States to survey and divide lands held in common by Indian tribes and allot them to Indian individuals. Any "extra" land was to return to the U.S. government, which could then give it to settlers, lumber companies, mining companies, and railroads. On some reservations Indian agents became the largest landholders in the region. Reservations, once places for Indians and Indians only, became a checkerboard of Indian land, white farms, and federal lands. As of today, on Leech Lake, like many other reservations, the tribe owns roughly 4 percent of the land within the reservation boundaries. The rest of the land is divided among county, state, federal, corporate, and private owners.

One of the most serious misconceptions about reservations is that they were a kind of moral payment: that the U.S. government, motivated by pity and guilt, "gave" reservations to Indians along with treaty rights, which functioned as a kind of proto-welfare program. This is not the case. Reservations and treaty rights were concessions negotiated for the right to settle and develop new land. People like Jerry Mueller and Citizens for Truth in Government don't like this arrangement. I think most Indians would be glad to abrogate our treaties. We will "give up" our reservations and our treaty rights, and all the non-Natives can move east of the Appalachians. Or if they don't want to move they can pay rent. It would be useful for most Americans to keep in mind that after they pass those mountains they are living, driving, eating, breathing, and walking on land that at one time or another was negotiated for, not fought for. More so than wars, agreements opened the part of America from the Appalachia to the Pacific to non-Indians. Reservations and their sovereignty are the remaining small result of those agreements.

All of this explains and yet does *not* quite explain Red Lake and why a white trespasser was arrested and fined by Red Lake Reservation conservation officers. Unlike most other reservations in the United States, Red Lake was not created by treaty. The government officially stopped making treaties with Indians in 1871. Red Lake Reservation was established in 1889 by a congressional act. In the years before—as tribes were encouraged and sometimes forced to the treaty table, reservations were established, and communities were moved—the Red Lake Ojibwe watched. They witnessed the treaties of 1825 (Prairie du Chien); 1836 (Michigan); 1837, 1842, and 1854 (Wisconsin and Minnesota); and 1855, 1863, and 1864 (Mississippi and Pillager Bands in Minnesota)—and they watched as the provisions of those treaties were ignored. They watched as faith was broken. Red Lake was forced to the treaty table in 1863 but was in a position of relative strength. The Red Lake people ceded some territory but retained their land around both Upper and Lower Red Lake. The treaty of 1863 did not create the Red Lake

Reservation. What it did was reduce the size of the Red Lake Band's territory. When the U.S. government quit making treaties with Indians in 1871, Red Lake still retained title to more than 3 million acres in northern Minnesota, and when the "allotment" provided by the Nelson Act was pressed on tribes to the south in 1889, Red Lake knew better than to agree to it. The Red Lake leaders rejected the proposition (though they ceded some acreage) and maintained that all land on the reservation should be held in common. One story has it that the old war chief Medwe-ganoonind (aptly, "He Who Is Heard Talking") was firmly against allotment. As the story goes, during a council meeting he slammed his war club (a club that he had used to kill not a few of his enemies) on the table and said, *If you think this is such a good idea, fine. If you want to vote for it, fine. But you've got to fight me first. If you win, you can vote yes.* No one wanted to fight him. Red Lake voted against allotment. This may be a legend, but what is not legend is that during the days when the federal commissioners were at Red Lake to push for allotment, the council ended up voting against the provision three times. Each time the council voted it down, the commissioners begged for a recess, during which time they threatened, cajoled, baited, and bribed the council members. Each time the issue came to a vote the council turned it down again.

In the early twentieth century, when the federal government once again tried to dissolve and diminish Indian control of Indian land, this time through a law that gave states criminal and civil jurisdiction on the reservation, Red Lake said no—even though that meant they could lose much of their funding for schools, hospitals, roads, and police protection. The reservation then built its own schools, paved its own roads, and built its own court, police station, and hospitals without state or county support and with little help from the BIA.

This is why Red Lake can and does retain complete control over its lands and its rights, and why officers Grolla and Nelson were within

their rights and acting in accordance with the spirit of tough independence particular to Red Lake when they uncased their assault
rifles, confiscated Jerry Mueller's boat, and fined Mueller. This wasn't
the first time the Red Lake Nation had fined a trespasser. In winter of
2002 a man landed his floatplane on Lower Red Lake, within the reservation boundary, and began fishing. The tribe confiscated the plane,
and the pilot had to pay more than $4,000 in fines and fees to get
it back. When Officer Grolla cited Jerry Mueller, Mueller was cooperative at first, as Grolla remembers it. But later, when he appeared in
Red Lake tribal court to argue his case, he was belligerent and hostile.
"If a Red Lake boat crossed the line and wasn't licensed through the
state, it would be the same thing," remembers Grolla. "Just the other
way around. But they act like we're terrorizing them. What they don't
understand is that the reservation is the only place Indians feel safe.
There's a story that my grandma Fannie Johns used to tell. That story
still makes me mad. She used to tell this story how they were coming
from Thief River in a wagon. It was Fanny and her grandma and her
uncle. Her grandma was alive during the Dakota Wars, that's how old
her grandma was. She didn't have an English name. Her Ojibwe name
was Ikwezens. And her uncle's name was Me'asewab. They were coming
from Thief River; they went over there by wagon to get supplies. They
couldn't make it back to the rez. There was kind of a rule that Indians
couldn't be off the reservation after dark. They went every month to
buy stuff like flour and whatnot, to sell blueberries. They were coming
back and they couldn't make the reservation. They ended up parking
alongside this trail, this wagon trail. They made a fire and made some
soup. They saw these lights coming from far away. They watched those
lights for hours as they got closer. They kept watching and these three
white guys show up in a Model A Ford. And these white guys started
in giving them shit. 'Hey, you want to sell your women,' saying things
like that. Giving them shit about being off the reservation. Her uncle

started getting pissed. He pulled out a lever-action rifle and said if they didn't leave he'd kill them all. These guys took off. Fannie and her grandpa tried to sleep but her uncle stayed up all night, keeping watch, on the lookout for the white guys. I just hated that. I hated it that my grandma got terrorized just for being Indian and being off the reservation. When it got light they packed up and drove the wagon as fast as they could back to the rez. And guys like Mueller and other guys like that are telling me that Indians are terrorizing *them*. It pisses me off that they cry around about stuff like that."

There still exists a lot of hostility between Indians and whites in northern Minnesota—especially between Red Lake and its white neighbors. But the waters Mueller was fishing on were troubled for other reasons, too—related to Red Lake's sovereignty. Sovereignty means that you can determine your own lives, but it has a downside: you also have the latitude to destroy them. The one industry that Red Lake could claim in an otherwise economically depressed region was the commercial fishing of walleye pike. The walleye pike is unique to North American waters. It is the Minnesota state fish, and by the 1990s Red Lake was the last remaining natural fishery for walleye in the United States. The Red Lake Band had overfished the lake, and the effect was catastrophic, both economically and culturally. Until that point, the walleye was the principal resource of Red Lake and its dominant cultural icon. Much of Red Lake's material and social culture was based on the harvesting and use of walleye. This continued slowly until the fishery collapsed and was shut down in 1997.

A distinctly New World species, walleye are found throughout Canadian and northern American waters. They can be found in lakes and rivers in cold northern areas and get the name "walleye" because of the way their eyes reflect light, like the eyes of cat. They school during the spring spawning, which usually occurs in late April or early May in Minnesota, and a little later in colder waters farther north in

Canada. The rest of the year they hunt alone, though groups of wall-eye will congregate in productive habitat like sandbars, rock piles, and the edges of weed beds: places where small bait fish congregate. Their eyes allow them to see in cloudy or disturbed water, giving them an advantage over their prey. They are not fussy fish, like brook trout or brown trout. You don't need to be an analyst to catch them, worrying over presentation, lure color, or insect. They are, however, excellent fighters and are considered by many to be the best-tasting freshwater fish on the continent. Moreover, they don't grow to an impressive size and aren't even really a "pike." Walleye belong to the Percidae family— technically, this makes them perch. They live, on average, nine years and grow to a weight of about five to seven pounds and a length of twenty-four to twenty-eight inches. The largest walleye ever caught was forty-two inches long and weighed twenty-five pounds. The old-est walleye on record (age is determined by measuring the layers of bone—like the layers of a pearl—on a special bone in their head called an otolith) was twenty-nine years old at the time of its capture.

These statistics don't really compare to those of true pike—known as northern pike and muskellunge—which are found in northern waters across America, the British Isles, Scandinavia, Russia, and Siberia. These monsters can grow up to six feet long and weigh well over thirty pounds. The largest pike on record weighed seventy-seven pounds. They are ferocious fish that will attack and try to eat just about anything—from their own young to frogs, mice, and ducklings. They have teeth, like walleye, but bigger. One friend of mine describes them as being 50 percent teeth and 50 percent appetite. They are also, unlike the walleye, a storied fish. The hero of the Finnish epic the Kalevala made a musical instrument out of the jawbone of a pike. The U.S. Navy named a total of five submarines after the pike, and an entire class of Russian submarines from the Soviet era, the Victor III Class, was nick-named "Shchuka," Russian for "pike."

Nor does the walleye measure up to the sturgeon, which still surfaces from time to time in our larger and deeper lakes. This prehistoric fish is found throughout America, Europe, and Asia and can grow up to eight feet long. Some sturgeons caught in America are estimated to be more than 200 years old. Frederick the Great released a great number of sturgeons in Lake Gardno in Pomerania in 1780. Some of them were still alive in 1866. John Tanner, during his travels in the 1790s, was canoeing up the Mississippi with a party of Ojibwe warriors when they all leaped out of the canoe and charged through the shallow water. He thought they were under attack. Rather, they had spied a sturgeon grounded on a sandbar. The warriors beat it to death with their clubs. It took four men to lift it into the canoe. Once back in the village they cut it up and fed an entire village of over 200 Ojibwe for a week.

But Minnesota loves its walleye. Minnesotans and nonresidents came together in 2006 to buy 1,371,106 fishing licenses and used them in Minnesota's 5,493 fishing lakes and 15,000 miles of streams. Although panfish like bluegill, crappie, perch, and sunfish are the most commonly caught fish (with an annual harvest of 64 million pounds), most people come to Minnesota for walleye. Sport anglers take 35 million pounds of walleye annually. And the state of Minnesota restocks its 3.8 million acres of fishable waters with 250 million walleye fry (newly hatched fish), 2.5 million walleye fingerlings (infant fish), and 50,000 walleye yearlings every year. The financial statistics are staggering: more than $1.58 billion is spent every year by anglers, most of them trying to land a walleye or two.

Walleye also appears on most menus in the state, usually fried, sometimes herbed, rarely baked or poached. It is delicious, even if you don't like fried fish. It has a clean taste, and firm, white, flaky flesh that comes off the spine in thick, moist shingles. The meat near the tail, where the rib bones and other substructures disappear, is the best part—the firmest, sweetest, most delicious freshwater fish this side of trout you will ever taste. It is difficult to buy the fish anywhere outside the state, and expats often order it from online retailers just for a taste of home.

The walleye has also been implicated in a high-level culinary intrigue that some have called "Walleyegate." In 2004, Minneapolis-based KARE 11 News went "undercover" to expose a "walleye scam" being perpetrated in restaurants near Minneapolis and St. Paul. Evidently, the news program had been tipped off that many of the restaurants advertising walleye on their menus weren't serving walleye at all.

Walleye retails at about five dollars a pound, but a European fish called zander—which has the same texture, size, and flavor—sells for two dollars less per pound. For a restaurant like, say, the swanky Tavern on Grand in St. Paul, which sells 50,000 pounds of walleye a year, the switch could mean more than $100,000 in savings. KARE's reporter ordered "walleye" at about twenty restaurants in the area and sent samples to a laboratory in New York that specializes in testing fish and animal DNA. In half the cases, the results came back as zander, not walleye. One wonders if the switch is important enough to merit such careful undercover work; after all, no one could tell the difference. But according to their DNA, zander and walleye went their separate ways at least 12 million years ago, and "species substitution" is illegal under U.S. law. Restaurant managers mostly refused to talk on film, saying only, "No comment." One manager, however, did say that he had been assured by his vendor that what he purchased was walleye. Zander, he was told, is a different name for walleye. He went on the record as saying that his company was "embarrassed" but had been "led astray." Even the Ojibwe community of St. Croix was selling zander as walleye in its casino in Turtle Lake, Wisconsin.

It seems ironic that Indians, long imagined (by ourselves and by others) as "stewards of the land"—that is, as possessing, by virtue of culture or blood, a unique and wholesome relationship with the natural world—are, in numerous cases, primarily responsible for the destruction of the ecosystem that gave us life.

When Ojibwe first came to Red Lake in the 1600s—encouraged by the fur trade to expand and control new trapping grounds, and engaged in wars to the east, north, and west—the lake was a paradise. There were certain requirements that a place needed to meet in order to be suitable for settlement, and Red Lake met them all. It had abundant wild rice beds, diverse forests (a mixture of pine and hardwood excellent for building), easily navigable water, and a recurring and stable source of protein: the walleye. There are many kinds of fish in the world, and all contain protein, but not all are easy to harvest with primitive methods. Some, such as northern pike, are so widely dispersed throughout a lake that it is impossible to catch them in large enough numbers to feed a village. Others, like trout and eelpout, run and live so deep that retrieving them with nets or traps is difficult. Walleye are the perfect fish for surviving on medium-size inland lakes. They don't live deep in the water. They spawn at regular intervals in very shallow water. They are big enough to satisfy. They school up rather than spread out. Other large Ojibwe settlements were supported by other fish; the settlement at Sault Sainte Marie on the narrows between Upper and Lower Peninsula, Michigan, is one example. This community lived off the whitefish that ran in the cold current. Some explorers wrote that during the spawn (which occurs in the fall) it was possible to walk from one side of the Sault to the other on the backs of the fish. The Indians of the northwest coast have salmon. The plains tribes have buffalo. The Ojibwe have fish. Red Lake, in particular, has, or had, walleye. Like the buffalo for the Blackfeet, the Dakota, Nakota, Arikara, Cheyenne, and Nez Perce, the walleye gave the Ojibwe of Red Lake life. And so, after a series of bloody wars, the Ojibwe drove the Sioux west and took control of Red Lake.

Fishing at Red Lake occurred at a subsistence level for about 400 years with little change in the technology used to harvest the fish. They were speared from a canoe by torchlight in the shallows and netted and noodled (lifted out with the hands) in small streams during the spring spawn. Spears were made of pliable, sharpened deer and porcupine bones. Nets were woven out of twine made from the fibrous innards of stinging nettle stalks. The canoes were made of birch bark. In the 1800s iron replaced bone. Commercial twine replaced nettle. In the 1900s canvas and wood canoes replaced birch bark. By 1917 fishing was done from the decks of motorized boats. Nets were remarkably strong and much lighter. It was at this time that the first commercial fishery opened at Red Lake.

During the final years of World War I, there was a food shortage in the United States. The federal government saw that fish, such as the walleye at Red Lake, could be an easily harvested and renewable food source. In violation of Red Lake's sovereignty, which the band was not in a position to enforce very well at the time, the federal government established a state-run commercial fishery in the village of Red Lake. It was one of the largest commercial fisheries in the United States. Hundreds of thousands of pounds of walleye were caught in Red Lake, dried, and shipped south by railcar. In 1930, as a result of some hard lobbying by Red Lake leaders, the fishery was turned over to the Red Lake tribe, and the Red Lake Fisheries Association (RLFA), a fishing collective made up of Red Lake Band members, was founded. The RLFA issued licenses and quotas from the fishery, to whom members would sell their fish. Everyone would receive money for poundage sold as well as a dividend of profits from the export of the fish to wholesalers in the region. Whenever fishers exceeded their quota, all they had to do was apply for a supplement, which was never denied. Then they could go out and get more fish.

Beginning in the 1970s the lake started on a boom-and-bust cycle, which should have been seen as a warning sign that the lake was trembling under the pressure of fishing. Some years the fish were caught by the hundreds of thousands, as they had been for centuries. In other years the fishing wasn't so good. No one listened to the lake—not the Red Lakers netting fish in the south and not the sport anglers catching them with hook and line in the north. No one listened to other lakes where the same thing had happened.

There are two other large, shallow sandy lakes in Minnesota that once supported huge fisheries—Lake Winnibigoshish on the Leech Lake Reservation and Lake Mille Lacs, closer to Minneapolis. Both lakes were overfished and eventually collapsed; they yielded next to no walleye—but not before the same erratic pulse, the same boom-and-bust cycle, was evident. Neither lake has ever come back to the levels of fish and fishing it once supported.

Fishing continued on Red Lake in the 1970s and 1980s as before. There seemed to be no end to the fish. By the early 1990s the RLFA membership had swelled from 200 to 700. The annual harvest stood at 1 million pounds, with an estimated additional 1 million pounds of walleye sold on the black market. Gary and Jane Bymark own a resort on the northern shore of Red Lake, off the reservation. Gary said in an interview that he watched pickup trucks drive past with walleye mounded up in the back so high he could see them from behind the bar. He also remembered Red Lakers coming into the white-owned resort to sell fish: "Like when you're sitting at the bar here, and any one of them Indians come in and say we got walleye for a dollar a walleye, cleaned and everything, they're going to buy them. Two or three guys would come in here and walk out with a hundred walleyes."

A few hundred walleye were small change. One former fisherman told me he would gut his fish, pack them in the trunk of his car, and drive the five hours to Minneapolis, where he sold the fish to the Asian markets. The Hmong were the best customers, he said. They wanted the whole fish—head, fins, tail—not just fillets. So it was easier and you got more poundage. He'd dicker with them and threaten to cross from north St. Paul over to Minneapolis and sell them to the Chinese and Koreans instead. The Hmong would hurriedly buy the entire load at three dollars a pound: three times what he was paid by the RLFA.

Fish came to function as a kind of currency. In the early 1980s my mother, a lawyer then in private practice, was paid in fish; one client gave her 500 walleye fillets and his JVC stereo to settle his bill. "If you didn't have a job, set nets, sell fish," says Greg Kingbird, a spiritual leader and lifelong resident of Ponemah. "Make enough money, sit back for a few days. Run out of money, go set again. That was a way of life. You could go out there any day, get something to eat." Also, the sport fishing on the north end of the lake was out of control. Ed Hudec, a resort owner near the town of Washkish on the north shore of Red Lake, remembers seeing 10,000 boats on Upper Red Lake during the fishing opener in mid-May.

All this came to an end in 1996. That was when the last mature and healthy year-class of fish was taken from the lake. Instead of millions of pounds, fishermen were able to take only 15,000 pounds in total. It was a disaster. The fish were gone. In 1997 Red Lake stopped commercial fishing, and a year later it closed subsistence fishing as well. In 1999 the state of Minnesota followed suit and closed state waters in Upper Red Lake to sport fishing. A moratorium was in effect. The band and the state would try to bring the fish back.

Red Lake's sovereignty had, in some ways, led to this. The band could determine—without consulting the state or anyone else—how much fish could be taken and in what ways and by whom. And, as many Red Lakers admit, greed was allowed to run its course.

So there is sovereignty, but of a special kind. Tribes can't keep standing armies (though some have done so). They can't issue their own currency (though some have done this, too). Most can't have border patrols and can't require passports (though some, including Red Lake, do or did). In July 2010, the Iroquois national lacrosse team—which has been traveling to lacrosse tournaments around the world on Iroquois Confederacy passports for thirty years—was barred from traveling to Britain on these passports because of newer restrictions stemming from the Patriot Act. The team refused to use U.S. passports and in the end missed competing in the championship of the sport the Iroquois invented.

When Floyd "Buck" Jourdain was voted in as chairman of Red Lake in 2004, he saw the plight of the fisheries and what it meant for Red Lake—for its economic health and its sovereignty—as the biggest challenge facing the tribe. Instead of pulling in and protecting the reservation from outside scrutiny, the Red Lake Band launched an aggressive program, along with the state of Minnesota, the federal government, and local resources, to restock the lake. It was a long process. The participants assessed water quality, breeding habitat, and genetically tested fish to find which strains were best suited to Red Lake's waters. They had to enforce a strict ban against fishing on Upper and Lower Red Lake. Between 1999 and 2004 Red Lake and the state of Minnesota dumped more than 105.2 million walleye fry into Red Lake. By 2004 the fish were reproducing on their own. And hook-and-line fishing (not commercial netting) reopened on Red Lake in 2005.

It was in these troubled waters that Jerry Mueller and his son-in-law crossed onto Red Lake Reservation. After Jerry Mueller's boat was confiscated in May, Citizens for Truth in Government threatened a blockade of Red Lake unless the tribe effectively gave up its sovereignty. Many people, from Republican hopefuls to white anglers and

resort owners, were still upset at what they saw as Red Lake's mismanagement of its waters. Michael Barrett and Doug Lindgren leaned on
the federal government to intervene—clearly trying to make Red Lake
a campaign issue in the elections during the fall of 2006. The situation came to a head on August 14, 2006, when Michael Barrett, the
Republican candidate for the U.S. House of Representatives from the
7th District, scheduled a speech at a fund-raiser in Bemidji. The fund-
raiser was held at the Rotary Pavilion on the Bemidji waterfront, where
Indian burial mounds had been razed in the 1920s to make room for a
fairground. About forty-five people sat on folding chairs in the pavilion while forty more, mostly Indian, stood outside, ready to question
Barrett about Red Lake. Barrett—a pharmacy manager—didn't show
up. He had planned to announce his desire for the federal government to enforce a 1926 decision by the U.S. Supreme Court that the
state of Minnesota had jurisdiction over a drained lake bed within the
ceded territories but not on the Red Lake Reservation itself. It was an
obscure ruling that in no way spoke to the sovereignty of Red Lake.
Barrett, Lindgren, and Citizens for Truth in Government had been
using this case as ammunition to shoot down Red Lake's sovereignty
despite the response by the state and federal government that it didn't
apply.

Although Barrett didn't show up, Doug Lindgren did. He raised
the issue and got into a shouting match with the Red Lake Nation
tribal historian and tribal secretary Kathryn "Jodi" Beaulieu, who
called Lindgren and his position racist.

Other Republicans present tried to backpedal and distance themselves from Barrett and Lindgren. "He went about it in the same way
Mike is going about everything—head down and head first, like a bull
in a china shop," said the chairwoman of the Beltrami County Republicans, Kath Molitor. Mark Kennedy of the U.S. House of Representatives was surprised by the hubbub and didn't know how to answer

questions about Red Lake's sovereignty. He said he'd never been to Red Lake but would love to visit. This gave the fiery Red Lake treasurer, Darrell Seki, the opening he needed. Seki is from Ponemah, is a fluent speaker of both English and Ojibwe, and is not known, generally, for holding his tongue or for keeping his opinions to himself. He's a fighter, not a diplomat—and with his severe face, shaded glasses, and glossy hair, he cuts an imposing figure. "Any non-members are welcome to come to our lake," he said in response to Kennedy, "and I hope they bring their equipment, because our DNR [Department of Natural Resources] needs equipment. Tell the non-members to come to our lake—we'll arrest them. We'll take their equipment, too." He concluded by saying, "It's our lake, it will stay our lake. We, as a Tribal Council, will protect our lake and our people. All the lands are ours and we are going to protect them." One got the feeling that Seki had stopped just short of saying "by any means necessary." What was clear was that Lindgren and Barrett, under the mask of favoring "fairness" and opposing "special rights," were trying to turn Red Lake into a campaign issue. Red Lake Reservation, with nearly 10,000 members, is a huge voting bloc in the region and has the highest voter turnout in the entire county: according to some statistics, more than 90 percent of Red Lakers go to the polls. Of these, 90 percent vote Democratic. Reservations, after all, are covered by congressional districts, county districts, and sometimes local government as well. And while enrolled band members of tribes can vote in tribal elections, they are also U.S. citizens and can vote in the same elections as their non-Indian neighbors.

As these campaign issues raged, there were other elections under way that summer. Buck Jourdain was running for a second term as tribal chairman against the tribal secretary Judy Roy. On July 19, 2006, Jourdain defeated Roy by a margin of seventy-one votes. Shortly thereafter, a Red Lake tribal member, Archie King, filed a complaint with the General Election Board alleging that Jourdain had bought votes and had used tribal funds for his campaign. The board agreed and ruled that a new runoff between the candidates was in order. Jourdain not only denied the allegations but said that the General Election Board did not have the right to call a new election. As for the complaint, Jourdain said that the "election was fair and my campaign was conducted in accordance with all election laws." Furthermore, he argued, "According to the Red Lake election code . . . all challenges must be submitted and received within five days of the public posting [of election results] by the General Election Board." The election issue was covered in the local paper, in the *Minneapolis Star Tribune,* and in the *New York Times.* Ultimately, the candidates squared off again. Jourdain won.

What is clear is that, taken together—the mismanagement of the lake and the fish, problems with the police force, election disputes—all missteps and even the perception of incompetence, let alone corruption, do threaten the sovereignty of a place like Red Lake. Whenever something does go wrong—and things go wrong all the time— someone raises the issue of sovereignty and suggests it should be done away with. But then again, all nations make mistakes. During the lobbying scandal involving Jack Abramoff, the Enron affair, Iran-contra, Teapot Dome, and the Whiskey Ring, to name a few, no one said, "Well, clearly the Americans can't manage their own affairs; it would be best if the United States reverted to British control and became, once again, part of the British Empire." And people often forget: the only reason there were fish to overfish in the first place (and the only reason the fish have been able to come back so strongly) is that since Red Lake is a closed reservation, there is no development on most of its shoreline—there are no sewage treatment plants, no resorts, no houses perched along the shore, no vacationers pulling up the bulrushes and cattails, no fertilized and pesticide-drenched lawns. Everyone has Red Lake and its leadership to thank for that.

No wonder that Mueller was not cut any slack: the boat was taken, he was summoned, and Red Lake stood its ground. Reflecting back on the case, Grolla seems proud to serve Red Lake and the community he calls his own. "We've got a mind-set, you know. It stretches all the way back to when we fought the U.S. government, when we fought the Sioux. We're used to warfare. We're used to fighting. That's who we are. People talk about how we're a gentle people, you know. How we respect everything. We do, but we've had to fight for it. It's kind of a curse sometimes, you know. I mean, hypothetically, let's say a girl gets raped Back of Town [a neighborhood in the village of Red Lake] and then her brothers take after the guys who did it, beat them up, burn their house down. Then the perp's family comes after the girl's family and on and on it goes. They fight until people are in the ground and nothing is left standing unless you catch them and arrest them and stop it before it really gets going. That attitude, that fighting attitude, goes back to Chief Bagonegiizhig and Changing Feather, back to those guys. Maybe it needs to change. But it's kept us alive, too. We're alive because we don't back down. There's a message in that, maybe."

In the end, Jourdain was reelected, the Republicans lost their elections, and the Democrats won (largely because of the support they received from Indians in northern Minnesota). There was no flotilla of angry fishermen. Citizens for Truth in Government has not been able to persuade the state of Minnesota or the federal government to change its attitude to Red Lake, which still exists on a government-to-government basis, as all sovereign nations relate to one another. Jerry Mueller appeared in Red Lake Tribal Court in October 2006. He probably felt the way Indians on the rez feel all the time: surrounded, outnumbered, and unloved by people different from himself. He argued his case, and his defense was based on "Officer, I didn't know and I'm sorry." He lost. He paid his fine, and if he has fished on Red Lake since then, he has probably stayed far away from the reservation boundary. Terry Maddy was wrong. Red Lake can have its fish and eat it, too.

Sean Fahrlander and his son Aatwe, 2009

2

"Just dump it in," Sean is saying to his brothers Marc and Mike. The light is fading, and the wind is coming strong off the big lake: Lake Mille Lacs. It's April, and the ice has retreated from the shore but the water is soupy with it. When the wind pushes the crushed ice up against the larger unbroken plates out in deeper water, it makes a raspy tinkling sound.

Sean is tall, with large hands, perfect for gripping nets. He was a basketball star in high school, joined the navy, and worked as an air traffic controller on an aircraft carrier. I don't know if the job was good for him. "You wouldn't have recognized me back then. My shit was squared away A-1 tight. I was *correct*. Everything in place. Not like now." Not like now. His hands shake ("Goddamn allergies," he says). He is nervous ("Goddamn steroids, they really fuck me up"). He is a little high-strung ("PTSD is a bitch, man, a real bitch"). He also talks a lot, more than most people and certainly more than most Indians. In a rush, his words tumble over themselves, each one apparently anxious to reach the finish line—your ears—before the next. He's an excellent ricer, and can fillet a walleye faster than anyone else I know. ("Talk to a Chippewa and you'll end up talking about two things: fish and beaver.") Be that as it may, Sean's the only Indian I know who is conversant on topics ranging from storytelling to how to tap a maple tree, the meaning of life, how to hit an alternator with a hatchet so it works, the design of the National Museum of the American Indian, *Meerkat Manor* on Animal Planet, ancient Greek warfare, what's wrong with Indians today, string theory, how to tell the best "drunk story," and Genghis Khan. I think the idea of *not* knowing something hasn't occurred to him yet. When you talk to Sean the conversation always finds its way back to Sean. He is, however, generous with his time and energy. Life is much better with him in it—and that's not something you can say about everyone. Once I bought a decrepit Airstream in Wisconsin. He helped me load it onto the back of a twenty-foot beavertail trailer. We got it strapped down and he looked at me sideways: "You'll never make it back to Minnesota alone. I'm going with you."

"How are you gonna get home?"

"Fuck if I know. Just let me run home and grab some underwear and I'm good to go."

He was right—I couldn't have done it without him.

Sean can find something funny in just about every encounter, and he has an agile mind. He's just over forty and his hair is receding a little and is peppered with gray. His laugh comes easily except when he's "in a mood," at which time he'll say, "Don't fucking talk to me, I'm in a mood." And so you don't.

"Fuck no, not yet. Got to fix this little bastard. Little bastard bounced off on the way over here. Little bastard. Fucking transducer." That's Mike, Sean's brother, as he tries to fix the fish-finder on the stern of his sixteen-foot Lund. "Little bastard" is his favorite phrase and he is free with it; he'll call everyone—white and Indian alike—a "little bastard" as often as he uses it to refer to fish and motors.

The wind pushes its way through our clothes. We're on Indian Point, on the west side of Lake Mille Lacs. It's getting dark but if I squint I can see the floats attached to other nets bouncing on the waves. No one else is setting, and the only light comes from the headlights of the reservation game warden's truck, staffed by two non-Indian reservation conservation officers, making sure we obey the letter of the law as spelled out in the agreement between the Mille Lacs Band and the state of Minnesota at the end of a decade-long legal battle. They are also protecting us from non-Indians who, until very recently, gathered at boat landings like this one and heckled Indians, spit on us, and held up signs that read "Save a Walleye, Spear an Indian" and—one of my favorites—"Indians Go Home."

The transducer on the fish-finder and depth gauge has broken off and Mike is still trying to rig it up right. His brother Marc, a large man with large strong hands wearing a SpongeBob stocking hat, leans out the door of his Ford F350. The Cummins diesel throbs under the hood. He takes his foot off the brake and the dually tires in the back inch down the ramp toward the lake.

"Just ditch the boat in the lake and let's go," says Marc. "It's getting dark."

"Yeah, fuck it, we don't need it. The water's like, what, six feet? We'll just go by the other floats," offers Sean.

"I installed this little bastard so we could be exact," says Mike. "I mean, like, exact. I didn't hump around and do all this shit just to guess. I want some fucking walleye. I want to get some of those slimy bastards in the net for sure."

Finally Mike fixes the transducer and hooks the fish locator up to the battery and they're ready: Marc slips his truck between the rocky banks and slams the brakes so the boat goes skipping off the trailer while Sean holds the bowline. The tires of the Ford churn rock and gravel as it climbs away from the landing, earth that has been churned by Indian tires and Indian feet for years with the same goal as the three brothers have: to net some walleye and feed their families. Marc walks back down from the truck and he and Sean and I get into the boat while Mike tries to push us off. But Marc must weigh at least 240 pounds and Sean 210, and the addition of my 170 pounds means that the small aluminum skiff is grounding out. Mike jumps into the lake up to his knees, heaves, and the boat is free, Marc yanks the engine to life and within minutes they are yelling and swearing and giving each other shit as they drop in their 100-foot net. The three brothers— all colorful speakers, all amazingly gifted with fine mechanical ability (Mike, a mason, can mentally calculate, down to the block, the number of cement blocks for the basements he builds, and Sean is a mean stonewright in his own way, too)—have gathered to net fish. Marc drove all the way from Colorado. He owns his own construction company, based in Colorado Springs. He comes back to Mille Lacs every spring to net walleye with his brothers and, this year, to hunt in the first Mille Lacs turkey season. The birds have made a comeback. He's brought along half a dozen calls, camo, inflatable decoys, and his shotguns—all brand new. Mike's come over from Brainerd, and Sean from Wisconsin. They are all Mille Lacs enrollees and they are back on the reservation none of them grew up on to net the fish that is theirs. "Why bother?" I ask as we're idling back near shore. "Why go to all the trouble for a few fish?"

"Well," Sean drawls, as he thinks it over, smoking, resting after the rush to get the net into the water: "Let me answer your question with another question: Why does a dog lick his dick?"

As the fish gather every spring, so does Sean's family—to visit, to hang out, to argue and fight, and to exercise their treaty rights. As I drove down to Mille Lacs to meet them it was hard not to notice how the place has changed since casinos. The roads were nice, and the houses tucked back into stands of old-growth maple and oak were spacious. The cars parked in the yards were quite new, tending toward Buicks and Chryslers. I made a wrong turn, missing the road to Sean's mother's house. Instead, I turned by the Vineland Indian Chapel, just below the water tower, emblazoned with the seal of the Mille Lacs Band of Ojibwe Indians—the state of Minnesota in outline, with an arrow passing through the heart of it, which is exactly where Mille Lacs is: a little bit north and west of Minneapolis. A few old shacks clung to the hilltop in the shadow of the water tower. They were falling in, the roof boards were rotted out, and tar paper was waving in the wind. All of them were small, none bigger than sixteen by twenty feet. I was surprised no one had burned them down. Maybe the tribe kept them standing to remind themselves of the hardships it had faced during the past century. Until recently the tribe had experienced the kind of Indian existence one usually thinks of, but worse.

Once I'd straightened myself out, I found myself on long, winding, suburban-feeling roads (with curbs and fire hydrants) that snaked back amid the maples. The new houses are enormous—three bedrooms, two baths, double attached garages—with vinyl siding and landscaping. All the streets have Ojibwe names: Noopiming Drive, Ziigwan Lane. The elders on Mille Lacs get their houses free. So do veterans, and there are many veterans at Mille Lacs.

Bonnie's house is creamy yellow, the second house on the right on a small cul-de-sac ending in a large swamp. Sean said I would see a small boat on a trailer in the driveway and another big boat parked out front. The big boat is a twenty-two-foot Bayliner with a waterskiing deck, a berth, and a sporty white canvas cover over the wheelhouse. Marc drove it up from Colorado, and since they had nothing else they used it to net the year before.

When I'd walked in the door I saw Sean and Marc wrestling on the living room floor. Marc outweighed Sean by at least forty pounds and had him on his back. Mike and their other brother, Jay; Marc's wife, Holly; and their mother, Bonnie, half-watched the wrestling match and half-watched *Ghost Rider*. The flames from Nicolas Cage's digitized skull licked Bonnie's enormous flat-screen TV. Bonnie barely seemed to notice that her sons, all in their forties, were trying to rub each other's faces in the carpet until finally Sean said, "I give! I give!" Marc wouldn't get off him till Bonnie said, "Let him up, Marc. You're hurting my little boy." Holly, pregnant, went into the kitchen to make some lunch.

Everything is big at Mille Lacs, except the reservation itself. A smattering of small parcels scattered over east central Minnesota, Mille Lacs is close to, but shies away from, Minneapolis and its crawling, clawing suburbs, which are eating up the nearby farmland. Mille Lacs Lake is huge: covering about 132,000 acres or 206 square miles, it is the second largest in the state and one of the largest in the United States. The Ojibwe name for the lake is Mizizaga'igan, "It Spreads All Over." The Sioux who lived there before the Ojibwe called it Mde Wakan, "Spirit Lake," and this is what the Dakota of Minnesota still call themselves, the Mdewakanton Sioux.

The lake was settled and contested, lost and won, many times before the Dakota and then the Ojibwe settled there. It has been continually inhabited for at least 9,000 years, a fact attested to by huge archaeological sites and a particularly impressive and perplexing altar composed of more than fifty bear skulls, uncovered during a highway expansion project.

The first European to see Lake Mille Lacs was a Franciscan priest, Father Louis Hennepin. In 1680 he was traveling, mapping, and baptizing his way through the region when he was taken captive by the

Dakota. He spent five months as a captive at Mille Lacs. During that time he described the lifestyle of and the region inhabited by his captors. He was struck by the wealth of the land and the people. One thing he noticed was that the Dakota, rather than living in tepees, built earthen lodges like those the Arikara and Mandan later adopted in the West.

Two hundred years later it was still possible to see what attracted the Dakota and why they fought so hard to keep the lake to themselves. The lake "lies imbedded in deep forests," wrote the Ojibwe historian William Warren in 1885. "Its picturesque shores are skirted with immense groves of valuable sugar maple, and the soil on which they grow is not to be surpassed in richness by any section of country in the northwest. The lake is nearly circular in form, though indented with deep bays, and the view over its waters broken here and there by bold promontories. It is about twenty miles across from shore to shore, and a person standing on its pebbly beach on a clear calm day, can but discern the blue outlines of the opposite side, especially as the country surrounding it is comparatively low and level. Its waters are clear and pure as the waters of Lake Superior, and fish of the finest species are found to abound therein. Connected with it is a string of marshy, or mud-bottomed, lakes in which the water is but a few feet deep, and wherein the wild rice of the north grows luxuriantly, and in the greatest abundance. Possessing these and other advantages, there is not a spot in the northwest which an Indian would sooner chose as a home and dwelling place, than Mille Lacs."

Legend has it (and it probably *is* only a legend) that the Dakota were driven from Mille Lacs because of a lovers' quarrel. Sometime in the 1600s a Dakota man and an Ojibwe man liked the same Dakota girl. The Dakota and Ojibwe had been fighting off and on for centuries, but during the time of this love triangle these tribes had been enjoying a lasting, if uneasy, peace. The girl chose the Ojibwe man, and the jealous Dakota lover killed him. This in itself didn't lead to war; as William Warren suggests, "it only reminded the warriors of the two tribes that they *had once been enemies*." Not long afterward, an Ojibwe chief from Fond du Lac, to the north, allowed his four sons to travel to the Dakota village at Mille Lacs to visit their Dakota friends. On their way back, one son was murdered. The remaining three brothers asked if they could go and visit again, and the father said yes: most likely, their brother had been killed by mistake. But another brother was killed on the second trip. They visited again. A third was killed. Only one brother was left, and he wanted to go again, despite the murders of his brothers. The weary father said sure, the three brothers had probably all been killed by mistake. Off went the fourth brother. He never returned. The father, overcome by grief, said to all who would listen, "An Ojibwe warrior never throws away his tears." He planned and plotted his revenge and two years later led a huge war party against the Dakota. The Ojibwe wiped out a number of small villages and the few Dakota survivors retreated to the main village on the big lake. The Ojibwe attacked again and instead of simply relying on the few guns they had and their bows and war clubs, they threw bags of gunpowder down the smoke holes in the Dakota lodges. Many hundreds of Dakota burned to death. The surviving Dakota gave up the lake and retreated west and south. However, it would be another 100 years before all the Dakota left northern and central Minnesota. The lake is as beautiful and rich today as it was when the lovers' quarrel set off that chain of events.

Mille Lacs is drained by the Rum River, named by early explorers with a sense of humor but still earlier known as Wakha' or "Spirit River." Many people now think of the name "Rum" as a pretty bad joke. Bogus Brook, a tributary of the Rum (which eventually flows into the Mississippi), is reputed to have been a backwater hideout for bootleggers during Prohibition. Many of the tourists who come to Mille Lacs in the summer are from Chicago. It is said that Al Capone had a house on Mille Lacs, and that he also had a hideout in Lac Courte Oreilles in Wisconsin and at Leech Lake, north of Mille Lacs. It is also said that he had an Indian mistress with whom he was very much in love; some say she was from Mille Lacs, others say she was from Lac Courte Oreilles, and still others say she was from Leech Lake. Everyone wants to claim Al Capone. The casino at Mille Lacs is called Grand Casino, and it is indeed big.

Despite (or perhaps because of) the abundance of natural resources Mille Lacs was almost a reservation that wasn't. In 1825, when representatives from Mille Lacs signed the Treaty of Prairie du Chien (along with about 1,000 other delegates from the Ho-Chunk, Sac, Fox, Menominee, Dakota, Iowa, and others), they were a force to be reckoned with. The meeting had been organized by the United States and was primarily a treaty not between it and the tribes but rather among the tribes themselves. The United States, having gained control of the area after the signing of the Treaty of Paris in 1783, no longer had to contend with the British. Now it had to deal with Indians. And at the time, Indians controlled the whole region. Trade and settlement were hampered by constant aggression between the Dakota and Ojibwe tribes along the Minnesota River, the dividing line between their territories. They fought over hunting and trapping rights—each anxious to control more resources than the other. The U.S. government was caught in the middle and feared that continued intertribal warfare would jeopardize the fur trade in the region and the trade routes through it. The United States was the supplicant; the Indian tribes were the power in place. The Treaty of Prairie du Chien established an uneasy peace between the warring tribes.

Circumstances, however, changed quickly on the frontier. By 1837 the fur trade was wobbling and about to crash. Animals such as the beaver, muskrat, and otter had been trapped to near-extinction within the domain of the Ojibwe in Wisconsin and Minnesota. The Ojibwe, still strong, still a powerful military force, looked east and saw more and more white settlers. They looked west and saw that the Dakota had adopted the horse, had colonized the plains, and were growing stronger. They were being squeezed, and there was nowhere the Ojibwe tribes in the Great Lakes region could expand their land base. Also, there were no caches of natural resources outside their control that they could bring under their control—no additional rice beds, maple groves, cranberry swamps, or untapped trapping grounds. Starvation was, for many, only a season away. The Ojibwe saw this, and when the United States wanted them to come to the treaty table again in 1837 they said yes. Chiefs from Leech Lake, Gull Lake, Swan River, St. Croix River, Lac Courte Oreilles, Lac de Flambeau, La Pointe, Mille Lacs, Sandy Lake, Snake River, Fond du Lac, and Red Lake all traveled to the town of St. Peter in present-day Minnesota. It was an impressive array of personalities and power. Present were the chiefs Flat Mouth, Elder Brother, Young Buffalo, Rabbit, Big Cloud, Hole in the Day, Strong Ground, White Fisher, Bear's Heart, Buffalo, Wet Mouth, Coming Home Hollering, Cut Ear, Wood Pecker, White Crow, Knee, The Dandy, White Thunder, Two Lodges Meeting, Rat's Liver, First Day, Both Ends of the Sky, Sparrow, Bad Boy, Big French-man, Spunk, Little Six, Lone Man, Loons Foot, and Murdering Yell. All of them were decked out in their finest attire and sported the scalps they'd won in battle and eagle feathers notched or colored depending on how they'd killed the enemy (bludgeoned, split down the middle, or stabbed). They brought warriors with them, armed with bows, guns, scalping knives, and war clubs. They entered singing. The white repre-sentatives brought maps, whiskey, and money and started talking.

The U.S. government presented its case: it would trade land for money. So while the bands who signed the treaty would give up, on paper, the right to establish villages or homes in large tracts of land including half of present-day Wisconsin and part of central Minnesota, they would retain the right to live in the region and hunt, fish, and trap within and to the entire extent of their former homelands. In addition the government promised to pay the bands the following, every year for twenty years:

$9,500, to be paid in money.

$19,000, to be delivered in goods.

$3,000 for establishing three blacksmith shops, supporting the blacksmiths, and furnishing them with iron and steel.

$1,000 for farmers, and for supplying them and the Indians with implements of labor, with grain or seed, and with whatever else might be necessary to enable them to carry on their agricultural pursuits.

$500 in tobacco.

This didn't seem like a bad deal as far as the chiefs were concerned. First, and most important to them, they were assured that they could hunt, fish, and trap as they had been doing, without interference or restriction. From the perspective of the chiefs it didn't seem that they were losing much of anything: they could still live, work, and travel within their homeland, and there was a financial bonus of twenty years during which they wouldn't want for much. This seemed to quell any concerns they had about the encroachment of whites from the east and the hard border with the Dakota tribes to the west. It seemed like a win-win for the Ojibwe, and they signed the treaty without being able to see the full ramifications of what they'd done. No mention was made of logging in the treaty. Little did they know that they would lose much and wouldn't regain much of it until more than 150 years later, by which time (according to the logic of the U.S. government) all the Indians should have been either assimilated or dead.

The tribes weren't able to see the full scope and importance of logging in their ceded territories, and there was no mention of it in the treaty. But the virgin white pine forests of the upper Mississippi would fuel the growth of Minnesota, Wisconsin, and Chicago for the next fifty years. And the United States wanted not just some of the pine but *all* of it.

Another point that the tribes involved didn't understand was a small but key phrase written into the treaty: "The privilege of hunting, fishing, and gathering the wild rice, upon the lands, the rivers and the lakes included in the territory ceded is guaranteed to the Indians, *during the pleasure* [emphasis added] of the President of the United States." The president whose pleasure was in question was Martin Van Buren, and as regards the treaty he left well enough alone. But presidents (and their pleasure) change. In 1850 Zachary Taylor canceled the clause in the treaty of 1837 by presidential order. Taylor had spent forty years in the military and seemed to quite like fighting and killing Indians. During the War of 1812 he defended a fort from an attack by Tecumseh. He fought Indians again during the Black Hawk War and was the one who accepted Chief Black Hawk's surrender. He fought Indians again in Florida during the Seminole Wars. It's hard to judge such matters, but it seems he had a low regard for life—he spent most of his own life taking away the lives of others. So it's no wonder he tried to do away with what few rights remained with the Mille Lacs Band.

The effect was disastrous. The Indians of the upper Mississippi, who had been living in relative security, suddenly saw the land drop away from them on all sides. It was as if they were now living on islands. They were told they had no rights to hunt, fish, or gather off their reservations. The vast forests of the northern United States were disappearing day by day. These were desperate times.

In the 1840s, on the heels of the 1837 treaty, the U.S. government tried to do to the Ojibwe north and east of Mille Lacs along Lake Superior what had been done to the Cherokee in North Carolina, Kentucky, Tennessee, Florida, and Alabama in the 1820s and 1830s: removal. And this was done for the same reasons. Large and valuable mineral deposits, mostly of copper and iron ore, had been discovered in the Lake Superior watershed, and the government wanted them. In 1850 President Zachary Taylor ordered the removal of the Ojibwe living near the ore deposits to new homes in the West. The ostensible reasons for removal were to prevent "injurious contact" between Indians and whites, to move the Indians out of the reach of whiskey traders, and try to concentrate the Ojibwe into one or two small areas so as to better "civilize" them.

Chief Buffalo and others tried to enable the Ojibwe to stay in their homeland and cited the treaty of 1842, which guaranteed them access to their land and the right to stay. In a cruel move, the governor of Minnesota Territory and the subagent for Indian affairs for northern Wisconsin moved the site for annuity payments and services (these included food, blankets, traps, and money) from La Pointe (present-day Madeline Island near Bayfield, Wisconsin) to Sandy Lake (just north of Mille Lacs). They did not provide any way for the Ojibwe of Wisconsin to get to Sandy Lake, a distance of 300 to 500 miles from Ojibwe settlements in the disputed area. Faced with starvation or death, the Ojibwe of Wisconsin paddled and walked to Sandy Lake, where the promised payments failed to appear. More than 630 Ojibwe men, women, and children starved, froze, and died of disease at Sandy Lake in the winter of 1851.

In part because of the callousness of this maneuver and also because of hard lobbying by various chiefs, the removal order was suspended. And in 1852 Chief Buffalo, then over ninety years old, led a delegation to Washington, D.C. He traveled by canoe and train for months until he reached Washington, where he presented President Millard Fillmore with a list of grievances. Fillmore had become president after

Taylor died of gastroenteritis; the best thing that ever happened to the Wisconsin Ojibwe might be that Taylor died of stomach flu—a fitting disease after so many Indians had suffered similar deaths. Fillmore, who grew up in poverty, the second of nine children, was much more sympathetic to Indians than Taylor had been. He agreed with Chief Buffalo's claims, and promised that annuities would be paid in Wisconsin rather than at Sandy Lake. Chief Buffalo would not agree to Fillmore's terms until permanent reservations had been established in Wisconsin for his people. Fillmore agreed. Permanent reservations were made for the Mississippi and Lake Superior Ojibwe bands. Other rights were included in the treaty as well—these bands would have the right to hunt, fish, and gather up to 100 percent of the available resources in order to maintain a modest standard of living within the treaty area. This, in effect, gave them an easement to all the land of northwestern Wisconsin and northeastern Minnesota, regardless of what happened to that land later. Fillmore's last words before dying—directed at his soup—were the same sentiments expressed by the Ojibwe chiefs he treated with so fairly: "The nourishment is palatable."

The Mille Lacs Band went back to the table again in 1855 and signed another treaty with the government, trying to salvage what it could of its rights and sovereignty. The band members were guaranteed 60,000 acres at the southern end of Mille Lacs Lake. But while they were assured a homeland on the southern portion of the lake, the north half was opened to logging—and the loggers weren't necessarily willing to stop at the reservation boundary. Then 1862 arrived.

To the south of Mille Lacs, along the Minnesota River, the old dividing line between Dakota and Ojibwe tribes, the former enemies of the Ojibwe were experiencing similar difficulties. More and more white settlers were creeping into the fertile Minnesota River valley with the encouragement of the U.S. government. Just as to the north loggers were claiming more and more forest, farmers were squatting

in larger numbers in Dakota territory. The Dakota were facing starvation. The promises made by the U.S. government regarding treaty
annuities and food had proved empty. There is some disagreement
about whether the conflict was a spontaneous development or a strategic decision. Either way, the Dakota, having had enough and realiz-
ing that the United States was tied up in a war with the Confederacy,
which the Union might very well lose, decided it was time to kick all
the whites out of their territories. Such was the situation when, on
August 17, 1862, a Dakota foraging party attacked a farm near Acton,
Minnesota. Three men and two women were killed.

The Dakota quickly convened their leaders, who decided that the
settlers and the U.S. Army would be sure to come down on them. So
they went on the offensive, with the Dakota chief Little Crow in the
lead. The next day, August 18, a party of Dakota warriors attacked the
Lower Sioux Indian Agency near Redwood Falls, killed all those present, and took control of the agency. A relief party had been sent from
Fort Ridgely. The Dakota surprised them and killed them all. Attacks
continued over the next week. Fort Ridgely was besieged and the settlement of New Ulm was attacked. New Ulm was so badly burned
that the residents who survived the attack fled. The Dakota killed all
the men they encountered—settlers and soldiers alike—and took the
women and children captive. General Sibley sallied forth from Fort
Snelling at the head of a contingent of 1,400 soldiers. They chased
Little Crow up the Minnesota River and a standoff ensued. Meanwhile, some Ojibwe bands, mostly Pillager Band warriors from Leech
Lake, decided to lend support to the Dakota and swept down from
the north.

But not all Dakota or Ojibwe thought war was a good idea. Some
Dakota near Shakopee didn't fight, and many protected their white
neighbors. Likewise, the Ojibwe at Mille Lacs decided that they would
not join the Pillagers. What's more, they refused to let the Pillagers

pass through their territories and sent them back north, thereby protecting their neighbors. The Dakota and Ojibwe who refused to fight might have done so out of neighborliness and out of self-interest, feeling that their relatives would be defeated and judgment would be harsh. They were, and it was.

When the conflict was over, between 400 and 800 whites were dead, along with many more Dakota. It was the largest loss of civilian life as the result of a "foreign attack" on U.S. soil until the attacks on the World Trade Center on September 11, 2001. Three hundred Dakota warriors were sentenced to death. Eventually thirty-eight were hanged at Mankato, in what was the largest mass execution in the history of the United States. In the wake of the conflict the U.S. government abrogated all of its treaty obligations to the Dakota in Minnesota, and a conflict that began because of hardship led the Dakota to a century of the most abject living conditions on the margins of American life during a time of unprecedented prosperity among their white neighbors. Some of the Mdewakanton Dakota near Shakopee who hadn't been removed and the Mille Lacs Band of Ojibwe seemed to fare well: during subsequent rounds of treaties they were each given assurances of their continued existence and land as a payment for their noninvolvement in the violence of the preceding year. As for Little Crow, he was shot by a white farmer near Hutchinson, Minnesota, on July 3, 1863, while picking raspberries. His skeleton and scalp were put on public display in St. Paul, Minnesota, until 1971, when they were repatriated to his grandson.

But the assurances and land that both bands received were short-lived. Business as usual resumed shortly. The Department of the Interior authorized private companies to cut timber on Mille Lacs Reservation, against the terms of the treaty Mille Lacs had signed with the U.S. government. Five years later they were still cutting, and white settlers had begun farming the areas that had been cut over. Mille Lacs

Band members complained to the government, to no avail. This tension continued until the Nelson Act turned land held in common by many tribes into smaller parcels allotted to individual band members, with the "extra" parcels given to white lumber companies and farmers. Many Indians lost their allotments because they were not educated about such things as loans and tax forfeiture. Many from Mille Lacs were removed to the newly established White Earth Reservation to the west.

The story of relations between Indians and whites in the Midwest and West during the early nineteenth century is a story of war: armed conflict, forced removals, and death marches. Whatever lessons the federal government might have gleaned from the Seven Years' War and the French and Indian War—that Indian tribes were powerful and could mount powerful resistance to white encroachment, and that even if weak, they were better dealt with at the negotiating table—seemed to have been forgotten. But as bloody as Indian history was in nineteenth century, during the twentieth century the warfare waged between Indians and whites was of a quieter kind—instead of guns the combatants carried petitions; instead of scalps, people held aloft legal briefs.

In 1902 government representatives traveled to Mille Lacs to negotiate an agreement with the Mille Lacs Band for damages done to the reservation and its citizens during the timber grabs over the preceding fifty years. The negotiations were a disaster. Many from Mille Lacs emerged from the meetings convinced that the government would never give them justice. Disgusted, they moved their families to White Earth. But a few, led by chiefs Migizi, Shabashkung, and Wadena, held on and refused to move. They paid the price: in 1901 a posse lead by the local sheriff attacked the village at Mille Lacs, burned all the shacks and wigwams to the ground, rounded up all the villagers, and chased them out so a developer could claim the land. It took another three years for Chief Migizi to get promises of redress (in the form of forty-acre lots for the band members) from Congress, and another twelve years for the lots to be assigned. By then Congress decided that forty-acre lots were too big. Most of the Indians who stayed in Mille Lacs got five-acre land patents instead.

And there they remained: penniless, without support, without the hope of fair treatment. While the lake itself became a destination for vacationers from Minneapolis and Chicago, the Mille Lacs Band members who had endured broken promises, and every sort of indignity and violence, hid and huddled in the woods nearby.

A newspaper article in the *Minnesota Star* dated Monday, March 27, 1939 (alongside a dire front-page article about the Germans), shows that the twentieth century hadn't been kind to Mille Lacs. "A century ago the Chippewa Indians roamed the plains and forests of Minnesota lord of all he surveyed. Today, in a squalid settlement near Isle, Minn., near Lake Mille Lacs, 60 members of that once famed tribe attempt to eke out an existence on a rocky, 40-acre hillside unfit for cultivation. Their settlement consists of 11 tarpaper shacks, many of them floorless. Most of them cook, eat and sleep in the same room. Their total income is about $414 a month, or around $7 apiece." Within two years twenty-five Mille Lacs Indians would be serving in every theater of World War II—Guam, Iwo Jima, North Africa, Italy, and later Normandy and Belgium—while at home their families were starving. By contrast, though life was hardly easy for them, the Indians who agreed to move to White Earth Reservation (from reservations in Minnesota, North Dakota, and Wisconsin) had schools, businesses, homesteads, and their own newspaper. But that door closed in the 1920s—even if they'd wanted to, those from Mille Lacs and elsewhere couldn't have moved to White Earth any longer and received any kind of allotments or assistance. Even so, fifty years later the move to White Earth seemed to many to be not that bad an idea.

Sean's family bears the mark of each and every one of the cataclysmic shifts that make up the story of Mille Lacs Reservation. In the 1880s, during the allotment period when Mille Lacs Indians were encouraged to move to the newly established White Earth Reservation, many left. There were promises of homesteads, farming equipment, seeds, blacksmith shops, schools, and churches. All of these were fine incentives. White Earth also provided a fresh start. Sean's great-grandfather John Shingobee (southern Ojibwe for spruce) didn't leave Mille Lacs, but John's brother Tom did. "Some say there was an argument about a trapline," explained Sean. "They say Tom might have killed a man. Others say it was over a woman. Maybe you should just say 'There were reasons to leave' and leave it at that." Tom's daughter Josephine was Sean's grandmother. Tom Hill was the first chief at Mille Lacs elected under the Indian Reorganization Act (IRA) government in 1934. He was hit by a train on the way to a ceremony at Lake Lena. By the time Sean's mother, Bonnie, was born to Frank Shingobee and Josephine Hill, times were tough. Josephine was left to raise her children on her own. She drank a lot. The county nurse and missionaries interceded, took Bonnie away from her, and moved to White Earth to start a mission. So even though that branch of the family didn't relocate, Bonnie ended up at White Earth anyway. And it was there at White Earth, and Minneapolis and Duluth, that she raised her eight children—John, Dawn, Denise, Dana, Jay, Marc, Sean, and Mike. Bonnie didn't live at Mille Lacs until she came there to work at the casino in the late 1990s. Her children grew up mostly at White Earth.

⁂

It's fair to say that most Indians didn't know about the treaty rights they had for the first half of the twentieth century. Until 1934 most reservations were still controlled by the Bureau of Indian Affairs (BIA),

Indian agents, and missions. Tribal government was often a matter of coping with unilateral federal policy—gradual, democratic change was a luxury that most tribal governments didn't have. On many reservations that had been allotted and fractured by the Nelson Act and the Dawes Act and opened up to white business interests, such as logging and mining, Indians struggled to survive. With Indian boarding schools in place, Indian parents didn't even have control over the destiny of their children, much less an understanding of or energy to fight for their treaty rights. Nor did Indians even have their own lawyers. The county nurse, social workers, missionaries, and Indian agents occupied their attention, as did the constant search for food on a dwindling land base. Life was largely an issue of mean survival until 1934.

With the passage of the Indian Reorganization Act (IRA) in 1934, constitutional government came to many reservations. The IRA, also known as the Wheeler-Howard Act, is considered by some to be the most significant piece of legislation for Indians in the twentieth century. It signaled and made concrete a major shift in Indian policy. Its primary architects were John Collier and Felix Cohen. When the borderline socialist Collier was appointed commissioner of Indian Affairs by Franklin Delano Roosevelt in 1933, things began to change, if only temporarily, for Indians. He had strong pro-Indian opinions, formed after visiting Taos pueblo in 1920; he referred to it as a "Red Atlantis" because of the ways in which the individual was served and meshed with the political structure. It was a happy, perfect place in Collier's mind. Collier wrote passionately about his plans for Indian renewal:

> In all our colorful American life there is no group around which there so steadfastly persists an aura compounded of glamour, suspicion, and romance as the Indian. For generations the Indian has been, and is today, the center of an amazing series of wonderings, fears, legends, hopes.

Yet those who have worked with Indians know that they are neither the cruel, warlike, irreligious savages imagined by some, nor are they the "fortunate children of nature's bounty" described by tourists who see them for an hour at some glowing ceremonial. We find the Indians, in all the basic forces and forms of life, human beings like ourselves. . . . Just as we yearn to live out our own lives in our own ways, so, too, do the Indians, in their ways.

For nearly 300 years white Americans, in our zeal to carve out a nation made to order, have dealt with the Indians on the erroneous, yet tragic, assumption that the Indians were a dying race—to be liquidated. We took away their best lands; broke treaties, promises; tossed them the most nearly worthless scraps of a continent that had once been wholly theirs. But we did not liquidate their spirit. The vital spark which kept them alive was hardy. So hardy, indeed, that we now face an astounding, heartening fact. . . . No longer can we, with even the most generous intentions, pour millions of dollars and vast reservoirs of energy, sympathy, and effort into any unproductive attempts at some single, artificial permanent solution of the Indian problem. No longer can we naively talk of or think of the "Indian problem." Our task is to help Indians meet the myriad of complex, interrelated, mutually dependent situations which develop among them according to the very best light we can get on those happenings—much as we deal with our own perplexities and opportunities.

We, therefore, define our Indian policy somewhat as follows: So productively to use the moneys appropriated by the Congress for Indians as to enable them, on good, adequate lands of their own, to earn decent livelihoods and lead self-respecting, organized lives in harmony with their own aims and ideals, as an integral part of American life. Under such a policy, the ideal end result will be the ultimate disappearance of any need for government aid or supervision. This will not happen tomorrow; perhaps not in our lifetime. . . .

In looking at the Indian picture as a social whole, we will consider certain broad phases—land use and industrial enterprises, health and education, roads and rehabilitation, political organization —which touch Indian life everywhere, including the 30,000 natives of Alaska for whose health, education, and social and economic advancement the Indian Service is responsible. Lastly, this report will tell wherein the Indian Service, or the government's effort as a whole for the Indians, still falls short.

So intimately is all of Indian life tied up with the land and its utilization that to think of Indians is to think of land. The two are inseparable. Upon the land and its intelligent use depends the main future of the American Indian. . . . A major aim, then, of the Indian Service is to help the Indians to keep and consolidate what lands they now have and to provide more and better lands upon which they may effectively carry on their lives. Just as important is the task of helping the Indian make such use of his land as will conserve the land, insure Indian self-support, and safeguard or build up the Indian's social life. . . .

In 1887, the General Allotment Act was passed, providing that after a certain trust period, fee simple title to parcels of land should be given to individual Indians. Individual proprietorship meant loss— a paradox in view of the Indian's love for the land, yet an inevitable result, when it is understood that the Indian by tradition was not concerned with possession, did not worry about titles or recordings, but regarded the land as a fisherman might regard the sea, as a gift of nature, to be loved and feared, to be fought and revered, and to be drawn on by all as an inexhaustible source of life and strength.

The Indian let the ownership of his allotted lands slip from him. The job of taking the Indian's lands away, begun by the white man through military expeditions and treaty commissions, was completed by cash purchase—always of course, of the best lands which the Indian had left. In 1887, the Indian had remaining 130 million acres. In 1933, the Indian had left only 49 million acres, much of it waste and desert.

Since 1933, the Indian Service has made a concerted effort—an effort which is as yet but a mere beginning—to help the Indian to build back his landholdings to a point where they will provide an adequate basis for a self-sustaining economy, a self-satisfying social organization.

Collier's missive was bold and poetic and changed reservations forever. The Wheeler-Howard Act effectively put a stop to the loss of land through allotment and unfair land-sale practices, closed down the boarding school phase of Indian education in the United States, and returned the rule of reservation and tribal life to Indian hands. Called the "Indian New Deal," the IRA ushered in an era of self-determination and self-rule. As part of the Wheeler-Howard Act, the IRA encouraged the formation of tribal constitutions. Still, the IRA was largely scripted by the BIA. The constitutions adopted by many different tribes (despite large cultural and historical differences) were either provided by the BIA or drafted in response to a list of suggestions provided by the BIA. One hundred eighty-one tribes voted to accept the IRA; 77 voted to reject it. If tribes wished to adopt the IRA they were obligated to let tribal councils employ legal counsel, get a majority vote from the tribe before agreeing to any major land sales, and officially authorize the elected tribal council to deal on a government-to-government basis with local, state, and federal authorities. These new tribal constitutions established a governing council (elected district representatives; basic election rules; the process by which to choose a chairman, secretary, treasurer, etc.) that seems quasi-corporate and quasi-municipal. Many of these constitutions have similar, and tragic, flaws—no separation or balance of powers, no judiciary, nothing resembling a bill of rights. Ironically, the author of the IRA was a passionate advocate of Indian rights, a young lawyer named Felix Cohen, whose book *Handbook of Federal Indian Law* is something akin to a bible among Indian law professionals and students. Cohen recognized that "tribal constitutions, after all, are not an innovation of the New Deal. The history of Indian constitutions goes back at least to the Gayanashakgowah (Great Binding Law) of the Iroquois Confederacy, which probably dates from the 15th century. . . . So, too, we have the written constitutions of the Creek, Cherokee, Choctaw, Chickasaw, and Osage nations, printed usually on tribal printing presses, constitutions which were in force during the decades from 1830 to 1900." Yet, despite his own knowledge, Cohen drafted the IRA and made suggestions for tribal constitutions along the lines of local government. Tribal governments "were to be like town governments, except that they would have federal protection and their special rights." The political science professor David Wilkins notes that the bibliography for Felix Cohen's article on tribal constitution refers more than seventy-five times to matters such as "city planning," "health and sanitation," and "licenses." No wonder early tribal constitutions have a municipal feel. There is little or no discussion of treaty rights—the very issue that would come to occupy a large part of the discussion of Indians and reservations in the late twentieth century. Treaty rights lay dormant because they were not a part of the general restructuring of tribal government and because many reservation populations, including those at Mille Lacs, had been treated so poorly for so long that few pressed for their treaty rights. They were certainly not something BIA officials and traders and lumbermen were keen on reminding Indians about, either. But then, after tribal governments began running their own show and

84

deviating from the BIA script in the 1950s, and after the civil rights movement and the American Indian movement of the late 1960s and early 1970s, people began wondering what their rights were, not just as Americans but as Indians.

And then Fred and Mike Tribble decided to test the limits of those rights. In the winter of 1974 the Tribble brothers, members of Lac Courte Oreilles Ojibwe reservation in northern Wisconsin, stepped off the reservation where it cut through the middle of Chief Lake. They cut a hole in the ice and began spearing fish. They had informed the Wisconsin Department of Natural Resources (WDNR) of their intention to spear fish before they left, and the WNDR was there to greet them. The Tribbles were arrested, as many Ojibwe had been arrested for game and fish violations in the past and as other Indian activists in Washington state and Michigan were as well: to deliberately create a test case for their rights. Then they sued the head of the WDNR, Lester Voight. They claimed that the treaty rights secured by Chief Buffalo had never been extinguished. The right to hunt and fish by whatever means necessary wherever necessary was a property right secured by their ancestors, and they were the heirs to it. Other Ojibwe from adjacent reservations in Wisconsin joined the fight for both on-reservation and off-reservation treaty rights. In 1978 Judge Doyle of the Federal District Court ruled against the Ojibwe of Wisconsin. Meanwhile the Ojibwe continued to fish. White protesters formed the action committees Stop Treaty Abuse Wisconsin (STA/W) and Protect America's Rights and Resources (PARR), and they networked to prevent Indians from exercising their treaty rights. Dean Crist, who owned a pizza shop in Minocqua, Wisconsin, and was one of the founders of STA/W, began selling Treaty Beer and funneling the proceeds into STA/W. The newly elected governor of Wisconsin, Tommy Thompson (later secretary of health and human services under George W. Bush), addressed STA/W and PARR in Wausau and said that he supported them, that he thought the treaties were wrong, and that he'd fight against the treaties. Doyle's ruling was appealed in 1983 and the 7th District U.S. Court of Appeals overturned it. The appeals court ruled clearly and decisively that when the Ojibwe in Wisconsin signed the treaties with the federal government they in no way relinquished their off-reservation hunting, fishing, and gathering rights. Wisconsin appealed but the U.S. Supreme Court declined to hear the case. The case was settled in 1985, when the 7th District Court ruled that the Ojibwe in Wisconsin had retained the right to hunt and fish anywhere within the territory they had ceded, even on private land.

With their rights affirmed, tribes in Wisconsin began fishing in earnest. Lac du Flambeau Reservation became a hot spot, and boat landings where Ojibwe fishermen were exercising their treaty rights became battlegrounds. On April 26, 1987, at the boat landing on Butternut Lake, thirty miles west of Lac du Flambeau, protesters opposed to the treaties began throwing rocks at Ojibwe fishermen. A few hundred protesters had gathered at the landing as the fishermen set out at dusk. By the time they got back sometime before midnight there were about 500 protesters at the landing. They heaved fist-size rocks over the heads of the state police and conservation officers who were there to protect the Indians. "We were backed up against the water," remembered the tribal leader Tom Maulson, an advocate of the treaties. "That cop from town was saying to the protesters that it was an illegal gathering, an unlawful gathering, and those guys were telling him to get fucked and that they were going to kill us."

"Save a Walleye ... Spear an Indian" became the rallying cry for the many non-Indians who gathered at boat landings to protest against Indians' fishing rights. Indians in Wisconsin were subjected to almost continuous harassment. Fishermen (and -women) were shot at. When "Save a Walleye—Spear an Indian" wore out, protesters got more creative: "Save Two Walleye—Spear a Pregnant Indian" appeared on bumper stickers. In 1987 Bruce Currie and his friend Pat Coughlin of Solon Springs, Wisconsin, set off two pipe bombs at boat landings. No one was injured, but both Currie and Coughlin were convicted and sent to prison. After his conviction Currie said, "I'm not prejudiced against Indians. . . . I don't know them. . . . They don't know me. . . . I'm not an Indian hater. . . . We were just goofing around with it." One man, Wayne Valliere, remembered, "I would find the loudest one [protester] and walk right up to him and let him know that I wasn't afraid of him. They would think, 'This guy is crazy,' and they would quiet down. You can't be afraid of them. My wife was spit on. I took out my handkerchief and wiped it off her face. I wanted to gut that guy just like a deer. I usually carried my hunting knife with me and it's razor sharp. I could gut him pretty quick." Indians from Lac Courte Oreilles, Flambeau, Bad River, and Red Cliff kept fishing, but children weren't allowed to go out at night.

Eventually the furor died down. Biological surveys and studies showed, conclusively, that off-reservation spearfishing had no large or lasting effect on walleye populations and so tourism wouldn't suffer in any way. Dean Crist and STA/W along with several county sheriffs were convicted in a federal civil rights case: the prosecution claimed they had violated the civil rights of Wisconsin Ojibwe when they tried to prevent the Ojibwe from fishing. Crist was ordered to pay $275,000 in legal fees on behalf of the people he had wronged. Many turned away in distaste from the whole issue because of the ugly racism that had marked the conflict. And, in a turnaround, many people who had protested against the treaties came together with Ojibwe activists in Wisconsin to protest against the development of the Crandon Mine near Crandon, Wisconsin, and Mole Lake Indian Reservation. The Crandon Mine is one of very few sites in the United States (and certainly the largest of them) that contain metallic sulfide. One by-product of metallic-sulfide mining is sulfuric acid. Afraid that the mining and ore-processing waste would damage the environment and walleye fisheries in northern Wisconsin, Indians and sport fishermen banded together to fight it. In 2003, funded largely by casino profits, the Sokaogon Ojibwe and Forest Potawatomi bought the mine for $16.5 million and closed it down.

From 1974, when the Tribbles first speared a fish, to the early 1990s, when most of the trouble over treaties in Wisconsin died down, many tribes around the country followed the example of the Wisconsin Ojibwe. Treaty rights (both on-reservation rights and off-reservation rights reserved explicitly in treaties) were pressed in Washington and Oregon regarding whaling and the salmon harvest. In Michigan claims were made for commercial fishing rights in the Great Lakes. Tribes in the southwest fought for access to sacred sites and fought against the commercial development of sacred mountains, such as Mount Graham in Arizona. Water rights and hunting and fishing rights were argued in and out of court. Not every tribe was as successful at securing its rights as the Wisconsin Ojibwe, but many were.

The Mille Lacs Band, closely allied to the Ojibwe Indians at Lac Courte Oreilles, Lac du Flambeau, and St. Croix (they were all signatories of the 1837 and 1854 treaties), saw what their relatives to the east had achieved and, marshaling their resources, made a similar claim for their own treaty rights in 1990. The Mille Lacs—enduring, patient, and stubborn—sued the state of Minnesota. The basis of their suit was that the state was violating their treaty rights by interfering with their hunting, fishing, and gathering rights. It took four years for the District Court of Minnesota to affirm Mille Lacs treaty rights. A wonder: Indians had won again. The state appealed to the 8th Circuit Court of Appeals.

Around this time Sean's mother, Bonnie, moved back to Mille Lacs. She got a job at the casino and later at the tribal museum. Sean followed her to Mille Lacs.

He had been working and living farther north. In the mid-1990s he was the cultural coordinator for the Northwest Juvenile Center: "I'd been working at the Northwest Juvenile for a while, what was it? Three years, from 1995 to 1998. So while I was working with the kids there in Bemidji I started going down to Mille Lacs. My mom was living there then. And I'd never met any of my mother's people. I knew I had a slew of uncles and aunts that I never knew. And so, around 1995, I was following the Cass Lake football team real close, they were having a great season, doing really good. And besides—I'd quit drinking and that's where all the sober people were. They went to watch football and basketball and shit like that. And I went down to Pine River for a regional match. I was just watching the game and the ref comes up to me and he says: 'I know we never met. And you're too young to be him but you look just like my best friend from high school.' Who? 'Ken Shingobee. From down at Mille Lacs.' Anyway, so I went to go find him. They were never lost, you know. I was. I was the one who was lost. That began a period of discovery, of rediscovery, for myself. And I went to the drum ceremonies down there. And popped in here and there. Wherever I went down there people recognized me because I looked like old Tom Shingobee and Kenny, too. And that PR job opened up at Mille Lacs and so I moved down there for that. I got to wear a suit and go to meetings and travel around. It was fun. This was 1998. They hadn't resolved that fishing case yet. The decision came down in 1999, but people were fishing. I'd grown up fishing—at the resort in Cass Lake where I was fostered and with Warren, setting nets. I knew a lot about fish."

While he was at Mille Lacs Sean saw the controversy around fishing and hunting, and having learned to net walleye with his adopted family on Leech Lake he thought about getting involved. Between 1990, when Mille Lacs filed suit, and 1999, when the suit was settled, it was a tense time. The Supreme Court had refused to hear the Wisconsin treaty rights case—in its opinion the court of appeals had issued a definitive verdict. But it chose to hear the Mille Lacs case and ruled five to four in favor of the Mille Lacs Band of Ojibwe. The reasoning was much the same as in the case in Wisconsin: the Ojibwe had never relinquished their off-reservation treaty rights spelled out in the 1837 treaty; and the state of Minnesota and the Mille Lacs Band of Ojibwe were ordered to work out limits, quotas, and seasons together. Before the ruling came down everyone was afraid that Mille Lacs boat landings would look just like those in Wisconsin—packed with Indian-hating protesters. As the case wound its way up the chain, Mille Lacs opened up its first casino in 1991 and, later, a second casino in Hinckley. Given that Mille Lacs was close to both Duluth and Minneapolis, the casinos began making money almost immediately. The money helped buffer the band from the actions of their white neighbors and bought them some measure of protection in the form of lawyers, influence, police, and conservation. Among other things, it eventually bought a bank. In 1996, when the elected tribal officials tried to get bonded by Onamia Bank (bonding is necessary by law in order to receive antipoverty funds), they were refused. Within a decade they bought the bank that had turned them away, along with one other bank and a holding company.

Casino money brought a lot of the twentieth century to Mille Lacs in a rush. It brought paved roads; modern housing; a new clinic; elder housing; a tribal school; and a museum planned, operated, and staffed in partnership with the Minnesota Historical Society. It also brought a great legal team and almost unlimited resources to the battle the Mille Lacs people were fighting to recover their treaty rights. They hired teams of lawyers, many of them with experience and expertise gained from working on similar cases in Michigan and Washington state. Indians hadn't begun the fight to restore rights in court in the 1970s or the 1990s: the Cherokees had fought for this as far back as the 1820s. But lawyers and deep pockets wouldn't necessarily do the trick. This wasn't the early 1970s. Public sentiment and court disposition were different. These were no longer entirely liberal times. Reagan and Bush had done their best to stack the courts. The Senate was Republican even if Clinton was not. The social climate was also different. Resort owners and anti-treaty groups (all of whom professed to be "pro-Indian" but anti-treaty because, according to them, treaties weren't "fair" and actually hurt Indians) formed a strong opposition to Mille Lacs. The Mille Lacs Band wasn't sure of a good outcome and was afraid that if it lost it would lose everything. So in 1993 Mille Lacs proposed a kind of settlement like those that had been negotiated at other reservations in the 1970s and 1980s. At that time, tribes for whom off-reservation hunting and fishing weren't as important as they were for Indians from Lac du Flambeau and Lac Courte Oreilles opted to lease some of their treaty rights. That is, in exchange for money, typically a percentage of sales from state hunting and fishing licenses and of gas and cigarette taxes, they agreed not to exercise those rights or not to press them in court. Mille Lacs proposed a similar settlement, but the resort owners, sport fishermen, and anti-treaty warriors (such as the Minnesota Vikings' former head coach Bud Grant) leaned on the legislature and the proposal was killed. Its opponents were certain of victory and wanted to leave Mille Lacs with nothing. So once again Mille Lacs stood firm. Once again the band members refused to move. And once again, they won. In 1999 the Supreme Court handed down a decision in favor of the Mille Lacs treaty rights. The vote was five to four. The court affirmed that Mille Lacs had the right to hunt, fish, and gather both on and off the reservation (but within the treaty area set aside in 1837) in order to maintain a "modest standard of living."

Working with the state, the Mille Lacs Band continued policing its own members, issuing permits, and setting harvest levels.

The casinos continued to make money hand over fist. The band bought more land and hired more conservation officers. And the fishermen and anti-treaty people who fought so hard at Mille Lacs often stayed in the casino and resorts owned by the band. It was a sweet victory: the fishermen slept in Indian beds, ate Indian food, stared out of Indian windows, bought Indian gasoline, and watched as Indian fishermen practiced age-old methods of gathering fish—with nets and spears.

Sean has a different theory about racism in Minnesota (he has a lot of theories about a lot of things). "One thing I've got to say," he practically shouted over the phone. "The rednecks in Minnesota are more subtle than those Wisconsin rednecks. There was never any of that overt stuff when we were fishing at Mille Lacs. Down there it was like how it was in Cass Lake when I was growing up. No one said much overt. It was kind of live and let live—maybe because the people in Minnesota are better Christians than in Wisconsin or wherever. But it was still there. You knew it when they looked at you. They looked at you and you knew what they were thinking: you were less. In their eyes you were less. I remember one time. I had been away in the service for a year. I'd done basic and went to my A school and was doing air traffic control on an aircraft carrier. I'd been at sea for six months. I saw combat in the Mediterranean. I had a major attitude. I mean, Christ, I just spent six months on a boat with five thousand other guys. Anyway, so I went home and me and some high school buddies from Cass Lake went into Bemidji to shoot some pool and drink and whatnot. I go in there and I'm shooting pool, just shooting pool with my buddies. We're out of beer so I walk up the bar to get another pitcher and there's these two guys sitting there. I walk up to the bar and there's these two red- necks. If you saw them you'd know what I mean: jeans, logging boots, those Red Wing boots, thick wallets sticking out of their pockets, and honest to God both had flannel shirts on (I shit you not), and three days' beard. So I step forward to try and reach the bar and they close in, lean into each other. I try to walk around to the left and the guy on the left leans to the left. I say OK and walk to the right and the guy on the right leans that way. By now I'm pissed. They're big boys, big redneck boys. But I'm in a mood. I mean shit: I was solid, topped off at about two hundred twenty, hard, you know. At sea there's nothing to do but eat, shit, sleep, work, and lift. I step right between them with my arms real narrow. I reach the bar and I pop my elbows out and knock those fuckers right off their stools, both of them. And then I order a pitcher. They're picking themselves up and saying, 'What the fuck? What the fuck is your problem?' And I say, 'What the fuck is *your* problem?' And then they say: 'Why don't you guys go to one of them Indian bars?' And I was like: That's fucking it. I wasn't about to take that shit, not after serving in the military and in combat (and besides I had a fair amount of alcohol in me). My buddies looked up from the pool table (I won't name them because they are now persons of importance over in Leech Lake, but you know who they are). I threw down the pitcher and we started in. And my one buddy said, 'Sean, holy shit! We got to get out of here!' Eventually I had one of those guys from the bar out on the street. I had him pinned against the curb and was pounding the shit out of him right there in the street. But my buddy pulled me off and we ran down the alley and sat out the rest of the night at Keg-N-Cork, down in the basement so the cops wouldn't see us. We didn't get caught. But that's how the racism was, you know? Subtle like that."

Sean stated his theories about racism in a nutshell, a coconut shell: "It was subtle like that in the military, too. It was the strangest thing: when I got on board, there's five thousand guys. And I'm working with this other air traffic controller, his name was Mike Jenkins. Strangest fucking thing: here we are halfway around the world, on a boat, working the same job. And he's from Deer River and I'm from Cass Lake. He's Indian. I'm Indian. Both his parents spoke Ojibwe. We grew up thirty miles apart but never knew each other. They called him Little Chief, which pissed him off. They started calling me Big Chippewa. That lasted about two hours. And then they noticed I didn't give a shit so they stopped. It wasn't any fun. I told them: there's a boundary you can't cross. I just ain't going to put up with any shit. I told them: I'll follow the rules and report your shit to the superior officer. We can do it that way. Or, if not, I won't follow the rules and it'll be just me and you and we can deal with it that way. Your choice. This was around the time that that one Indian guy, a marine, sold secrets to the Russians. You remember that?"

I did not. I checked it out. And just in case you think Sean was making stuff up: Clayton Lonetree, Winnebago and Navajo, was a U.S. Marine stationed in Moscow at the American embassy. He enlisted in the Marine Corps in 1980 and entered the Marine Corps Security Battalion Guard school, a rigorous, elite training program in which he was instructed in espionage and counterespionage techniques. Lonetree was given top secret security clearance and was assigned to the U.S. embassy in Moscow in 1984. While working as an embassy guard he was entrapped by a Soviet officer named Violetta Seina, whose cover was that of a translator and secretary in the embassy. Sources interviewed later acknowledged that she was a "presence"—five foot nine, with gray eyes and shoulder-length brown hair. They began dating and Seina introduced Lonetree to her "uncle Sasha," who persuaded Lonetree to become a friend of the Soviet Union. He gave the Soviets detailed blueprints of the embassy and a burn bag containing more than 100 documents about U.S. arms reductions in Western Europe. Eventually he turned himself in. He was tried and sentenced to twenty-five years. The sentence was reduced to fifteen years of which he served nine. He was released in 1996.

"Anyway," continued Sean as though he had absolutely nothing to do that day, that week, or that month, "his lawyer mounted a really stupid defense. Like: he did it because of what the government did to his people. I mean, that's stupid. It was more like: for the first time in his life he's getting some nice, slick, grade-A, white pussy. So this was going on, and when you're at sea there's not much to do, like I said, so you sit around and do a lot of philosophizing with the guys. And they asked me about this and I said, 'A man does what a man does.' And then they say, 'What about the government? What about what it did to your people?' I was raised by Warren Tibbetts, remember, a tried and true AIMster. And so I told them *all* about the treaties. I told them it really pisses me off. I told them about 1854 and 1837 and the Nelson Act and the Dawes Act. I told them it was illegal to practice our religion until the American Indian Religious Freedom Act in 1978. An Indian couldn't even buy a drink, legally, until 1953. We weren't even citizens till a bunch of Indians fought in World War I and were given medals by the French and nothing by their own country and because of that they passed the Indian Citizenship Act in 1924."

Once again, Sean had his facts right. Until 1924 Indians existed in a kind of official limbo. Some Indian women had become American citizens by marrying white men. Others had been naturalized through military service in World War I. Still others had become American citizens as part of treaty agreements or special statutes. But the majority of Indians were not American citizens and were not allowed to become naturalized in the same manner as immigrants to America were. Doctor Joseph K. Dixon, a proponent of assimilation, wrote: "The Indian, though a man without a country, the Indian who has suffered a thousand wrongs considered the white man's burden and from mountains, plains and divides, the Indian threw himself into the struggle to help throttle the unthinkable tyranny of the Hun. The Indian helped to free Belgium, helped to free all the small nations, helped to give victory to the Stars and Stripes. The Indian went to France to help avenge the ravages of autocracy. Now, shall we not redeem ourselves by redeeming all the tribes?"

The Indian Citizenship Act was passed in 1924, in part because so many Indians had served in the armed services during World War I, and in part because of U.S. assimilationist policy. Indians were now American citizens and tribal citizens—one did not preclude the other; they belonged to the U.S. nation and their respective tribal nations, too, one identity overlapping the other. Citizenship in the United States is a questionable kind of "redemption," made for questionable reasons.

As for religion, it had been government policy since the Ghost Dance craze in the nineteenth century to forbid Indian religions. This prohibition, though loosely enforced, was supported by missionaries. Authorities sometimes went so far as to confiscate and destroy religious items, physically disrupt ceremonies, and imprison religious leaders. By the mid-1970s no one seriously stopped Indian ceremonies or religion any longer. But Indian religion was sometimes difficult to practice because sacred sites were on private land or in national parks and it was illegal to possess some religious accoutrements such as eagle feathers, eagle bones, and peyote. The BIA's Circular 1665 of 1921, officially in effect until 1933 but unofficially heeded until much later, explicitly forbade the practice of Native American religions: "The Sun Dance, and all other similar dances and so-called religious ceremonies are considered 'Indian Offences' under existing regulations and corrective penalties. I regard such restrictions as applicable to any dance which involves . . . the reckless giving away of property . . . frequent and prolonged periods of celebration . . . in fact, any disorderly or plainly excessive performance that promotes superstitions, cruelty, licentiousness, idleness, danger of health, and shiftless indifference of family welfare. In all such instance, the regulations should be enforced."

The circular was amended in 1923. The amendment somewhat "softened" the tone of the original circular: "Indian dances be limited to one day in the midweek and at one center of each district; the months of March, April, June, July and August being exempted (no dances in these months). That none take part in the dances or be present who are under 50 years of age. That a careful propaganda be undertaken to educate public opinion against the (Indian religious) dance." The American Indian Religious Freedom Act (AIRFA), passed in 1978, formally put a stop to the suppression of Indian religions.

Sean continued: "So I said, 'How the fuck do you *think* I feel?' I said, 'I'm always wondering what the government is going to do to me next.' And then they ask the obvious question: 'So what are you doing in the navy? Why are you serving, then?' And they don't see it. They didn't see it till I said it, and I said, 'Hey. This is still my fucking country. My Turtle Island. Get it?' And they did. They got it after that."

In 1999 after Mille Lacs won its case, Sean called his brothers and said: "Man. We got to do this. You got to come down here and do this." So, despite protesters, anti-treaty rednecks, and the rest, Sean and his brothers began fishing. Still, even after they'd won the case they were nervous about racism, though you'd have to be pretty foolish to take on Sean and Marc and Mike.

"Oh, we didn't get all that really bad racism about netting like they did in Wisconsin," Sean assures me. "But that group led by Bud Grant, PERM, they'd show up at the boat landings and take pictures. But they didn't protest. At that time you couldn't put in or pull out without a rep from GLIFWC and a state warden and a cop there. It was tense. Nothing overt. But there was that subtle undercurrent of hatred. One time we were pulling out on a landing. We had three nets. A great big tub of fish—me and Marc and Mike. And we see some people coming from some houses nearby; there's lots of white people living near that landing. And I see they got cameras. And I'm thinking, 'Ahh-hhhhhhh, fuck. Here we go.' So they come up and the one guy, he's young, in his twenties. He says, 'How are you guys doing? Can I take a look? We've been living here, our family has, for like fifty years. We've seen you putting in here. We recognize the boat. We just wanted to say good luck. Hope you're doing well. We hope you get a lot of fish and think its pretty cool you're doing this stuff.' I about fell out of the boat. No doubt he recognized us: we were using Marc's boat. The USS fucking *Minnow*—his cabin cruiser. In six feet of water! He's got those dual props on his inboard, that spin in opposite directions, you know, to reduce cavitation (you know: that's the forming of air bubbles) and they cost about fifteen hundred apiece. And every year he grinds the props on the rocks. One year he got them refurbished. But a couple of times he had to totally replace them. First time we took that boat out I was standing up there and I started singing: *There once was a sailing ship, a mighty ship was she . . .*"

After we set the nets we went back to Bonnie's house and watched movies and smoked in the garage while Mike tried to fix the running lights on his boat. The game wardens worked for the tribe, but if his lights didn't work he would get fined. They might not even let him back on the lake to gather the nets. Mike's boat is a small, clunky, sixteen-footer with a twenty-horsepower motor. I stared out the open garage door at Marc's Bayliner: the USS *Minnow*. "Let's just use that," I said.

"We did, man!" said Sean. "Last year. We dropped that fucker in and pulled nets with it and everyone at the landing looked at us like we were fucking crazy."

"We were fucking crazy," said Mike. "Crazier than fuck."

"Yeah. We were bottoming out. We had to use those little ladders for water-skiers attached to the back. We had to hang on to those and pull from there. The boat is so high up you can't reach the water from the deck. We had that thing full of fish. And it was windier than shit and we were blowing into shallow water. It was fucking nuts."

We woke up the next morning at four o'clock bleary-eyed and grumpy. Sean, Mike, and Marc stumbled toward the coffee and once everyone had some we got in Marc's truck and headed back to the lake. There is something magical about being on a big lake before dawn. Everything exists as stored potential. It was cold. The ground was still frozen. Great plates of ice, some of it several feet thick, rubbed against each other out in the lake as though anxious for things to begin. We dumped the boat in. Mike tried to start the motor, cursed, tried again, cursed, and it coughed to life. The brothers were anxious to get their nets in before the northern and muskie started hunting. Since they hunt by sight they tend to move around at dusk and dawn, when the bait fish can't see as well as they can. No one much wants these fish; they don't taste as good as walleye and when they hit the net their instinct is to roll rather than twist. A big northern or muskie can rip a hole in a net yards wide, and it can take hours to untangle them.

Mike was in the front and pulled the floating line toward the boat. At first it came up easily, too easily. "Fucking bastards," he muttered. But then, after a few yards of net were in the boat, Mike began to strain.

"Watch out, boys!" he said. "Here come the slimy bastards now!"

And sure enough, one walleye, two, a cluster of four. Sean stood behind Mike, stripped the net as it came in, and threw the fish into a tub mid-thwart. Marc piloted and was largely silent. By the time we were done with the first net a tub stood in the middle of the boat filled with forty-two walleye, some of them still gasping, others turning their eerie eyes toward the sky. The second net held fifty walleye and one northern. By the time we got back to the landing everyone was cold and excited, looking forward to filleting but dreading it, too: it's tough work and ninety-two fish are a lot to handle.

Marc turned the boat around and headed back to the landing. The creelers were there—tribal employees who along with the game wardens count and measure the fish, note it against the licenses held by the tribal members, and add it to the overall tally. They want to be very sure that they don't exceed the quota of fish set jointly by the state and the tribe. In the seventeen years since the Mille Lacs Band began exercising its treaty rights in earnest, it has never once exceeded its quota. The band members are very careful to play by the rules, to take less than what they are licensed to take as a way of avoiding criticism and conflict. Not that it always works.

As it often happens, nets are set in the spring, when there is still ice on the lake. When the wind shifts or a storm comes up, the ice moves in great crushing sheets and rolls right over the tops of the nets, which are pulled from their weights by the force of the ice and deposited sometimes miles away. Such conditions happened in 2007, and ten nets were lost on the west side of Mille Lacs. The subtle racism that Sean talked about wasn't far behind, though it was mostly confined to online forums—which rednecks seem to like precisely because anonymous online forums don't require accountability, factual argument, respect, or understanding. One poster (identified as "Chief No Net") wrote, "Why are Native Americans allowed to net fish? How about hunting buffalo . . . is that still legal?" Zach, from Kansas City, Missouri, wrote, "I believe they should let them keep all the fish they want, after all before the Europeans came they did that. But they should be only allowed to use spears and canoes just like they used before the Europeans came, only fair." Of course there are Indians online, too. A poster from St. Paul retorted, "Hey, you, wasichun . . . what part of TREATY don't you understand? The Native people exchanged millions of acres of prime land for the right to fish. Don't like the deal? Give the land back! Feel free to send the keys to your house to the closed Anishinabeg Tribal council, and don't let the door hit ya' on your way out!"

The sad thing is that in this argument neither side understands what a treaty is and how treaty rights work. Indians aren't "allowed" to hunt or fish. It isn't a matter of "permission." To cast treaty rights as "special rights" is to suggest that they are in some sense an expression of pity or a payment for wrongs done or a welfare system for Stone Age people. But treaty rights were not "given" to Indian people because of past cruel treatment or because of special racial status. Nor were treaty rights "given" to Indians in exchange for land, as the Indian poster claimed.

Rather, when Indian bands signed treaties (and no new treaties have been signed since the end of the treaty period in the 1870s), they *reserved* land, which became reservations, and they *reserved* rights. Treaty rights are rights that the Indians who signed treaties always had, rights they explicitly reserved when they signed their treaties. In addition to rights specifically reserved in the treaties (such as those for hunting and fishing in the 1837 treaty signed by Mille Lacs) there is an understanding that rights not explicitly given up are still reserved, though this is implied more so than stated. A tribal lawyer I know had this to say: "It's just like when you enter into a contract with someone to, say, mow their lawn. You are exchanging your time and labor for money. You reserve all your other rights, unless explicitly stated otherwise. So, you agree to mow the lawn and you reserve the right to, say, not get fucked up the ass. Just because you didn't specify, when you agreed to mow someone's lawn in exchange for twenty dollars, that you didn't want to be fucked up the ass doesn't mean that you implied or understood that you gave up the right not to get fucked up the ass. It's assumed—that's what 'other rights reserved' means." A good example, that. The long and short of it (as Sean might say) is that the government doesn't "give" rights to anyone—Indian or other. Americans enjoy rights under the Constitution and in particular under the Bill of Rights that are not "granted" by Congress, the president, or the government.

It has been argued that the U.S. government entered into treaties with Indian tribes because it didn't imagine that the tribes would be around much longer. The government assumed that Indians would either be dead or be totally assimilated in the very near future. Just as the Indians who signed the treaties couldn't foresee the full impact of their decisions, neither could the U.S. government. The United States was mainly after three things: timber, farmland, and settlement. The idea never occurred to the government that fishing with rods and lures for a small inland species, which wasn't nearly as nourishing or tasty as saltwater staples such as cod, would someday generate billions of dollars in revenue. This was nothing like the future it imagined for the heartland: grain, timber, towns, mines.

Most tribal treaty rights in the United States involve hunting, fishing, gathering, water rights, and travel. That is, most tribes were anxious to have explicit language protecting the rights that affected their daily survival—their search for food and shelter and their religious purposes. In most cases treaty rights like hunting and fishing become complicated because, by and large, each state has its own hunting and fishing laws that control bag limits, harvest methods, and seasons. This is not something the federal government controls unless a species in question is protected, or, like waterfowl and salmon, crosses state lines in an annual migration. So, as with gaming, an agreement reached between sovereign nations becomes complicated on the level of local and state government.

Take, for instance, the Puyallup Indians who live near Tacoma, Washington, on Commencement Bay. They had been fighting for their treaty rights since the 1950s, long before the Tribbles stabbed some fish on Chief Lake in Wisconsin in 1974. They were routinely arrested and beaten up by game wardens, sheriffs' deputies, and city cops. Children were arrested along with adult protesters. Boats were rammed and fishermen and -women fell in the water. The local and state newspapers refused to run ads paid for by the tribe explaining their situation. Television stations refused to broadcast any story on the issue. The whole media apparatus of the state of Washington shut them out. Salmon were already on the decline, and salmon brought in a lot of tourist dollars and were commercially fished by many outfits in Washington state. The Puyallup's claims could jeopardize all of that. But then, in 1964, Marlon Brando accepted an invitation from the tribe to help publicize their plight. And in the spring of 1964 the portly actor and a local Indian shoved off from shore in a small skiff. They managed to catch one small salmon. But one was enough. They were both thrown into jail. The Indian was charged. Brando was not. Still, the action had its effect: the world began paying attention to tribal treaty rights. The Puyallup won their case in court a decade later. "Marlon Brando was the first person of non-color to step forward to help us," remembered SuZan Satiacum on the evening of Brando's death. "Marlon Brando was ahead of his time."

It is easy to see why non-Native outdoorsmen care about treaty rights: they think these impinge on their own rights to hunt and fish. Treaty rights create special limits, harvest methods, and seasons for Indians that seem unfair to non-Indians. And it is easy to see why those who serve the sportsmen, those who are involved in the $11 billion tourism industry in Minnesota, care as well. Every boat, motor, trailer, gas station, restaurant, campground, motel, RV park, and grocery store up and down this food chain is affected by rises and drops in tourism, and every time there is a rise or drop in tourism most people in the industry see a walleye in the calculations. The same goes for other species of fish and game that Indian tribes are allowed to catch exclusively or with much greater ease than non-Natives.

But part of the antipathy toward treaty rights might not have any-thing to do with industry. Many of the protesters at boat landings in Wisconsin and those who belonged to anti-treaty organizations in Minnesota were, like their Indian neighbors, relatively poor. Also like their Indian neighbors, they are not making money off the fish (Mille Lacs Band members are prohibited from selling their walleye on the market). Most of them seem to be upset by what they see as "special rights" or unfair (and hence, in their words, un-American) advantages. However, what they don't understand about treaty rights related to fishing extends equally to what they don't understand about their own rights. Contrary to what anti-treaty groups believe, non-Natives don't have the right to fish and hunt. They do have, presumably, the right to life, liberty, and the pursuit of happiness. They have a right to an attorney. They have the right to remain silent. Fishing and hunting, however, are *privileges*. These are privileges for which they must pay. In most cases they pay in the form of hunting and fishing licenses, state duck stamps, and the like. And if they are convicted of a felony those privileges are taken away, sometimes permanently.

In one of the ironies attending the issue of treaty rights, anti-treaty groups (some of whose proud constituents belong to the John Birch Society and Posse Comitatus) have made the claim that they are fol-lowing the teachings of Martin Luther King Jr. when they protest against the "special privileges" given to Indians—and that they are doing their best to give "equal rights to whites" throughout the Mid-west. Their most strident claim is that Indian fishing methods—with spears and nets—are tantamount to raping the land. This is a fairly odd claim, given the history of the previous 500 years. It is also espe-cially odd given the fishing statistics in contested waters. For instance, in Mille Lacs the yearly quota for netting and spearing in 2010 was about 13,500 pounds. Initially, in 1997 the quota was set at 40,000 pounds annually and was intended to move upward until it reached

50 percent of the catchable stock. In contrast, the annual reported take of sport fishermen on Mille Lacs is about 1 million pounds. Steve Smith, a water quality expert in Minnesota, maintains that it is impossible to take 1 million pounds of fish from any lake annually and still have a healthy fish population. Those who fish and practice "catch and release" are also part of the problem; statistics from the Minnesota Department of Natural Resources suggest that one-third of all fish caught and released in shallow warm-water lakes such as Mille Lacs die. But the claim is made anyway—that Indians are raping the land. The claim was echoed by Jesse "The Body" Ventura when he was governor of Minnesota and was asked about the suit filed by the Mille Lacs Band in 1990. He responded, "If those rules apply then they ought to be back in birch-bark canoes instead of with 200-horsepower Yamaha engines with fish finders." He went on to say (showing that he had no knowledge of how treaty rights work) that he also had a "natural heritage" giving him special rights. "My heritage as a frogman is DuPont fishing. I would question why I can't DuPont fish," he said, referring to the method employed by the navy SEALs of throwing a grenade into the water and collecting the stunned fish. It's strange logic. If every agreement between governments locked the signers into the technology in use at the time of the treaty we would be living in fairly backward conditions. But I think it is safe to say that many Ojibwe would go back to using wooden spears and birch bark canoes if non-Natives simply fished with cane poles from shore, with bits of pork rind on the end of their hooks, only as far west as the Ohio River.

In a very strange turn of events, the white supremacists who chanted "Timber Niggers!" and "Indians go home" at boat landings are on the same side as many environmentalists regarding treaty rights. The Makah Indians from Neah Bay, perhaps the remotest point in the lower forty-eight states, are in such a bind. When the gray whale was taken off the endangered species list and was, in fact, once again thriving, the Makah planned to continue their ancient practice of whale hunting, not really for sustenance as much as for cultural and spiritual reasons. In 1998 the annual Makah Days celebration was approaching a showdown with environmental groups. Their police force of five officers, usually sufficient security when the tribe held a picnic, canoe races, or a small powwow, was deemed insufficient as the Sea Shepherd Society began to assemble a fleet to blockade the Makah's first ceremonial whale hunt in generations. Some estimates suggested that 20,000 protesters would show up to stop the Makah. As it turned out, the gray whale migration was late and no whale was harvested. By the time the Makah killed a whale in 1999 the protesters were deterred by the Coast Guard, which detained their boats if they approached within 500 yards of the Makah whaling canoe. Protesters did succeed in stopping the whale hunt in 2000 by driving skiffs close enough to spook the whale into diving. The Makah whale hunt is still hotly disputed today.

As the Makah show, Indians as well as whites care about treaty rights in a way that extends beyond economics, though treaty rights saw many Indians through the dark years of the twentieth century. For instance, at Mille Lacs, with two successful casinos, an expanding land base, and well-funded infrastructure (largely because of the casinos) the Indians care deeply about their right to fish even though it doesn't bring them any money. Fishing is, as with the Makah, a part of their heritage and identity, not just an issue of economics or class. The same is true at the other end of the spectrum: when the state of Wisconsin offered to settle with the Lac du Flambeau Band of Ojibwe in Wisconsin in the 1980s, the offer was refused. Flambeau was then and is now incredibly poor. And the offer was a good one. If we do the math (the amount offered versus the number of fish speared in a year by Flambeau members), the settlement would come out to about $3,000 per fish speared. At the time no more than 13 percent of Flambeau tribal members speared fish, and of those who speared most spent only one or two nights doing it and usually harvested no more than two dozen fish per family. The tribe put the issue to referendum. The members, as noted above, rejected the state's offer.

"Look at it this way," offers Sean. "When a white person dies the children inherit whatever their parent left them. Money. Houses. Investments and retirement money the parent didn't get a chance to spend. Well, they didn't earn that, did they? I mean, their parent earned that. Well, our treaty rights are like that. Our grandparents and great-grandparents worked to keep our land and our rights and we get to benefit from that. That's just how it works. If Chief Migizi or Shabashkung or whoever had called it quits and moved to White Earth we wouldn't even have a rez. But they stuck it out. They stayed when the world was against them. And because of that we have casinos and our fishing rights and our communities and our ceremonies. It's our inheritance. Why isn't that fair?"

⤡

We're done with the nets for the day. They were pulled, stripped, and reset. The fish were filleted, packaged, and frozen. Another good day. Everyone went back to sleep for a few hours and now it's midafternoon and Marc and Mike are standing in the middle of the narrow dirt trail we've been walking along.

"Is it or isn't it?" asks Marc.

"I think it is. I can definitely see that little bastard moving."

They crane their necks and squint against the sun. They're watching a black speck move back and forth 400 yards up the road. Marc, Mike, and Sean have traded their slickers for camouflage, their nets for shotguns, the tubs of fish for decoys. They are hunting turkeys in the very first reservation turkey season. Turkeys, once nearly extinct in Minnesota and Wisconsin, have made a dramatic comeback in the last twenty years, thanks to the efforts of conservation groups across the country. The road we're on runs through the middle of land recently purchased by the Mille Lacs Band—3,600 acres of swamp and scrub reserved exclusively for tribal members as a hunting preserve. They call it "the 3600." Mille Lacs and most other landowning reservations can set their own hunting seasons and limits for the game on their land. They can also control access. Some tribes sell hunting or fishing permits to non–band members. Mille Lacs doesn't.

"It most definitely is. I can see that bastard's beard from here," says Mike.

"Well, get the fuck down, then," says Sean, "Turkeys can see better than you can. What is this, a Mille Lacs ambush?"

Since neither Sean nor his brothers have ever hunted turkey before, there has been lots of opinion thrown around for hours—about hunting methods, patterns, and species habits and habitat. Most of the information has come through hearsay and somewhat directed searches online between checking nets and watching Bonnie's flat screen. In terms of the ratio of meat to money spent there aren't many activities more expensive than hunting turkey. Blessed with keen eyesight, excellent hearing, vast intelligence, and a suspicious nature (not unlike Sean's mother-in-law), turkeys require a stealthy approach. They also require a lot of gear. Calls (mouth calls, box calls, slate), camouflage (gilly suits, face masks, and gloves), guns (twelve-gauge loaded with four-shot), and decoys are all considered required.

In years past game wardens in this area might have prevented Mille Lacs Indians from hunting. Now the two white game wardens employed by the tribe from whom Sean and his brothers purchased their permits were helping. Avid turkey hunters themselves, the wardens told Sean, Mike, and Marc that they'd seen turkeys roosting by the powwow grounds and had seen at least two flocks over at "the 3600." They advised Sean how to set up his decoys and they seemed generally excited that Sean and his brothers might be the first Mille Lacs hunters to get a turkey. How times change.

We'd hunted all afternoon with no luck—we saw lots of tracks pressed into the frozen clay and a few callbacks and one approach across a cornfield, but nothing had come close. But then, as we're walking back to the truck we see them step out of the woods 400 yards distant. Marc and Mike weren't so sure at first, so they just stood in the middle of the road. But Sean whispered and yelled, and Marc, Mike, Sean, and I hunkered down in the ditch. We stuck our hands out and staked down our decoys where the turkeys could see them. Marc and Sean began using their calls.

We didn't seem to have any effect at first. We could barely see the turkeys over the ditch grass but they just seemed to mill and peck at the ground, oblivious of the calls. But then one stuck up its head. And then the rest. After five minutes they began moving closer. And closer. The flock came all the way down the middle of the road, drawn by the sound. When they got 100 yards away they really came into focus. The late afternoon sun hit the one in front—a large tom with an eleven-inch beard. Behind him were at least twenty hens and a few jakes. They wanted the tom—the Mille Lacs Band and the state of Minnesota allow only the harvest of toms, in order to preserve the population. Marc rubbed his box call gently. The tom stood tall and began prancing sideways toward us, and then he turned to the other side. His chest feathers were puffed out and trapped the sun. They were beautiful—streaked with bronze, copper, and gold. His tail was fanned out completely, and he seemed to fill the entire road. His caruncle was puffed out and bloodred. As Marc rubbed his call the tom pranced, lifting his legs high enough so we could see his spurs, and strutted, switching from side to side. It was one of the most beautiful and exciting things I have ever seen.

When he closed to forty yards, then thirty, Marc began whispering, "Shoot, Mike. Take him. Take him, goddamn it. Shoot, shoot!"

Mike paused and then shot. The covey jumped. Birds were flying in every direction around us. Mike shot again and the tom flopped down to the edge of the water in the ditch.

"Holy shit! You got him," shouted Sean. "You got him! You got him!"

The brothers ran forward and collected the turkey from the ground. They all took turns holding it, turning its body this way and that, examining the beard and the tail feathers, the shrinking caruncle. They looked at each other and smiled and high-fived one another. After a quick smoke we set off into the setting sun, down the road back to the truck, to go once again out on the cold water of Lake Mille Lacs and pull plenty from the deep.

Judge Margaret Seelye Treuer in robes.

3

It is minus twenty-two degrees Fahrenheit when my mother and I pull into the Tribal Court building at Bois Forte Reservation in far north-eastern Minnesota. It's hard to tell, but sober business goes on inside the low-slung, graceless structure. We walk in. Everyone looks serious: the tribal cop at the entrance, the staff in the office, the Indians waiting in chairs and standing around in the cramped hallway. They are all serious. And they are all deferential toward my mother. It's understandable. She's the judge.

But they don't know her as I do. They don't see the disorder of her bedside table or the way she can never locate the lids for her many dozens of travel mugs. They didn't see the look of excitement—or was it predatory glee?—when, during our drive to Bois Forte, a partridge wandered onto the frozen road to peck at salt. "Swerve, Dave! Hit him and we'll be eating partridge tonight!" They don't see the worry that attends her thoughts about her remaining siblings, and the sorrow that clings to her memories of Barb, Sonny, her cousin Mikey, and her father, all of whom died too soon, and not in peace. They didn't hear her fussing over me when I was in high school and college and began drinking and smoking pot: "Barb said that when she smoked marijuana she could feel her soul leaving her body. It just left and never came back. That's what happens. You'll lose yourself. You'll lose yourself completely." What they do see is a formidable woman. A formidable Indian woman who will sit in judgment over them and hear their crimes.

Once inside the building she goes to her chambers (the term makes the space sound grander than it is—just a room directly across from the main entrance with two desks and lots of files scattered about) and I go to the courtroom to wait. The courtroom is small. (So is the reservation, which is one of the smallest in Minnesota.) There are vinyl-covered brown chairs and wood-paneled walls that make the courtroom look, to me, like someone's basement den from the 1970s. I half expect to see a recliner, a wet bar, and a disused foosball table against the far wall. The American flag and the Bois Forte Reservation flag stand, exhausted, in the corner. The bench is slightly raised. Everyone is quiet, dressed in work clothes, jeans, parkas, and Caterpillar and Sorel pac boots. Lucille, the court administrator, who cooks lunch every day there's court, says, "Caps, caps! Take off your caps." The people pull them off in a hurry and stuff them into their pockets.

"All rise," she says. And my mother wafts into the room from a back door and takes her place at the bench. It is a strange thing to doff my cap and rise when my mother enters the room. And I get the feeling that every time she walked into my bedroom or the kitchen or the living room or wherever, I should have been standing with hat in hand, a supplicant before her. The bailiff brings the papers over and while he goes over the docket with my mother, Lucille squints at the huddle of Indians in the gallery, leans back, leans forward again, and says:

"You there. Is your hair blue?"

"Yes, ma'am. I colored it for fun," says a teenage boy who, later, will appear before the bench to face charges.

She laughs. "Oh, I wasn't sure. But I thought it was blue. Or purple. You know, purple for the Minnesota Vikings."

"No, ma'am. I am a Packers fan."

With the docket sorted out, my mother reads everyone's rights en masse. It must give her some pleasure to do so. For most of the people facing charges and for most Indians everywhere, it wasn't until recently that we felt as though we had any rights to speak of. Certainly not rights administered in an Indian court presided over by an Indian judge, or defended by Indian lawyers and prosecuted by Indian lawyers, or facilitated by an Indian bailiff. One of the things I am only now beginning to realize is how deeply any one law, any congressional act, or any Supreme Court ruling can affect everything else. As common as the Bois Forte Tribal Court seems, as down-home (if not homey) as it might be, there is a seething mass of history that props it up—the legacy of the Bureau of Indian Affairs (BIA), the Major Crimes Act, the policy of allotment, and the Dawes Act—and sets the act and the actors in motion. Tribal law is notoriously tricky; each thread is tied to another and to another and it seems almost impossible to figure out sometimes. But one thing uniting all the disparate forces that come together in my mother's tribal court is the issue of power and powerlessness.

Memories of the kind of powerlessness that Indians felt in the face of the law run close to the surface for her and for many other Indians. My mother remembers very clearly, and narrates with a force of anger surprising because the subject itself is both so old and so commonplace for Indians of her generation, how the state game warden confiscated her family's rice one fall. At Leech Lake, the Indian children started school in late September, after participating in the wild rice harvest. The area schools hated this arrangement, of course, because their funding was based, in part, on their average daily membership (ADM), which was compiled at the start of the regular school year. Wild rice—which grows naturally in shallow streams and along lake edges—ripens in late August and mid-September. There are about three good weeks when it is possible to harvest it. This is usually a family affair. Everyone, from young children to the old, gathers at boat landings and campgrounds and shoves whatever kinds of homemade boats are available—duck boats, canoes (if people are wealthy enough to own any), flat-bottomed boats made of plywood—into the rice. One person pushes the boat or canoe through the rice with a long tamarack or cedar pole tipped with a Y-shaped tree fork or (again, if people are rich) a metal duckbill. The person doing the pushing is like a gondolier. The ricer in the bow bends the rice stalks over the gunwales of the boat with one wooden knocker and hits or "knocks" the rice with the other one. The ripe rice kernels drop into the bottom of the canoe; the unripe rice stays on the stalks, and when it is ready you can rice the same area again. The knocker alternates between the left and right sides. Meanwhile the poler slowly pushes the canoe along through the rice beds—if the boat goes too fast, the knocker won't have a chance to reach out and bend the stalks; if it's too slow, you won't get much rice in the boat. If the crop is a good one and if you stay at it all day, a two-person team can expect to harvest about 200 pounds of green rice—sometimes a lot more, sometimes a lot less. Most people keep some rice for themselves, either finishing it the old-fashioned way (by roasting it over a fire and dancing on the parched rice to loosen the hulls and then winnowing it) or sending it to a rice finisher who does the same thing but with a wood-fired mechanical parcher and winnower. Most of the rice is sold. In the 1950s, when my mother was growing up, this was, for many, the single major source of cash income for the year. If not the only source, it was certainly the largest. In the 1950s green rice (rice that was knocked and sacked but not parched or winnowed) fetched around one dollar per pound. This was a lot of money. My grandfather, grandmother, mother, aunt Barb, uncle Sonny, and uncle Davey could make $600 a day if the rice was good. A rice season could yield a few thousand dollars—the cash needed to buy clothes, shoes, kerosene, flour, lard, bullets, roofing material, everything they needed to stay dry, warm, and fed for the winter. Ricing was a big deal. The harvest mattered more than any other. The rice mattered more than fish, more than furs, more than farming. It was the one tribal resource, in Ojibwe country at least, that was controlled and protected throughout the centuries when other treaty rights languished. By the 1950s, however, ricing, too, had eroded and the state had illegally assumed control of the rice beds.

One fall Dinah Stangel, her parents, my great-uncle Diddy Matthews, my mother, and some others drove around to the northwestern corner of Lake Winnie to rice on Raven's Point and Rabbit Lake. There was no good way to get to the spot, because the wind was blowing hard and kicking up waves that would have swamped their canoes and boats, so they drove down an old tote road and dragged their boats through the trees and across bogs to get to the rice. They got a lot of it. But by four in the afternoon the wind had not let up. It was blowing out of the south and waves as high as four feet were crashing into Raven's Bay from the main lake. My mother and her ricing partner Dinah Stangel were fourteen years old and both skinny as snakes. They were almost finished when the ricing pole broke. They had one oar and began using that to get back to the landing, and then that broke. Their homemade flat-bottomed duck boat was not intended for open water or for use in that kind of weather.

"I don't know how we did it," my mother remembers. "I totally thought we were going to die. We were lost in the rice. We were both so short we couldn't see over it. We didn't know which direction to go. I don't think I've ever been so scared in my life."

Somehow they met up with Dinah's parents and my mother's uncle and aunt, and together they ventured out into the big lake and crept along the shore until they reached a public landing, West Winnie Landing. It was deserted except for one old white man camping out in an Airstream trailer. It was well past fishing season and all the tourists had gone home. The man saw them come in off the lake, saw what kind of shape they were in, and invited all six of them in. He turned up the heat and gave them all soup.

"I don't know what that old-timer put in his soup, but it was the best damn soup I've ever tasted. Ever then. Ever since. Anyway, since it was such a long way around by boat to get the cars the men decided to walk around and get them and drive them down to the landing. It took them a couple of hours. When they got back they had the game warden with them. The way they used to do it, they'd open a lake for ricing for a couple of days and then close it, and open it again or open another one. So every day you'd hear where it was open and where it wasn't. Well, Winnie was closed that day. And this state warden says, 'Lake's closed today. I'm going to have to take that rice.' And we'd gotten a lot of it. It had been a real good day. So he took something like ten or twelve sacks of rice. He couldn't even close the trunk of his car. And he drove off and we had nothing. Fucking asshole."

It was more than fifty years ago and she's still mad about it.

"Damn right I'm mad. That was our life. It was our life he put in his trunk and drove over to the rice buyer and sold."

"He sold it?"

"Of course! What the hell else was he going to do? We didn't know our rights then. We didn't know, nobody knew, that a state warden has got no jurisdiction over Indians on their reservations. Back then they thought they were the law. And no one knew any better. We didn't know any better. I almost died getting that rice and then he took it."

*   *   *

My mother's experiences of powerlessness as a young Indian woman aren't far from her mind as the first case is called. A skinny middle-aged woman stood before the bench, practically buried in her parka, which she hadn't taken off, either because in her nervousness she'd forgotten to or because she was still cold. She faced five charges, all of them alcohol-related. She pleaded guilty to all the charges. My mother glanced down at the papers in front of her and then back at the defendant. "Did you complete treatment?" "Yes, your honor." "Looks like you did. You look better. Seems like you're doing something right." She suspended the jail time and the fines and ordered the defendant to complete community service. When it was over the woman's lawyer leaned over and whispered in her ear, "Good job."

The second case involved a girl who shoplifted from the convenience store on the reservation. The next case was related to the one before. Evidently the two young women took eight dollars' worth of hamburger from the freezer. After stealing the hamburger they'd gone home and gotten into a fistfight with their mother and when the cops showed up they kicked and punched the squad car. The girls were charged with disorderly conduct, shoplifting, and domestic abuse.

After the charges were listed my mother paused again and looked straight at the defendant. "Did you apologize to your mother?" "Yes." "Are you on good terms now?" "Yes. Yes, your honor." "Have you been to treatment?" "Yeah, October. I did it in October." "Did you go on your own or did someone make you? Were you ordered to?" "I went on my own." "You look better now. Have you been staying away from booze?" "Yes, your honor." She pleaded guilty. The fines and jail time were suspended and she was ordered to complete another evaluation and to stay away from all parties and bars. My mother rarely suspends fines. Instead she requires defendants to do community service to pay off the debt.

Of the eleven cases that day, every case save one was, in one way or another, related to alcohol or drug abuse. One of the first cases my mother tried at Bois Forte involved a few men who were terrorizing one of their acquaintances. According to testimony, they forced a man to shave his face "dry"—without shaving cream or water. Purely sadistic and mean. She gave them all the maximum. And she told them, "I'm going to give you the maximum." The maximum penalty she can impose in her court under U.S. law is one year in jail and a $5,000 fine. Considering that some of the people appearing before her are so poor they steal eight dollars' worth of hamburger from a convenience store freezer, $5,000 is a lot of money. On that first day many at Bois Forte began referring to the new judge as "Maximum Margaret." Tribal courts such as Bois Forte, while limited in the kind of punishment they can dish out and also limited in what kinds of cases can be tried there, have fairly creative sentencing guidelines. She knows the price Indian communities and Indian people pay for the ravages of drugs and alcohol. She's lost several dearly loved relatives to alcohol and drugs. Despite the fact that my mother wears a black robe and sits on a raised bench and the other Indians appear before her—despite the fact that it would appear that she has the power and they don't—she has much more in common with them than I do. They seem baffled by life, somewhat defeated by it, confused by it. What "crimes" they've committed stem largely from this confusion. Just as confusing, just as baffling as the Indian lives that Indian trial courts are supposed to administer to and help, are the history and reach of the courts themselves. The complicated issue of tribal justice alone is enough to drive someone to drink.

All tribes had their own particular brand of tribal justice, and not in the ironic sense meant by phrases such as "Apache Justice," a story by Stanley Crane published in 1941, the title of a YouTube video showing three Iraqis being gunned down by a helicopter, and what is meant when you tie someone to a tree and beat him to death with a two-by-four—a punishment that comes up often on Web searches. The Ojibwe and many other clan-based societies had particular clans whose job it was to function as policemen and warriors. There are ceremonial positions such as "rice chiefs," known as "oshkaabewisag" (literally, "messengers"), whose job it was to ensure fair access to rice beds, the lifeblood of the Ojibwe people. Justice was, back in pre-reservation days, more flexible for us. We believed, and still believe, that when an Ojibwe dies a violent death, the soul is prevented from getting to the afterlife unless it is given some kind of justice. There were three ways this could happen. First, a family member could be put through a very elaborate ceremony to appease the soul of the deceased; in effect, the living could function as surrogates for the dead. Second, the offending party in the violent death could perform a "laying of gifts" on the family (literally covering up the living with heaps of valuables). Third, the dead could be appeased through revenge killing. Depending on the relationship between the deceased and the transgressor, the family chose one of these options. This helped preserve social order and compensated families who were both emotionally and financially bereft because of their loss. The system worked well. Murder was a rarity in Ojibwe country.

The Tonawanda Seneca of upstate New York, widely considered the most traditional Seneca community, not only has retained its traditional system of government in the form of longhouse ceremonies (involving a religious and political organization) but also adheres to a traditional form of justice, as does the larger Seneca nation. The Seneca nation's judicial branch of government consists of peacemaker courts, surrogate courts, the council, and two chief marshals. Each Seneca reservation elects the peacemaker judges, a surrogate judge, and a marshal. "The peacemaker and surrogate courts may apply tribal, federal, or state law to the case they are hearing, depending on the circumstances. Traditional law is still honored by the Senecas, especially in the regulation of property. For instance, individuals can own only surface property rights 'a plowshare deep.' Resources below that depth, such as minerals and oils, belong to the nation. In the case of gravel, which lies close to the surface, any sales profits are divided evenly between the individual owner and the nation."

And tribal justice extended to legal matters outside tribes, too. One of the treaties between the United States and the Choctaw was clear on this point. Article IV of that treaty, signed in 1786, reads: "If any citizen of the United States, or other person not being Indian, shall attempt to settle on any of the lands hereby allotted to the Indians to live and hunt on, such a person shall forfeit the protection of the United States of America, and the Indians may punish him or not as they please."

The Sioux had their own justice system as well, but it ran counter to mainstream ideas of justice. This dispute was one of the first intratribal conflicts and set the tone not only for Indian justice but for relations between Indians and whites well into the twentieth century. In 1881 the Brule leader Crow Dog killed the chief Spotted Tail. The murder was a fairly brazen act: "After leaving the council lodge Crow Dog was seen approaching Spotted Tail. He had his wife with him. He got out of the wagon and was stooping down when Spotted Tail rode up to him. He suddenly rose up and shot Spotted Tail through the left breast. The chief fell from his horse, but rose to his feet and made three or four steps toward Crow Dog, endeavoring to draw his pistol. He then reeled and fell backward, dead. Crow Dog jumped into his wagon and drove off at full speed toward his camp, some nine miles distant." Some say it was an attempt to seize power. Others maintain that Spotted Tail had offended Crow Dog's family. Spotted Tail had been a cooperative chief and U.S. officials wanted vengeance. Crow

Dog was arrested by the U.S. government and tried for murder. The Brule Lakota whom Spotted Tail represented tried Crow Dog according to their own sense of justice. They ordered Crow Dog to maintain Spotted Tail's widow and heirs for the rest of his life and banned him and his descendants from living in the community for the next four generations. This was acceptable to Spotted Tail's family. And the tribe upheld its own rulings. Even though Crow Dog's descendant Leonard Crow Dog became one of the most important spiritual leaders on the Rosebud Reservation, and arguably one of the most important spiritual leaders since World War II, he did not live in the village. Only in the last few years has Leonard Crow Dog's grandson been able to move back to the reservation. This ruling, however, was not acceptable to many whites. They cried that Crow Dog had gotten away with murder. The U.S. government agreed and the case of Crow Dog wove its way to the Supreme Court, which upheld Crow Dog's argument and ruled that state and federal governments do not have plenary power over tribes or jurisdiction over crimes committed by Indians against Indians on Indian land.

The federal government was not content with this. And as with the issue of Cherokee removal some fifty years before, it found a way around the Supreme Court's ruling. The Indian Major Crimes Act, passed in 1885, was the response. Murder, rape, grand larceny, and assault are a few of the major crimes covered under the act. These "major crimes" became, as a result of the act, federal offenses punishable only in federal courts. However, in order to administer justice for lesser offenses, the feds had already set up the Court of Indian Offenses in 1883. "Justice" is a term that must be applied loosely to the Court of Indian Offenses: in its charter were clauses that targeted Indian religions, referred to as "heathenish rites," and it was the hope of the commissioner of Indian Affairs that the courts would "destroy the tribal relations as fast as possible." For instance, in 1884, the Court of Indian Offenses at Red Lake enforced "rules forbidding plural marriages, dances, destruction of property following death, intoxication, liquor traffic, interference with the 'civilizing program,' and leaving the reservation without permission."

In 1881, when Crow Dog murdered Spotted Tail, many tribes already had Indian police—sometimes staffed by tribal members and funded by Congress pursuant to treaty—but tribes soon had courts as well, as clunky, corrupt, and guided by bad principle (like the Court of Indian Offenses at Red lake) as these were. "Indian offenses" is a concept fairly far off the mark of "Indian justice."

The justice system created by the Indian Major Crimes Act and the Court of Indian Offenses, which was hardly just, persisted more or less unchallenged until the Indian Reorganization Act (IRA) of 1934, which created constitutional governments with elected officials on many Indian reservations. Along with constitutions and elected officials came the sense that some sort of judiciary was necessary. Some tribes began to break away from the model of the Court of Indian Offenses and created their own courts, as difficult as that was. Smaller tribes, however, could not afford to start and administer their own courts and retained the services of the Court of Indian Offenses (more than twenty tribes still have CFR courts today). But change came slowly after 1934 and through the 1950s—it came as slowly as shifts in government policy came quickly. The Wheeler-Howard Act, part of the "Indian New Deal," was replaced in the 1950s with the policy of termination. The government was trying to rid itself of its responsibility to Indians once again.

🖎

It is easy to understand the animosity many Indians have toward cops, and why they feel they will never get a fair day in court. When my father worked for the BIA in the 1960s he saw a lot of brutality firsthand. As he went about his work at Leech Lake he began to hear stories about chronic abuse at the hands of law enforcement: beatings, rapes. "I talked to people and began to learn what was going on. Well, there was some obscure federal regulation or law that allowed government employees to register complaints directly with the Department of Justice; you didn't have to go through all the usual channels. So I collected affidavits. I interviewed people. By the time I was done I had twenty-four affidavits and I submitted a formal complaint to the DOJ. The one that sticks out in my mind is one older lady who was picked up for public drunkenness and brought back to the police station. According to her testimony she was bent over a squad car and raped with a billy club."

When the complaint landed at the Department of Justice, FBI agents were dispatched to Leech Lake. When their plane landed in Bemidji they radioed the sheriff's department (in Walker, seventeen miles south of Cass Lake) and asked the staff to find and collect all the officers named in the complaint.

"By the time the FBI agents made it to Walker," remembers my father bitterly, "every single one of the complaintants who signed affidavits had been found and threatened. They told them, 'The FBI is only going to be here a few days and when they leave we'll still be here.' All recanted except one or two of them. Next thing I knew I was called into the BIA area director's office. Mittelholtz was his name. He said, 'Paul Winslow, the acting area director in Minneapolis, called saying the U.S. attorney general wants to talk to you.' So I did what I was told. I went down to Minneapolis and met with Winslow. He said, 'Judge Miles Lord wants to talk to you.' So I met with Lord. He said, 'You're just doing this because you've got a personal grudge against the Cass Lake police for picking up one of your sons for reckless driving.' I told him, 'I've got no grudge whatsoever. My kid was driving recklessly and they arrested him and I agreed it was a good thing. That's why I let him sit in jail and didn't bail him out.' Lord paused. 'What will make all this go away?' That's how they did things then. So we made a deal. Judge Rollette, the county court judge for the reservation, was removed. He was a famous racist. He was famous for saying each and every time an Indian stood before him: 'You. You are lower than the dung of whales.' So they removed him. And they removed two of the three police officers named in the complaints. The two worst ones. The third retired. And then they fired me."

Before that, when my father moved to an abandoned farm on the edge of Leech Lake Reservation in 1953, he didn't know any Indians and hadn't given Indians much thought. Nor did he think about them very much when, after living in Milwaukee and Sheboygan while working for the AFL-CIO, he visited his in-laws (from his first marriage) on the north side of Cass Lake, on the Leech Lake Reservation. He fell in love with the place, with the land. "I loved the sand hills. The river channels. The feel of the land and the woods. The one piece of art my family had in Vienna, the one original piece of art, was a pastel of a river with trees. It hung in my bedroom and I stared at it every day and every night all through my childhood. All through those war years. The land up here, around Leech Lake, reminded me of that, of that painting. Maybe that's why I love this place so much. Anyway, I fell in love with the place. I was facing a transfer from Sheboygan to Detroit. I didn't want to go. I wanted to live up here. I was running from everything. From conflict. I found the property, bought it for two thousand dollars, which was all the money we had. And I got my teaching degree in Bemidji. But I couldn't get a job. Finally, after a lot of looking I started teaching high school English on the rez."

While he taught at Cass Lake he came to know many Indian families. The majority of his students were Indian. He was shocked by the attitudes of many of the teachers, the police, and the other powers that be in a small town like Cass Lake. The town itself, in the middle of the reservation, was very mixed, but all the stores and all the positions of power were occupied by white people. "I was appalled at conditions and attitudes and so I wrote an ill-considered, heated letter to the commissioner of Indian affairs, Philleo Nash."

My father knew Philleo Nash from his labor union days in the late 1940s and early 1950s in Wisconsin. Nash was an interesting man. He came from a well-to-do Wisconsin farming family (they farmed cranberries near Wisconsin Rapids), was trained as an anthropologist, and found his way to Washington, D.C., where he worked for the Roosevelt and Truman administrations and became friends with Eleanor Roosevelt. Like Eleanor Roosevelt, he was deeply concerned about racial problems in America. While in Washington he and his wife, Edith, founded the Georgetown Day School, one of the first integrated schools there. When Nash received my father's manifesto, he telephoned. "Well, you think the BIA could do things better?" he asked. "Yes, I do." "OK, then. The ball is in your court. I'll hire you and see what you can do about things."

It would have been hard for anyone to change the BIA at that time. Created in the 1800s to deal with the "Indian problem," the BIA was, tellingly, under the auspices of the War Department. It was in charge of treating with tribes, administering allotments, dispersing funds, settling disputes, and overseeing day-to-day operations at reservations and forts across the American West. It had been, since its start, notoriously corrupt. Eventually the BIA was transferred over to the Department of the Interior, but it couldn't shed much of its reputation as a powerful and damning (if not evil) force. As of 2010, Congress was considering a settlement for claims brought against the Department of the Interior and the BIA. The settlement under consideration is for $3.4 billion—a small amount, considering the alleged $150 billion the Department of the Interior and the BIA illegally withheld from Indians over the last ninety-five years. The money withheld is for timber, oil, and land leases. "Over the past 100 years, government record systems lost track of more than 40 million acres and who owns them. The records simply vanished. Meanwhile, documents were lost in fires and floods, buried in salt mines or found in an Albuquerque storage facility covered by rat feces and a deadly hantavirus. Government officials exploited computer systems with no audit trails to turn Indian proceeds into slush funds but maintain plausible deniability," suggests a recent article in the *Atlantic*.

It wasn't until the 1990s that an Indian, the Menominee activist Ada Deer, was put in charge of the BIA. And after her, there was the Ojibwe entrepreneur Dave Anderson (owner of the Famous Dave's BBQ chain). In the 1950s, remembers my father, the BIA controlled everything. "You couldn't get anything done without their approval," he says. "They controlled everything. They controlled the land and collected rents. All fees were paid to them. And they paid out the money. All leases, all business deals, all disputes. . . . It went through them. Even the tribal council meetings were controlled by them. The tribal council wasn't allowed to meet unless they had BIA approval. And even then they controlled the agenda because they were in charge of giving out gas and meal vouchers and a small per diem for the tribal council members. The tribal council was made up of poor reservation people. They couldn't make meetings if they didn't get a little money for gas and for lunch. And so the BIA made damn sure that their agenda was on the table and they got the vote they wanted. Or no gas. No lunch. No meeting. It was like that. They were smooth and polished and sophisticated. It was a sophisticated kind of control. But it was control."

Enter my father. He was the least likely person for the job: he came from a family of socialists and was a borderline socialist himself. He worked for years as a labor organizer in Wisconsin. He was not BIA material as far as control and paternalism were concerned. But he was Philleo Nash's protégé. He had the ear of the commissioner of Indian affairs. And so the area superintendent, Mittelholtz, generally left my father alone; he might lose his job if he stood up to Nash.

One of my father's first jobs for the BIA was to do a kind of census in the reservation village of Ball Club. There was a nationwide program dedicated to making sure the elderly were signed up for the newly created Social Security benefits. Not a lot of seniors knew what they were entitled to receive from the government in their retirement, least of all Indians, and a program was launched to find tribal elders and give them information. What my father found deep in the woods around the reservation shocked him. "I expected to see the poverty and the disease and all that. But what I found was a totally atomized society. Scattered. Old couples living off by themselves in the woods with no water and no food and no money. Their kids gone. Gone away to the cities or to boarding schools or just lost. There was no one looking after them. All this talk about community, community, community you hear around and about Indian country. It wasn't there. There was little community to speak of. Community and family systems had been destroyed—as a matter of policy by government and church—so there were just scattered people all over the place."

Such was my father's impression of Ball Club and other small villages and settlements on Leech Lake, White Earth, and Red Lake. But villagers remember it differently; Bena, Ball Club, Inger, Ponemah, Oak Point—these places were still cohesive and functional. Bena, for instance, was the only district on Leech Lake that voted against the Indian Reorganization Act back in 1934 even though it was accepted by a majority of the council.

A little while later Ball Club was once again on my father's radar. There was a complicated program in place to deal with malnutrition. Ball Club was a village of a few hundred people, all Indian, at the eastern edge of Leech Lake Reservation. There was a school lunch program in place, but it was manifestly unfair. As my father remembers it, the children whose families lived on trust land (tribal land) got the free lunch. But those who did not live on tribal land did not get the free lunch. It was creating a weird kind of class conflict in a community where every member was poorer than dirt. This division was tearing the community apart.

"My plan was very simple. It came from my union days. You get all the parties involved in one place—the BIA, the county, the reservation leadership, the state board of education—and that way when one of them passes the buck they have to pass it to someone else in the room. And you bring a tape recorder so it's all on tape. Someone will hang for it and someone will have to eventually take responsibility. The all-Indian parents' organization asked the usual questions and the usual nonanswers were given. But they kept asking and the official people kept passing the buck. One of them, the one from the state, got mad and pounded the table with his fist. And one of the parents—I think her name was Dora—said, 'Hey. When you pound on the table like that you're hurting my tape recorder.' And then they realized that they wouldn't be able to leave until the problem got fixed. It got fixed. And the parent groups! They looked up and looked at each other and they were thinking, 'Hey, we've got power. *We* did this.'"

It was a small thing: making sure all the kids in one school got the same benefits. But it was a start, breaking the BIA's stranglehold on reservation life. My father's work brought him to all of the Ojibwe reservations in Minnesota, but most of his work occurred at the two biggest, Leech Lake and White Earth reservations. Leech Lake was bad, but White Earth was brutal.

In the late 1800s the feds tried to disband Mille Lacs, Fond du Lac, and Leech Lake reservations in Minnesota and Turtle Mountain Reservation in northeastern North Dakota. The Indians from these reservations, numbering in the tens of thousands, were promised farmland, schools, lumber mills, blacksmith shops, churches, seed, hoop iron, plows—in short, everything they would need to reimagine themselves as farmers. If the government had kept its promise, this would have been a good deal. White Earth Reservation is amazing country. The eastern parts near the headwaters of the Mississippi are full of rolling, hilly hardwood forests, and the western edge has rich, loamy soil not unlike the Red River Valley farther to the west (a river valley even more fertile than the Nile). And in the middle of all this are lakes rich in rice and fish. White Earth could have been a paradise. But the promises weren't kept. There were no lumber mills and no blacksmith shops and there was precious little farming equipment. Or at best there was none of this till sometime later. Meanwhile, the thousands of Indians from reservations all over Minnesota and from Turtle Mountain were left in paradise with nothing to work it. They were allotted their lands, which disappeared from underneath their feet because they defaulted on illegal back taxes or traded their land for enough supplies to get them through their winter. Tom Shingobee has in his possession a grocery receipt totaling seventeen dollars that his father had to settle by signing over his 160-acre farm. During World War I, when many of the men were away fighting in Europe, the timber stands were cut down by large timber outfits. One man remembers coming home to his beloved forests only to find a desert of slash and brush and not a tree in sight for miles.

In the 1950s, even after the Indian Reorganization Act, the "Indian New Deal," many of the Indian communities in White Earth still had barely anything to call their own. They had no water or phones or electricity. But the white farms on the reservation had been wired for electricity and phones through the Rural Electrification Administration (REA) with funds created by Congress as part of the New Deal. These lines had largely bypassed each and every Indian community in the region. When my father visited the village of Rice Lake, the village leaders pleaded with him to go to the REA office off the reservation in Bagley and get them electricity.

"No," he said. "I won't go to REA. You will go. I'll help you. But you go."

Rice Lake sent a delegation to the REA offices in Bagley. "I was there with them. And let me tell you, they got the same paternalistic runaround. 'Oh, we can't bring the wires in if we don't know how many of you there are.' Well, we had a census with us and we handed it over. 'Oh! There's that many of you!' After a lot of hemming and hawing the REA guys said, 'Well, it costs a lot to clear the right-of-way and we don't have the funds.' I asked them: if we clear the right-of-way—it was seven miles of trees and brush—will you wire it? 'Sure. We can do that.' But they didn't think it would ever happen. They had a real low opinion of reservation people. But a few weekends later we had a big potluck in Rice Lake. I got tools—brush hooks and axes and saws—from the BIA. And the whole village turned out. I mean women and men and kids. Absolutely everyone. And they cleared the right-of-way, all seven miles of it, in one weekend. That's all it took. And this meant a lot. It meant, for the first time, for the first time *ever:* light, toilets, heat. Real sanitation and light and heat for a village of three hundred people."

The real boon of electricity was the refrigerator. For many families the day an electric fridge arrived is remembered in fond detail, the way VE Day is remembered by many veterans. Refrigerators meant no more spoilage of meager supplies, no more rotten meat.

"This was before the War on Poverty," says my father. "I didn't do it. They did it. It was a powerful thing. That's how it happened: that's how the reservations broke the BIA, not the other way around. It happened in bits and pieces. Some of it was the civil rights movement. Some of it was a side effect of boarding schools. All those Indians who got sent to boarding schools were supposed to be whitewashed there, but it didn't always happen like that. A lot of them went back to their reservations and they had skills—as carpenters and accountants and farmers. And a lot of the vets from World War II came back. They knew how to operate heavy machinery. They knew how to organize. And all of this combined with Native grit. It changed things."

My father hastened to add: "It sure as shit wasn't AIM that did it. AIM was too polarized and too explosive to build anything. They couldn't build power lines or consensus or community. They just used people. They were all a bunch of Al Sharptons. And you can quote me on that. Make sure that gets in there."

The isolation and desperation of life on the reservation, largely aided and abetted by the BIA, still, fifty years later, bring tears to my father's eyes. But these conditions also brought joy. "Much of my life I was rejected. As a Jew. As a puny kid. A refugee in England. A refugee in Ireland. A refugee in the United States—and only a few years later I find myself working for good causes in the Indian community. It was a love affair. I was adopted, with tobacco and don't let anyone tell you different. I was at home, enfolded. I was at home in the Indian community not through some sort of James Fenimore Cooper romanticism but because I found people who loved me, and whom I loved. At first they respected my work. And it grew from there."

I suppose it's strange to find a Jew on a reservation. It's even stranger to consider that more white people than Indians live on the Leech Lake Reservation. This is true of many reservations. It is one of the lasting and most damning effects of the U.S. government policy of allotment, which began with the Dawes Act in 1887 and the amendments in 1891 and 1906. The Dawes Act was the enabling federal legislation, and the Nelson Act fueled the actual allotment of reservations in Minnesota. Section 1 of the Dawes Act authorized the president to divide collective tribal lands into individual sections. Each head of a household was to be granted a 160-acre parcel if the land was arable or a 320-acre parcel if the land was suitable only for grazing. Single individuals and orphans were granted eighty acres each and all other "single individuals" (minors, not women) were to be given forty acres each. The parcels of land distributed to Indian individuals were, under the act, to be held in trust for twenty-five years, during which time they were not able to sell it. Devastatingly, the "surplus" land (that is, the land "left over" after all the individuals in a tribe were given their parcels) was opened up for sale to non-Natives. So even as early as the 1890s, large reservations with Indian populations decimated by disease and warfare suddenly found their lands gone, and their near neighbors were the people who benefited from the dispossession. In all, during the forty-seven years the Dawes Act was on the books (the Indian Reorganization Act, passed in 1934, officially stopped allotment but did not formally rescind the policy), Native Americans lost more than 90 million acres of tribal lands, about two-thirds of the lands held by Indians when the Dawes Act was passed; Indians lost, roughly, land that equals the size of the state of California. Ninety thousand Native Americans were left landless and largely homeless. The problems of this kind of landlessness were felt well into the 1970s and are still felt today. During that time, many Indian families were found to be living in cars, under porches, and crammed eight and sometimes ten to a room in dilapidated shacks across the country.

To make matters worse, the Burke Amendment in 1906 took even more land out of Indian control. It instituted a process known as "forced patenting." Indians deemed "competent and capable" were given a patent in fee simple for their land. That is, the land was taken out of trust and they were given title, were now subject to taxation, and could sell their land. Those deemed "incapable and incompetent" had their lands automatically leased out at the discretion of the secretary of the interior. The processes by which Indians were deemed "capable" or "incapable" were largely subjective. In many cases (and land disputes at White Earth Reservation were often settled this way) government agents relied on the emergent field of eugenics to help them make a determination as to competence. Full-bloods were often deemed incompetent because they were full-bloods, whereas mixed-bloods were thought to have enough white blood to make them intelligent enough to understand the ins and outs of land ownership. But how to tell if someone was or was not a full-blood in an especially complicated community like White Earth Reservation whose population had been sourced from North Dakota, Mille Lacs, Leech Lake, and Fond du Lac? The secretary of the interior turned to two anthropologists: Dr. Alex Hrdlicka, director of anthropology at the Smithsonian, and Dr. Albert E. Jenks of the University of Minnesota. To determine full-blood status, Hrdlicka and Jenks had devised certain criteria: skull shape, distance between the eyes, color of teeth, nails, and gums. Their most interesting hypothesis was that if you scratched your fingernail across the chest of a mixed-blood it would redden (hyperaemia) more than if you scratched the chest of a full-blood. The effects of this policy and the determinations about full-blood, half-blood, and quarter-blood that were made in the 1920s are still felt today. Most of the "blood" statistics for White Earth were wrong then and were never corrected, and so thousands if not tens of thousands of White Earth Indians today cannot be enrolled and do not receive any of the benefits of enrollment. There were so many claims that land was illegally appropriated from White Earth tribal members that the White Earth Land Settlement Act (WELSA) was passed in 1986. According to WELSA, "The White Earth allotments and land claims controversy involved the individual property rights of Indian people who had received allotments (tracts) of land to be held 'in trust' by the United States government. The White Earth land claims involved over 1900 individual allotments and titles to over 100,000 acres of land, which were illegally transferred during the 1900s. The illegal transfers were accomplished through the use of mass quantities of liquor, falsified affidavits, mortgages on grocery bills, sales by minor children, and illegal tax forfeitures. Many of those illegal transfers were uncovered during a federal investigation during the 1980s. After the extent of the land claims [was] discovered and political pressure from the current landowners was applied, the federal government chose to pursue a negotiated political settlement to the land claims controversy. The White Earth Land Settlement Act (WELSA) was passed in 1986 extinguishing the White Earth land claims by retroactively approving the illegal land transfers. In exchange, WELSA provided that the allottees or their heirs would be compensated financially. The monetary compensation is to be based on the fair market value of the land at the time of taking, minus any money received by the allottee at the time, plus interest to date." But with many heirs (sometimes more than twenty) claiming the same parcels of land, what payments were made were so small as to change very little.

In the 1950s and 1960s as places like Ball Club got to make their own rules about how their children were administered to and as the people of Rice Lake at White Earth came to see they had the power to change their own lives, the grip of the BIA began to loosen in communities on reservations across the country. One skilled fighter confronting the BIA was Roger Jourdain, the first elected chairman of Red Lake Reservation. Just before my father worked for the BIA he found employment at Red Lake through the Community Action Program (CAP), which was funded in part by Lyndon Johnson's War on Poverty and was one of the more controversial aspects of Johnson's plan. It was a huge program designed to tackle local poverty problems with a cocktail of federal funds, foundation support, and local investment. The controversial aspects were the scale, speed, and unique features of the program that mandated local staffing and control. Jourdain, at Red Lake, was keen to get his hands on the CAP money, and so he and a few other leaders and my father submitted an application for funds through CAP. Their application was denied. The reason: not enough local buy-in. My father and three others got some money from the Minnesota Chippewa tribe and flew to Washington on the red-eye to see what they could do. They landed at six in the morning and spent what remaining cash they had on cab fare from the airport to the Office of Economic Opportunity (OEO), which oversaw the CAP program. They were too early. They went for breakfast, came back, and were told rather curtly by an administrator that there was nothing that could be done.

"Well," said one of the Red Lake representatives, "what next?" They had no money and little by way of encouragement.

"Why don't we walk down to the vice president's office?" suggested my father. "He's from Minnesota." Since they couldn't afford cab fare they walked from OEO all the way up Pennsylvania Avenue and announced themselves to the staff at Hubert Humphrey's office as a delegation from Red Lake Reservation. "We were met by some functionary," remembers my father. He came out and took one look at us and asked, 'What can I do for you?'—though it was clear he didn't want to do anything. He didn't even take us into an office to sit down or offer us water or anything. 'We came to see about our application for CAP money. We were denied and we want Humphrey to do something about it.'

"'What seems to be the problem?'

"'We applied. We have need. But we're too fucking poor to qualify. Is that what the War on Poverty is supposed to be like? You have to be rich to qualify?'

"That got his attention. He disappeared into the back. In a little bit Hubert Humphrey came out. We knew each other from his campaigning days in northern Minnesota. And he said, 'So what can I do for you?' And I said, 'We applied for CAP money. But we were told we were too poor to qualify—we can't afford the local buy-in because there's no damn money up there.' He looked at us and looked at his assistant and said to him, 'Do something about this, will you?'

"By that afternoon our application had been approved and we were on our way back to Red Lake. Just having CAP funded at Red Lake was a big deal. It meant health care and housing and social services. But it meant something much more, too," remembers my father. "For the first time there was a community program on the rez not funded by the BIA. Even the proceeds from fishing or timber sales were kept in trust by the BIA. But they had no part in CAP money. And the band got to hire its own staff, its own outreach workers, its own administration. That, too, was in part how the BIA stopped being the sole power and supreme controller of the purse strings on the rez."

In the town of Bemidji, Minnesota, many people are afraid of Red Lakers. Bemidji is the largest town in the area, with a population of 12,000. It is the county seat and the shopping and banking destination for most of the county. Indians live in Bemidji, and many of us go there either to shop or to appear in court or both. The next nearest town that is bigger is Duluth, 155 miles to the east. At one time Bemidji was *the* going concern. It sat at the junction of rail lines running north-south between Winnipeg and Minneapolis and lines that ran east-west between Grand Forks and Duluth. All the grain and timber passing through the north passed through Bemidji. And it is surrounded by Indians, literally— White Earth, Red Lake, and Leech Lake reservations form the points of a triangle in which Bemidji sits at the center, and the combined reservation populations outnumber the population of Bemidji two to one. Bemidji still has a "circle the wagons" kind of feel to it.

Nowadays, however, the circling of the wagons has more to do with the service-sector economy gutting local businesses. Most of the stores now hem the town instead of filling it out. At the city center or what's left of it, enormous cement statues of Paul and Babe stand facing west as they have done since 1937 at the carnival grounds, and just across the main street, at Morrell's Chippewa Trading Post, is an equally large iron statue of an Indian wearing buckskin breeches but no shirt. His hair is pulled back in two long iron braids and one arm is raised with palm out, in the old "How" pose so familiar to most Americans. For many years Morrell's iron Indian was the only Indian in town.

It's hard to say who's more savage: the Indian statue or Paul Bunyan. The Indian looks stoic (definitely not Ojibwe) but gentle, somehow, in his iron pose, wearing his iron pants, flexing his iron washboard stomach. The struggle between "the civilized" and "the savage" has been raging in Bemidji for many years. On October 25, 1966, Robert Kohl, a radio announcer on KBUN, Bemidji's only radio station, read an editorial about life on Red Lake Reservation. He described one particularly run-down home and said:

> The scene is typical of many a welfare home . . . dirt and filth, cats and dogs and flies, lots of kids . . . some retarded, some with emotional problems of a serious nature, but more in proportion than any families off the reservation . . . human irresponsibility at its zenith and it staggers the imagination to discover that we are trying to help these people with welfare money. . . .
>
> Perhaps that is where the welfare laws could be re-written . . . to help only those who are salvageable. . . . Perhaps we should never have lowered our sights to this level, perhaps we should have let nature take her course, let disease and malnutrition disrupt the reproductive process and weed out those at the very bottom of the heap. . . .
>
> They are so low on the human scale that it is doubtful they will ever climb upward. Their satisfaction level is so low that it corresponds to that of the most primitive of the earth's animals . . . food, comfort, and a place to reproduce . . . those are the three . . . and with our welfare dollars we provide a little food in the belly, some

kind of primitive shelter, and a place to reproduce, and this is all that is wanted, all that is needed, all that is desired.

They are satisfied . . . but who takes care of the offspring, including those with tortured and twisted minds raised in this environment? Is it really Christian, really human, to meddle with lives so primitive and basic? And what's the alternative? Spend thirty or forty thousand dollars per child to remove him from the element, educate him, only to look back and see the child population gaining on you through irresponsible procreation?

Is it any less heartless to sacrifice physically and mentally healthy young men in Vietnam or Korea to make the world safe for our political philosophy than it is to sacrifice these hopelessly morally and mentally indigent for our economic philosophy?

Ignoring the fact that not a few men from Leech Lake, White Earth, and Red Lake were at that moment serving in Vietnam, Kohl's comments were shocking for an entirely different reason. What is amazing is the extent of the belief that Indians don't read or listen to the radio. Comments about our lives float around us on the air and in print and it comes as a surprise that, in addition to being stoic and riding horses and skinning beavers, we read and we listen. Indians are compulsive newspaper consumers. So it was no surprise that the Red Lake tribal council heard that radio broadcast in 1966, recorded it, and played it at a regularly scheduled council meeting, which happened to be held that same day. At the time Red Lake was governed by an elected tribal council, led by Roger Jourdain, and backed by a council of hereditary chiefs, representing the original seven clans that made up the band. This was a powerful mix. And it was no accident that the joint council decided to fight; by far the largest clan on Red Lake is the Bear Clan. Since Red Lake had existed on the very western frontier of Ojibwe territory for so long, and was so long involved in wars and skirmishes with the Sioux, most of the Red Lake Band belonged to this warrior clan, the Bear Clan. By unanimous decision they decided to boycott businesses in the Bemidji area until Kohl was fired, and until the radio station broadcast a public apology. Leech Lake and White Earth reservations joined the boycott the following day.

The response to the boycott was predictable even if the effects were not. Some area residents came out in support of Indians: Elizabeth Rogers of Guthrie, just south of Bemidji, praised the "wisdom and courage of the Red Lake Tribal Council." Some did not: David E. Umhauer of Bemidji wrote, "I hope those Indians offended by the broadcast do boycott Bemidji. If they do, it will be a cleaner town." Cleaner or not, it was, almost immediately, poorer. "The boycott has been so effective and so thorough that over the week, for the first time since Bemidji became a community, Bemidji's streets have been practically devoid of Indians," reported the *Bemidji Pioneer*. No Indians spent any of their money in Bemidji. No one bought groceries, clothes, or equipment. Indians went elsewhere for construction supplies, heating oil, and gasoline. Tribal government offices on all three reservations refused to buy office supplies and business equipment. Many people canceled their insurance policies held by Bemidji brokers. Red Lake and the other reservations threatened to withdraw all tribal funds—obtained by government contracts, logging, and the profits from the Red Lake commercial fishery—from Bemidji's banks. Since Indians were universally acknowledged as being the poorest of the poor, marginal, without any clout to speak of, no one in Bemidji was concerned at first. But the tribal funds banked in Bemidji amounted to $2 million rather than the $500,000 that had previously been estimated. Local businesses, which had haughtily made Indians wait by the back door ever since Bemidji incorporated in 1896, began to feel the pinch immediately. And the pinch hurt more than they cared to admit.

Roger Jourdain also liked to write letters. As a child he had been sent to an Indian boarding school at Flandreau, South Dakota. He had worked as an operator of heavy machiney during World War II on the Alcan Highway. He was not afraid of a fight. And he was not afraid to write. He wrote hundreds of letters to local, regional, and national political figures. Each letter contained a statement about the radio broadcasts and a transcript of Kohl's editorial. And each and every envelope was hand-addressed by Jourdain himself in his neat boarding-school script.

Dear Sir,

The people of Red Lake Reservation have sought over the years to improve the economic and educational structure of the Reservation. Great strides have been made and particularly so in the last few years.

It is more than disappointing therefore when broadcasts are made reviving the ancient prejudices, resorting to the name calling of Indians, ignoring the good efforts of the many for the possible faults of the few.

We attach a transcript of a broadcast made over Bemidji Radio station KBUN on Tuesday, October 25, 1966, and ask for your careful examination of this. We do not consider ourselves as "sub-human, as animal like, or morally and mentally indigent." We trust you do not think of us in this fashion either. We will appreciate anything you, your office, and associates can do to persuade the management of a 20th century enterprise to outgrow the 19th century hate-the-Indian complex. This should be a time for working and building together, not a time for inflaming ancient racial prejudices.

It is unfortunate that such a broadcast would be made; it would be even more unfortunate if it were allowed to pass unchallenged. This broadcast is contrary to the mainstream American effort and the American struggle to build even better relationships between people. A healthy nation can not tolerate the singling out of one minority for abuse. We seek to enlist your support in our struggle.

The letters, written the day after the broadcast, were sent to senators Walter F. Mondale and Eugene McCarthy, Vice President Hubert H. Humphrey, President Lyndon B. Johnson, Mayor Howard Menge of Bemidji, and the president of the chamber of commerce, Carl Olsen. Later, identical letters were sent to dozens of state officials and legislators, local clergymen, business leaders, and anyone else Jourdain thought might be of help.

Within days the Brahmins of Bemidji were trekking up to Red Lake, where they met with the tribal council. Within a week they were begging Red Lake and the other reservations, Leech Lake and White Earth, to bring their business back. Within two weeks the radio announcer was fired and a public apology was made in print and over the air, and with it came the promise of fifty jobs for Indians in Bemidji. At that point no visible Indians (but a few invisible ones—Indians who were mixed enough to pass as white) worked in town. None. Not in government jobs, not in business, not even as checkout clerks at Luekens Village Foods or John's Super Valu, the two grocery stores. Red Lake changed that for all of us. Within two years 100 Indians were working in Bemidji.

Forty years later, everyone at Red Lake, Leech Lake, and White Earth remembers the days of the boycott. And though to an outsider it might matter little or seem like one small click of the wheel of social justice, it was the first time anyone could remember white people publicly apologizing to Indians not because they wanted to (well-meaning liberals have been apologizing to Indians for close to 500 years) but because they had to.

It was around this time—the late 1960s and early 1970s—that efforts began to establish tribal judiciaries beyond the Courts of Indian Offenses controlled by the BIA. But the courts, like the tribal governments from which they sprang, were complicated. Tribal governments after the IRA, loosely based on the organization of municipalities and cities, operating in accordance with constitutions that didn't necessarily conform to their cultures or their conditions, had an enormous responsibility and a dysfunctional relationship with the government.

Tribal government, like any government, has certain responsibilities. It must attend to the social conditions, economic status, public health, infrastructure, natural resources, and education of its people. But unlike many other kinds of government—the state and federal levels come to mind—tribal government has a highly codependent type of autonomy. A state can levy income and property taxes to pay for infrastructure such as roads, civic buildings, and schools. Tribes have the same responsibilities but they usually don't have the power to levy taxes. Or if they do, there is really no tax base to draw from and taxation is more or less politically impossible to achieve. Instead they have to negotiate with the state and the feds for educational funding, with the state and the feds for road improvements, with the feds for health care, and so on. They must maintain the health of their natural resources but they don't receive fees from selling licenses or lottery tickets (as the state of Minnesota does) to accomplish this. No corporation or HMO will build a hospital in the reservation; instead, most tribes rely on the Indian Health Service for medical care. Every executive decision puts the tribe in negotiation with one, two, or sometimes three different governments or agencies. Typically, the funding for tribal government comes from three sources—money and services owed to tribes as part of federal treaty obligations, tribally owned business enterprises, and federal and state grants for tribal projects. Tribes are rarely "free" to spend the money or to make their own decisions about resources, because all that money, or most of it, comes with strings attached. To make matters worse, the constitutions that largely empower these tribes are often very vague on separation of powers and responsibilities. There is language about elections and tribal courts, but when the two clash (say, in a contested election), the decision comes down to a judge who was appointed by the very tribal council about whom the dispute swirls. For most tribal governments there is no balance of power; on the contrary, power is very much out of balance. Such was the case at White Earth Reservation in the 1990s.

At the time it was controlled by one of the most powerful Indian leaders in the country, Darrell "Chip" Wadena. Wadena oversaw the advent of gaming on White Earth and held sway over the fractious reservation for more than twenty years. He drove a truck with a vanity license plate that read "CHIEF." The expensive bug guard over the lip of the hood had been hand-painted with the phrase "SUPER CHIEF." Brian Goodwin, a White Earth enrollee enraged by Wadena's thievery, happened across Wadena's truck in the casino parking lot, scratched off the C in "SUPER CHIEF," and replaced it with a T. And who says "counting coup" is a dead practice? When the casino was being built the bidding was rigged and contracts were awarded to construction companies that Wadena controlled or was a partner in. The contract for slot machines went to a company that Wadena had a stake in. When ballots for tribal elections were mailed out to White Earth enrollees who lived off the reservation, the packages contained flyers and information about Wadena and his campaign. Eventually the "super chief" became the object of a federal investigation, at which time he cried "sovereignty" and said that the government was trying to do away with tribal autonomy. But his was the kind of autonomy familiar to anyone who lived through the nepotism, fraud, and incompetence of the days when the Indian agent and the BIA were in charge. Wadena was con-victed of bid rigging and election fraud and served two and a half years in federal prison. In 2004 he ran for office again—there was nothing in the White Earth constitution at the time to prevent convicted fel-ons from running for or holding office.

Another example is Leech Lake, where there was a break-in at the tribal government offices. When the Bureau of Criminal Appre-hension (the top state-run law enforcement agency) was called in, its investigators found out that an undisclosed sum of money had been stolen from a filing cabinet. The money in that cabinet was used for paying tribal council members a per diem. The scam was this: the council members got their per diem (according to federal per diem charts) for every meeting they attended. But the council would call multiple meetings on a single day and the council members would get multiple per diems for a single "diem." That was a small scam com-pared with the one run by Alfred "Tig" Pemberton, Harold "Skip" Finn, and Daniel Brown. Together they formed a bogus insurance company, Reservation Risk Management, that succeeded in defraud-ing Leech Lake Reservation of millions of dollars, which they pock-eted. Finn (the tribal attorney and a state senator) resigned and was later convicted of conspiracy, theft, and mail fraud. He was disbarred, sentenced to five years in prison, and assessed a $100,000 fine. A cynic might say that after doing away with the corruption, mismanagement, and paternalism of the BIA and government agents, tribes took on the job themselves. Perhaps. But Wadena, Finn, and others around the country ended up in jail. And despite the design flaws of tribal govern-ment and the legacy of the abuse of governmental power on the part of federal and tribal leaders, tribes have managed to grow. With them, tribal courts have also grown.

As of today, there are about 275 Indian tribes and Alaskan Native villages that have courts of their own. But the paternalism of the 1950s lingers. Some of these courts and court systems are vast. The Navajo have six district courts and a seventh, floating judge who serves where needed. Supporting the courts is a police force of more than 200 officers. Other courts are small. Court is held in storerooms or modular buildings. In some places the tribal judge is also the prosecutor. Non-Natives can't be tried in these courts, but Indians from other tribes can be. Non-Natives who commit crimes on Indian land against Indians are still tried by the federal government, but tribal law enforcement can cite, fine, bar, ban, or expel them. The nonprofit Tribal Law and Policy Institute publishes a table on its Web site that tries to make sense of who can be tried, for what, and by whom in Indian country.

Type of Crime

	Major Crime as Defined by Major Crimes Act	All Other Crimes
Indian perpetrator, Indian victim	Federal and tribal jurisdiction	Tribal jurisdiction
Indian perpetrator, non-Indian victim	Federal and tribal jurisdiction	Federal and tribal jurisdiction
Non-Indian perpetrator, Indian victim	Federal and tribal jurisdiction	Federal jurisdiction
Non-Indian perpetrator, non-Indian victim	State jurisdiction	State jurisdiction

It seems simple enough, but an asterisk leads us to this: "Please note that this general criminal jurisdiction chart does not apply to jurisdiction where Public Law 280, 18 U.S.C 1162, or other relevant federal statues have conferred jurisdiction upon the state."

This means that the chart works, with the exception of states that have applied Public Law 280—civil jurisdiction legislation, passed in 1953, which some people consider the most destructive act of

Congress for Indian people in the twentieth century. In effect, PL 280 gave the states criminal jurisdiction over Indians and non-Indians on Indian land. These states include California, Minnesota (except Red Lake Reservation), Nebraska, Oregon (except Warm Springs Reservation), Wisconsin, Nevada, South Dakota, Washington, Florida, Utah, Montana, North Dakota, Arizona, Iowa, Alaska (except Metlakatla Indian Community), and Utah. Some reservations—Bois Forte, where my mother is judge—retroceded from PL 280 and reassumed jurisdiction over crimes committed on the reservation. So the chart above works for all the states except those with the most Indians and Indian reservations. Most of the time there is a complicated dance between federal, state, county, and tribal jurisdiction. If fairness is a mark of a good judicial system, one would think that clarity is also a virtue to be promoted. Some feel (and I am one of them) that PL 280 only passed on the crimes that the United States claimed it should prosecute under the Major Crimes Act, in effect making the states responsible for the jurisdiction claimed by the feds in the nineteenth century. This means that PL 280 might be seen as covering only major crimes—rape, larceny, murder, kidnapping—and that the rest, from petty crimes to whole categories of felonies, might be crimes the tribes have retained the right to try in their own courts with their own juries. This has not been tested widely but perhaps it should be.

That cold day in court at Bois Forte was, according to my mother, typical. Half the cases involved kids who were affected in bad ways. Nine of the eleven cases involved women. All of the cases except one were drug-related or alcohol-related and involved defendants who pleaded guilty and who seemed to be hanging on to the edges of their own lives. All the defendants who appeared before my mother seemed to have cobbled their lives together as best they could. They were underemployed; some had part-time jobs or service-sector jobs. Others made money doing seasonal work (ricing in late summer, picking balsam boughs in the fall, working on tribal projects). Their houses were partly funded by the BIA and the tribe and were often held together with whatever they could find at hand. Health care came partly from private insurance and partly from the Indian Health Service, but none of it seemed very comprehensive. Their families were fractured—in flux, separated, with some members incarcerated or scattered among various other relatives or foster families. When I think about the people who appear in my mother's court and in other courts around Indian country, their lives seem as checkered as the reservation land itself—which was made into a checkerboard by the Dawes Act. The idea of a checkerboard might very well be the best way to describe tribal justice and jurisdiction.

The land inside reservations such as Leech Lake and White Earth does resemble a checkerboard: the reservation boundary is the edge of the board, and within it there are squares of different colors—black for tribally owned land, white for non-tribal land owned by private individuals, counties, states, the federal government, and corporations. The rights of Indians and the jurisdictions of Indian courts form such a pattern, too. For instance, officers Grolla and Nelson could confiscate Mueller's boat at Red Lake. They could cite him and his son-in-law, could expel them from the reservation, but could not arrest them. There is some effort to change that, however. The struggle over the limits of tribal jurisdiction has been vicious, varied, and long-lasting. The Crow Dog case (which led to the Major Crimes Act) is but one example. More recently, in 1973, a test came again. On August 19, 1973, during "Chief Seattle Days," a celebration sponsored by the Suquamish Reservation, a non-Indian resident of the reservation was arrested by tribal police and charged with assault and battery. "Chief Seattle Days" draws a large and rowdy crowd, and the tribe had appealed to state and local law enforcement agencies for help in policing the event. Its repeated requests were denied. The tribe members were told that they would have to provide all the law enforcement and that they'd have to pay for it, too. So when Mark David Oliphant was arrested, he was arraigned in tribal court and transported off-reservation to Bremerton jail, where those arraigned in tribal court were sent pursuant to a lease agreement with the BIA and the state. A year later, another non-Indian resident of Suquamish Reservation, Daniel B. Belgarde, was involved in a high-speed chase on the rez. It so happened that Oliphant was a passenger in the car. The chase ended when Belgarde rammed a police car. He was charged, under the Suquamish tribal code, with reckless driving. Instead of facing charges Oliphant and Belgarde applied for a writ of habeas corpus; they claimed that the tribe didn't have jurisdiction over non-Indians. The case (as so many have) wound its way up to the U.S. Supreme Court. Even though the Suquamish never officially relinquished their right to prosecute wrongdoers as part of a treaty, and no congressional act had been passed that limited the Suquamish or their authority over their own affairs, the Supreme Court ruled that the Suquamish (and by extension other tribes) did not have jurisdiction over non-Indians. Tribes can hold non-Indians for serious crimes but only until those being held can be picked up by state, federal, or local authorities. This creates serious complications for tribes seeking to administer justice on their own lands, especially when we consider that Indians suffer physical violence at the hands of non-Indians at ten times the national average.

For instance, in Oklahoma, where Indian communities are scattered across many counties, law enforcement comes face-to-face with sovereignty in ways that don't help. Sexual crimes are the most difficult to deal with. Indian women in Alaska are two and a half times more likely than white women to be the victims of sexual assault. When Indian women are raped or assaulted by another Indian on tribal land the tribal police can intervene and arrest the perpetrators. Well and good. But they cannot arrest, detain, or investigate a crime perpetrated on an Indian woman by a non-Indian. It is a widely held sentiment in Oklahoma that local law enforcement is not as invested in solving rapes of and assaults against Indian women. The tribal police, who do want to act, can't. In one case, a Potawatomi woman was assaulted and the perpetrator was still hiding in her house when the police arrived. When the tribal victim's advocate showed up she found agents of four different law enforcement agencies on the front lawn, arguing about who had responsibility and jurisdiction.

Some tribes are trying to change this balance of power. In 2009 the Blackfeet tribal council passed a resolution calling on the Montana state delegation to Congress to sponsor a bill that would allow Indian courts to arrest and try non-Indians for crimes committed on Indian land. One council member—Rodney "Fish" Gervais, a strong advocate of the resolution and an activist for Indian civil rights—helped form the Montana Indian Civil Rights Commission. The Blackfeet Nation hosted the first conference to address issues of discrimination in towns bordering reservations. He said that many crimes against Native women committed by non-Indians go unpunished. Many drug runners use reservation lands to traffic drugs, and tribal police and courts administer justice with their hands tied. Some reservations, such as White Earth, are expanding their powers—White Earth has begun asserting jurisdiction in child custody and child support cases, even for non-enrolled children of White Earth Band members or for non-enrolled parents who are being taken to court for child support. Allotment made our land a checkerboard and as a result we lack complete control of the land; so, too, we lack complete control of our rights and our lives.

At lunch we retired to my mother's chambers and ate Lucille's soup. The soup was great, but court was a bit depressing. Still, it could be worse. As complicated and varied as the issues of jurisdiction can be for tribal members and tribal courts, and as shaky as they can be given the limits and history of tribal government, it is encouraging that Indians can appear in tribal court and be judged by their peers.

But it will be hard to change the mistrust many Indians have of government and policing. In a recent arrest report filed at the Cass County sheriff's office, an Indian man hitchhiking from Cass Lake to Bemidji was seen weaving over the white fog line that separates the shoulder from the roadway. A police officer witnessed the man stagger into traffic and stopped. He "asked how [he] was doing." But the man was combative and verbally abusive. "He stated that I was 'on Indian land' and began cussing at me." The officer continued to talk with the man and let him know he was concerned because he was walking in the roadway. Then the man lunged at the officer and grabbed for the officer's duty pistol. According to the officer: "I immediately struck [him] with the palm of my left hand on the left side of his upper torso. [He] released his grip and staggered backward. [He] then took a fighting stance and charged me. [He] swung his right fist at my face. I stepped to the side and took control of [his] right arm, and lowered him to the ground with a straight arm takedown." The officer then got the man into the back of the squad car. While in transit the man shouted at the officer all the way to the Cass County Jail. He stated: 'You fucking bastard! I'll get you! Fuck you, fuck you! Fuck you white boy.' "

In another incident an Indian man was stopped in Cass Lake for drunk driving. He could barely stand. He was searched, cuffed, and placed in the backseat of the cruiser. "I transported [him] to the Cass County Jail for Implied Consent and while en-route he stated I couldn't arrest him for DWI being he didn't take the test. That the Indians are going to have an up rising [sic] and kill the Whites. He stated that he was going to fuck me up at the jail when the cuffs come off. Upon arrival at the jail he stated all is good and shook my hand."

Charley Grolla says the same distrust of white law enforcement extends to white officers employed by tribal law enforcement agencies. "Some of the white officers have a tough time at Red Lake," he says. "I think to myself, they'd better not go alone, they'll start a riot. I mean, not that they are bad officers, they're not. They're good. But the green ones don't necessarily know Indians. And the Indians don't know them. So when the officer shows up they'll say, 'Hell, no. I won't go in with you. I won't get in the car.' And they'll make a run for it. But they say to me and Nelson and the other Indian officers, 'I'll go in with you, but not with that white devil.' Seriously! I've heard that 'white devil' stuff a lot. People say that shit!"

❧

Tribal courts are getting better—stronger, more impartial, and staffed by people with a lot of experience in the field. When tribal courts started, many of the judges, though they were Indian, had no formal legal training. It was hard to find Indian lawyers. Both problems have been amended in many places. Now ten of the eleven bands or tribes in Minnesota have lawyers as judges. The perception of unfairness that attended the early days of tribal courts has also been dispelled. This has been one of the greatest victories for the tribal court at Lac Courte Oreilles (LCO) Reservation and a personal victory for Brian Bisonette, the tribal secretary-treasurer for LCO.

Roughly 107 square miles in area and with more than 3,500 residents, LCO is one of the largest of the eleven reservations in the state, and one of the poorest. In terms of gross revenue it ranks as the third poorest in the state. Unemployment is high. Social problems abound. Milwaukee-based gangs like the Latin Kings were so entrenched at LCO that in 2002 the tribe declared a state of emergency. Dealing drugs there, and on other reservations, is easy, says Steve Hagenah of the Minnesota Bureau of Criminal Apprehension. He explains drug dealing on reservations in general this way: "It's easy for them to sell drugs on the rez. Gangsters buy drugs, mostly meth, from Mexicans in Minneapolis and drive it up to Red Lake and Leech Lake and White Earth, places like that. They then give free drugs to girls in exchange for sex and a place to stay. They keep the drugs in their cars. With no drugs on the premises it's hard to get warrants. When the cops get close they just close their trunks and drive away. It's easy. They've got no overhead except for gas." This is also true of LCO, which is a convenient place for drug dealers from Chicago, Milwaukee, and Minneapolis. In response the Bureau of Indian Affairs, the FBI, and the state of Wisconsin partnered with the tribe and together they worked to put a stop to the trade in crack and meth; their efforts led to the arrest of at least twenty-seven tribal members in 2004.

Brian Bisonette is on the tribal council at LCO. Bisonette is a good man for the job of secretary-treasurer. His hair is shaved on the sides and long on top and in back, styled in what some call an Ojibwe-mullet. He isn't especially tall, but he has long arms and strong shoulders. He walks slightly bowlegged. All in all, he has what I think of as the classical Ojibwe build: strong, balanced, not especially fast, more like a badger than a wolf. He speaks slowly, in a lilting voice that is like his gait. Even in English he sounds like a Wisconsin Ojibwe—these Ojibwe are known for being excellent talkers who speak slowly and musically. It is hard to imagine Brian getting really worked up about something or showing too much excitement. He chooses his words carefully. "Even to this day I don't honestly see myself as a politician. I got into politics because I believed in myself and I think I have vision. And I was concerned about the direction my community was going in. I didn't really have any desire for politics, not really, you know. I do know a lot in a lot of different areas. All in all I cared about my community and was encouraged by people I held in high regard, people I thought of as really intelligent. But I'd seem some of the decisions being made here and I didn't like them. It didn't seem like they had the vision or took the opportunity to delay their decisions and weigh all their options. A good example is as regards our land. At the time, around 2000, we used to issue land leases to any tribal member who met the criteria. The problem was that they were issuing leases scattered all over the place. Our reservation is small. We've got to think about a plan. They gave out residential land leases to tribal members but put them in areas that only benefited the leasees. They put those houses right on hunting and trapping grounds. They were giving a benefit to one person and everyone suffered the consequences, so I pushed a moratorium on leasing, and worked on a land-lease plan, a land-use plan for housing and development. It was situations like that—I've got a lot of experience and education—that was a motivator for me. I'd been passive, unconcerned, like the average tribal member. But I saw this stuff going on and I thought it could be made better. I got elected in 2003. Being the young naive guy I was I thought I could go in there and make all these changes. And then you try and it's a lot harder than you believe. The reality is that change will come, but it's incumbent upon you once you get elected to learn, to get all the information and be flexible and see all the options, and come up with alternatives. Since 2003 we've made some huge changes around here. Changes for the better. We've been supporting each other on the council. One of our biggest accomplishments was giving our tribal court autonomy. It was a first step in setting up a separation of powers. It was difficult. You had a council at that time which you could call 'old school.' They liked the concept of being the supreme court. They liked the power. It took a lot of debate. Even after the court codes were amended it still didn't sink in with some of the council members. I remember one of the first decisions the judge made affected one of the council member's family. He came running up: 'We need to overturn this.' Nope. Can't do it. Read the court codes. It took a lot of work. For the most part tribal courts have been perceived as kangaroo courts. Whatever decision the judge made could be overridden by the tribal council. My feeling is, it's all about fairness to everyone. Just because you are connected through friendship or you're a relative it shouldn't have any bearing. I mean, how fair is it if you and me go to court? You've got a case against me and it's iron clad. But you go into tribal court knowing my uncle is the chairman. How are you going to feel knowing the judge will decide in your favor and then I go to the council and change the verdict? That's crazy. That's not justice. We amended the codes to fix that problem. You can appeal a decision but not to the tribal council. You go to an appellate court made up of Wisconsin judges—so the decision goes to them and they are impartial. I love hanging my hat on that one."

Fairness is something that Brian Bisonette is clearly passionate about. No one expects fairness. Just after he was elected in 2003 he was gassing up his boat at the tribal trading post. A recent voter said something like, "It's nice to get voted in." "I told her—I've had this boat for years. I've always worked. I've worked my whole life and I'm good with my money. I'm careful with it. And so I can afford this boat. I don't get anything extra."

A lot of talent leaves reservations because there is no employment security. Few unions function on the reservation. There are few employment codes that are enforced. Brian's daughter was considering applying for a job on a neighboring reservation notorious for its corruption.

"I told her—there's no job security over there. Work here, at LCO. The pay isn't great, but at least you've got security here. Here you make less money and over there you make more, but you've got protections here. We have a tribal hiring committee that is independent of the appeals committee. Our tribe has lost a lot because it has violated its own employment policies. In the last few years we've gotten out of the business of personal personnel appeals. The number of personal appeals was outrageous. I didn't get elected to hear all these appeals. When you get politics involved, the hiring process and the appeals process get to be a joke. We amended the personnel policies and procedures. We've got appeals committee, hearing committee, screening committee. We have staff who have been appointed to serve in these capacities. The tribal governing board doesn't get involved in any of that anymore. We're keeping politics out of government. We're striving for fairness for our own people. If the system isn't fair, how can we lead?"

At places like LCO around the country tribal courts are getting more effective and bolder. They are beginning to establish juvenile courts, conservation courts, appellate courts, and so on. Constitutional reform is a reality at many places. And although jurisdiction, like the problems courts are trying to fix, is largely a checkerboard affair, Indians are beginning to change what is meant by "Indian justice."

And such changes don't affect just Indians. They might very well affect white people, too. Certainly the relationship between Natives and non-Natives is getting a little better than when anthropologists went around scratching the chests of Indians at White Earth. It is maddening to wonder how many thousands of acres of Indian land were lost because two guys went around White Earth Reservation in 1916 scratching the chests of my ancestors. I think it's safe to say that very few white people have ever lost their land because two academics showed up on their front stoops, scratched their chests, and measured their skulls. But as a result of this study, lots of white people came to live on Indian land and still live there, many generations after the passing of the Dawes Act. More white people than Indian people live within the external boundaries of Leech Lake Reservation.

Nett Lake tribal court is a long way from the paternalism of the 1950s. Court is wrapping up for the day. I was impressed—newly impressed by my mother. It struck me as totally strange and totally awesome to see a white lawyer defending Indian clients in front of an Indian judge. Among the more serious cases I heard that day was the case of the Boy with Blue Hair. He was Indian but not enrolled at Bois Forte. At Bois Forte the court has jurisdiction over all enrolled Indians of federally recognized tribes in the United States (but not Indians enrolled in tribes in Canada—even if the community is Ojibwe, too). If an Indian who is not enrolled is charged, like the blue-haired boy, he has to voluntarily submit to the authority of the court in order to have his case heard there. Otherwise it will be transferred to the county. The boy had lived all his life at Bois Forte. It was his home. He submitted and pleaded guilty. He was charged with disorderly conduct—vandalism. As he told the court, he was riding snowmobiles with his friends and he threw two eggs at a house from the back of the snowmobile he was on. He was caught almost immediately and he went back to the house to apologize and clean the egg up. The boy, age seventeen, was obviously nervous. His hands shook and there was a quaver in his voice when he pleaded guilty and explained himself to the court. I knew how he felt. Many times I'd had to stand in front of my mother and explain myself. It was never comfortable.

When he was finished my mother asked him, "Were you mad at those people? Did you have it in for them or were you just having fun?"

"Yeah."

"Yeah mad or yeah having fun?"

"Yeah, your honor, just having fun."

She perused his case file and looked down at him seriously from the bench.

"It says here you get A's and B's in school."

"Yes, your honor."

She sentenced him to $150 fine and fifteen days in jail but suspended the sentence and gave him ten hours of community service.

"And I want you to keep getting A's and B's in school. I want you to do something with your life. Do you understand?"

"Yes, yes, your honor."

"Good. I know your grandma. I know she looks after you. I don't want her to pay for what you did. I don't want you to be a burden and make her life harder. OK? You're smart. Do something with your life."

Visibly relieved, he thanked the court and left with his grandmother beside him.

By the time she heard the last case it was growing dark. Night comes early so far north in the middle of winter. Spring was still a few months away. I drove all the way back to Leech Lake while my mother ate sunflower seeds and drank coffee. There is a part of her that very much likes having a chauffeur.

As I drove between the pine-covered rock outcroppings and frozen creeks with nothing to light our way except our own weak headlights, I thought about my own transgressions as a teenager. I thought about how my brother, my cousins, and I not only "egged" houses but egged the church, the bar, the grocery store, and the priest's house—pretty much every significant structure in Bena with the exception of the post office. My cousin Delbert was much more daring than we were; he actually flung open the door of the Bena bar and hurled eggs inside. I remember seeing him standing in the rectangle of light that spilled from the open doorway. I was a way off but I heard shouts and I heard Delbert shout back, something like a war whoop, as he chucked the eggs in. He was always braver than I was. I was the one who threw the eggs at the rectory and somehow managed to break the front window there. We took off howling into the night. Later, having run out of eggs, we sat on the steps of the boarded-up community hall. After a while we saw someone stagger out of the bar down the street. He made his way into the middle of the highway and, using the dividing line, began walking toward us. He was very drunk. We began teasing him. "You old drunk!" shouted Dell. "Yeah," I said, trying to sound as tough as he was, "yeah, you old drunk." We thought this was pretty funny. When he drew even with us he paused and turned to look at us. It was my grandfather. "What are you kids looking at?" We ran.

The ride home was quiet. My mother and I were lost in our separate thoughts. I asked her, "How did you manage it?"

"Manage what?"

"I don't know. How'd you manage not to buy in to all the bullshit? All that Indian shame. All that shame your generation felt about being Indian. You never seemed to feel that and you raised us not to feel that way. How'd you do it?"

I was thinking of my own children.

She was quiet for a few minutes.

"Because I was the queen of Bena. I was the damn queen of Bena!" And then she laughed. "That's what everyone called me. I don't know why."

Dustin Burnette at Bemidji State University

4

When my brother Tony and I were kids we had two fishing buddies, Reagan and Patrick Morgan. They seemed a lot older than we were, though Reagan couldn't have been more than sixteen. There was no telling how old Patrick was. They were Leech Lake Indians, like us, but also not like us. Reagan was huge, stout, his body strong and soft at the same time. He had big hands and a big head, black hair parted in the middle and feathered back, thick tinted glasses, and bad acne. Patrick was the opposite: skinny, with a sharp face and short hair that always, no matter the season, tufted out from his head at odd angles. Patrick was handicapped. To this day I don't know what he suffered from, but he dragged one leg and his right hand curled up like a bird's wing against his chest. We never asked what was wrong with him and never teased him.

We rarely saw them at school. We never went over to their house. They never came to ours. But in the summer Tony and I would bike to the end of our dirt road and Reagan and Patrick would be waiting on their bikes, turning circles in the middle of the highway, and then we would all set off for the dam. Once we got there, Reagan, Tony, and I would fish. Reagan showed a lot of patience with Patrick, who usually did not fish with us for long. Patrick's attention would wander and then Patrick wandered after it.

Reagan always got his hands on contraband. He had candy, Cokes, and Snickers bars. Reagan always shared. There was a place on the river-bank near the fence where the riprapped stones had tumbled just so, creating a cave of sorts. It wasn't a real cave—it was no more than a foot in diameter and just slightly more than arm-deep. But you could hide things there. You could reach back with your hand and feel the cool damp stones. It was cold and slimy but all the same we were tempted to leave something of value in our cave to create the thrill of future discovery. So Reagan took one of his Cokes and placed it in the cave, and we covered the entrance with dead grass and a stick or two and left it there when we biked home in the afternoon. It was there the next day. No one ever found the things we left: lures, Cokes, a chocolate bar inside a ziplock bag.

Reagan also got his hands on other, more adult items. One day—it must have been in midsummer—Reagan and Patrick showed up at the dam. Tony and I were already fishing on the bank near our cave, under the shade of the willow and tag alder that sprouted from between the rocks. It was hot, but the spray from the river and the shade and the water that seeped from the riverbank kept us cool. Patrick wandered off to play somewhere else, alone. Reagan set up his pole, cast an unweighted twister tail into the water, and sat down between me and Tony.

You guys want to see something? he asked mysteriously. *Check this out.*

He reached into his thin nylon backpack and took out a magazine. His fingers fumbled a bit and tapped nervously on the cover. It was a *Hustler.* I was nine, maybe ten years old.

Reagan's jaw was a little slack, and he used both hands when he held the magazine. His eyes were far away, thinking on some other place.

This has it all. Everything's in here, he said. *Everything you need is right here.*

We fished and took turns reading the *Hustler*. At one point, with his rod braced against a willow and his line unfurling in the water, Reagan accordioned the centerfold and held it up. The sun came from behind the paper and I saw the river—the water spilling over the dam, the shadows of the diamond willow—through the woman's figure (which on the previous page was involved in weird ways with a clear plastic cane).

Hey, Dave. So let me ask you something. What's your favorite part?
I said nothing.
I mean, what's your favorite? Upstairs or downstairs?

A lot seemed to rest on my answer. I looked upstairs—pillowy, soft, full. I looked downstairs: confusing and vaguely dangerous. After some time, I said, Upstairs. I like upstairs the best. All the way.

Reagan snickered. *I figured,* he said disdainfully. *I like downstairs. There's nothing like downstairs. Nothing in this world.*

Reagan closed the magazine. We fished for a while longer, but nothing was biting, so we packed up our gear and biked back toward home, spread out along the highway from shoulder to shoulder, again with the sun at our backs. We parted at the intersection of our dirt road and Power Dam Road.

Tony and I pedaled south, parallel to the reservation boundary, until we got home, and if the boundary were in some way visually obvious, we would have been able to see it from the dining room window, where we would eat dinner with our younger brother and sister and our parents and then practice piano, play games, build a fort, or read, until it was time for bed. Reagan and Patrick pedaled straight toward the boundary sign, where they turned left to go to their house. I don't know what they did when they got there. I am certain they didn't practice piano. Reagan and Patrick did not, at that time, live with their family. I think they were foster kids in a white family. They might have been formally adopted. I don't know how long they had been there by that time or how long they stayed or even what brought them there.

⤝

Not far from where Reagan and Patrick and my siblings and I grew up was a place that welcomed lonely children and too often destroyed them. On the outskirts of Cass Lake, on the edge of the what some say is the worst housing tract in all of Indian country, sat a forlorn HUD house, no different in construction from all the others except that it is was painted pink. It's gone now, burned down. But while it stood it was known as the Pink Palace. The Pink Palace was a fairy-tale place, but twisted and grotesque, a place where you could go and get your heart's desire but forfeit your life. It was there that Heather Casey, a fifteen-year-old Indian girl, overdosed on drugs (mostly Klonopin, an antianxiety prescription drug), was raped while she was unconscious, died, and then was placed, naked, in a bathtub under cold water. She was then removed, was stuffed into the trunk of a car (she wouldn't fit, because rigor mortis had set in), and was driven to the IHS clinic a few blocks away where the police became involved. "She was," says the investigator in charge of solving her murder, "about the cutest little dead girl you've ever seen."

The HUD houses, like the one where Heather Casey died, and the neighborhoods made up of them, were conceived as part of Johnson's War on Poverty, launched in the 1960s. They brought twentieth-century housing to reservations across the country. Until that time most Indians on most reservations lived as best they could. Some had decent homes with running water and electricity. Most did not. Most

Indians on the reservation lived in shacks or cabins made of whatever was at hand—tar paper, corrugated tin, logs, scavenged lumber. Running water and electricity were rare. To listen to the stories of Indians who grew up in the 1950s and 1960s is to hear of hardships that almost seem fun in retrospect. Rene Gurneau of Red Lake remembers trying to fall asleep by counting the stars through the slits of the roof boards in her family's small cabin there. My mother, the eldest of five siblings, remembers sleeping two kids to a bed and having to take turns bathing in a galvanized washtub, the water turning brown and browner as each child stepped in, washed, and stepped out. Stories about winter trips to the outhouse belong to their own genre. "Oh," remembers my mother, "everyone had an outhouse. That wasn't special. Ours was a bad one, though. My dad never fixed anything. Not anything ever except for cars and then watch out, walk carefully! So the outhouse was missing slats in the door and the walls. When it was minus thirty you only went to the outhouse when you had to and you didn't take your sweet time. And of course the ground was frozen for half the year and with two adults and five kids . . . I mean, it was gross. It got pretty full. My grandma Izzie had the nicest outhouse in Bena: a two-seater and a third, lower seat, so kids could use it. All in tip-top shape." Helen Bryan, of Squaw Lake on the northern edge of Leech Lake, grew up much the same way—in a cabin with no insulation and no running water, built by her grandfather. When the anthropologist M. Inez Hilger conducted a survey on White Earth Reservation in Minnesota in 1938, she found that of the roughly 250 households she visited, well over half were merely tar paper shacks: rough stud walls covered in slab that was in turn covered with tar paper. Only eight of the shacks she looked at had wooden roof shingles; the rest used tar paper for the roof as well. Only one of the houses had a foundation (a log buried in dirt). The rest of the shacks were built directly on the ground. "A typical tar-paper shack as found on the White Earth

Reservation," she wrote, "consisted of a one-story framework of studding, the exterior of which was covered with rough one-inch boards of various widths. The cheapest lumber was usually gotten for covering, many times the first slats in the cutting of lumber being used. In several cases wooden boxes, used in shipping groceries and other supplies, were broken down and utilized. The boards, after being nailed to the studding, were covered with tar-paper, the latter being securely fastened with narrow slats of wood, or disks of tin. The extent to which wind and rain were kept from penetrating depended on the condition of the paper." The shacks were wet in the summer, cold in the winter, and made entirely of highly flammable materials. Dysentery, flu, pneumonia, and house fires were common. And this was how most people lived on most reservations from the turn of the century well into the 1960s. "You want to hear something really stupid?" asked my mother. "Someone got some grant from someone on Leech Lake. A grant for indoor plumbing, so they put toilets in about twenty shacks in Inger. No money for anything else. No money for things like interior walls. So they slapped toilets in the corners of these one-room shacks. This was in the 1960s. What did they think? Indians don't like privacy? No one used them, except for shelves. You'd visit someone and they'd have this toilet in the corner, piled high with magazines or papers or whatever. And everyone still used the outhouses." Although HUD tried to change all this, to change the way Indians lived, it only partially succeeded.

Armed with the latest research and outside experts, HUD built housing tracts (pronounced "tracks" by residents of these neighborhoods) on reservations across the country beginning in the 1960s. Larger tribes with more clout and better connections got more of the HUD funding. Small tribes were often overlooked. This new housing was the first step, for many Indian families, into the twentieth century. It came in the form of planned neighborhoods consisting, mostly, of split-level or rambler-style homes, arranged in either square grids or meandering culs-de-sac. It was believed that the suburban bioscape was the one most conducive to success and happiness. After World War II the logic was that communities built in culs-de-sac, with winding roads and no alleys, would reduce automobile traffic and so also reduce noise. Instead of a grid with streets and alleys (and lots of places for hoodlums to lurk) culs-de-sac and suburban developments would make it harder for crime to flourish because no one would simply be passing through; rather, anyone who was there would be there for a reason. This ignores the fact that crimes in a given place are often perpetrated by those who live there. The same planning logic that created the suburbs created the late-twentieth-century reservation housing tract across Indian reservations.

Where once there had been fallow fields or deep woods there were, suddenly, clusters of houses set cheek to jowl, with paved streets and gutters, but no curbs. Families signed up for housing and were assigned a house on the basis of a combination of first come, first served; lottery; and nepotism. Sometimes residents had to pay a small monthly rent; in other instances housing was free. Mostly the tribe was responsible for construction and upkeep. The good news was that for many families, the new houses were filled with luxuries—if not central air-conditioning, then at least constant heat, running water, a dedicated bathroom, electricity, and a roof that didn't leak. The bad news was that on large reservations, such as Leech Lake and White Earth (and this was true for large reservations across the country) that had many small villages located within their boundaries, the age-old structure of these communities—the geographical manifestation of family ties, old rivalries, kinship, and warring factions—was completely ignored. Families who had little to do with one another and who came from very different villages were suddenly neighbors. Sometimes this was fine. Sometimes it was not. And the houses were often poorly built.

Foundations were poured after and above the frost. Paint was hard to come by. Contractors skimmed. Sheetrock isn't always the best surface to put in houses for people who aren't used to it. At one time, most people who'd never been to a reservation imagined that Indians lived in tepees or wigwams. That idea gave way to the image of tar paper shacks and tin roofs. And now there is an image of HUD houses: decrepit ramblers with peeling paint, a dead car in the yard, kids in diapers running in the middle of the street without an adult in sight, weeds lining the road (instead of grass, flowers, or gardens), clothes-lines sifted over with dust. This is the stereotype, anyway, of HUD housing on Indian reservations—one that is sometimes true.

Many Indians today are still waiting for HUD housing. In 1995, after thirty or more years of HUD housing (and the disasters that attend those housing tracts), more than 40 percent of Indians in tribal areas live in what HUD calls "substandard" houses. "Substandard" is a euphemism for anything ranging from a plywood box (like the one Thelma Moses calls home on the Muckleshoot Indian Reservation in Washington) to a house with no bathroom. In 1996 the Navajo Nation declared a state of emergency. At the time, more than 80 percent of the existing homes on the Navajo reservation lacked running water, electricity, and telephones and more than 20,000 Navajo had no homes at all. Government estimates from the 1990s suggest that about 100,000 Indians across the country were waiting for HUD houses. And it's not that Indians across the country are waiting for handouts. Many Indians can't get loans—because of unemployment, which runs as high as 80 percent on some reservations, and also because they have nothing to offer as collateral; tribal land is held in trust and can't be mortgaged.

So Indians are still waiting for housing. The images of HUD housing, of life on a "track," are largely accurate with regard to many housing tracts on my reservation. From Tracts 33 and 34, just north of Cass Lake, to the more colorfully named tracts Mac Flats, Tooterville,

Fox Creek, and Porcupine Flats, life can be rough. But not all, not even most, Indians on my reservation live on tract. Many still live in their families' traditional villages—Onigum, Inger, Squaw Lake, Ball Club, Bena, Mission, Oak Point, Boy River, Federal Dam, and Sugar Point. Many don't live in villages at all but have, instead, built their own homes on dirt roads and long driveways in the deep woods both on and off the reservation. However, "track" has come to be the most recognizable portrait of rez life for most outsiders. Think of the long, moving color shots accompanied by "lonesome" sound tracks in movies such as *Thunderheart*, *Dance Me Outside*, and *Smoke Signals*. Indians who live or grew up on a tract have developed their own mythology about the place, a mythology based on violence. Dustin Burnette, a Leech Laker who grew up near Tract 33, remembers, "Yeah, I'd take friends to track in the summer, roll down the windows, and start blasting country music—you know Garth Brooks or something. And my friends would be like, 'Knock it off, man! You're going to get us killed!' And they'd duck way down in their seats and I'd whoop and holler and shit. It was fun." Country music does seem out of place on a track. But then again, so do Indians, in a way. If you squint hard enough to block out the trees and grass or the snow, you end up with a vision not of the north woods but of East LA, an East LA drawn from the movies. Colorfully painted houses falling into the ground, trash, burned-out cars. Track is hard. Even so, outsiders often don't feel, don't even recognize (no matter how often you tell them otherwise) that they are on the rez until we drive through a track. I once brought a reporter to the rez and she kept asking, *Are we on the rez yet? Are we there yet?* I kept telling her that yes, we were, but she didn't really believe me—until we drove through Tract 33 outside Cass Lake, and she was both scared and relieved that the rez was finally recognizable to her.

One resident remembered Tract 33: "I didn't feel safe in town, you know I was always looking over my shoulder and always when I parked my vehicle outside I was always checking on it to make sure nothing was happening." One former chairman of Leech Lake said, "Tract 33 was bad. . . . At night you can't sleep around here. There are cars racing up and down the street, and there are gunshots periodically and people coming to my door and knocking and wanting to come in, so I have to stay up and watch my house." One kid from track said, "I was involved, you know, in a lot of car thefts, just about anything from beatings from fighting to getting in them, starting to sell drugs. . . . Some of the people I grew up with, they are doing prison time for murder and I got other friends sitting in prison for attempted murder and these are the ones I grew up with and called, you know, my brothers. . . . It was a rapid change just from when I was growing up. . . . How bad it picked up. . . . People like me at the time . . . were actually scared."

There were plenty of reasons to be scared on track, whether you were young or old, passing through and blasting country music, or trying to get some sleep. Warren Tibbetts lived on Tract 34 just north of Tract 33. He had been around the block—twice, three times—and around the country as well. A veteran of Vietnam and an early and active member of the American Indian Movement (AIM), he had seen his share of conflict and violence. And he, admittedly, had instigated a lot of it. But he had settled down, quit drinking, quit smoking pot, and gotten his life together. He lived at the end of one of the culs-de-sac, where he raised his family and became an important part of a renaissance in Ojibwe culture and ceremony. Warren was thin and rangy and funny. He would sometimes take off into the bush for days at a time. If people needed a place to crash, to sleep it off, or to recover, he always welcomed them. On September 24, 2005, his neighbor Michael Francis Anthony Wind started things up. He was trying to get his dog to fight Warren's dog, goading both dogs with a rake or a broom. Warren, wearing his slippers, came out to stop the dogs (he really loved his dog) and to stop Wind. Wind, drunk, attacked him and stabbed him clean through the heart. Warren staggered back into his house and died on the kitchen floor in front of his daughter Dee and his niece Janelle. All of this came out of nowhere, on a typical night.

"It was just another day," says Shalah, the eldest daughter of Warren and Nancy Tibbetts. Shalah, twenty-eight years old, and brassy, is "a rez girl through and through till I die," as she puts it. It is impossible not to like Shaye; she is sharp and funny, and she can find just the right way to tease the people she likes: two parts fun and one part spice, so that you laugh instead of being offended. She is one of the least judgmental people I've ever met. She is dark but has freckles. She has a gap between her two front teeth. Her hair is always changing, from pink to red to brown to black and then back to pink. Her hair changes color and style even more often now that she's been living with her Guatemalan husband in Asbury Park, New Jersey, where she graduated from cosmetology school in 2009. But she's come home to Tract 34. "It's lonely out there. I mean, I like my husband's peeps. But they don't speak English. Neither does he. The only other Indian I met out there was the Indian from the Village people! It's true. I was in the UPS store in Asbury Park and this old Mexican guy comes in and the guy at the counter was real nice to him. He left and the guy says to me, 'You know who that was?' I say, 'Ummm, a Mexican?' 'No! that was the Indian from the Village People!'" Actually, Felipe Ortiz Rose, the Indian from the Village People, is Puerto Rican on his mother's side and Lakota Sioux on his father's.

Shaye is back at Tract 34. She and her husband, Pedro, came home from New Jersey because Shaye was pregnant and wanted to have her baby on the rez. I can hear merengue coming from the basement. The TV is on in the living room; *300* is playing. Shaye is doing Jordan Bush's hair. Janelle, Darlene, and Lindsey are waiting their turn.

It's prom night for some of the schools and they are all getting ready. The table where the girls are getting their hair done is littered with glasses, beading, jewelry projects, makeup, curling irons, straightening paddles, and a magnifying vanity mirror. The girls are already in their prom dresses. We're all sitting not far from where Warren died on the floor—not more than three feet away—but this place is teeming with life. The girls are excited. They have never looked more beautiful, more queenly. They tease Shaye and she teases them back and they smile into the vanity and perfect their makeup. When people describe families or communities as "close-knit" I think this is what they must mean. I would have to say that none of them can do without the other.

"It changed all of us," Shaye tells me as she begins to take the curlers out of Jordan's hair. "We all changed when my dad died. But my mom changed more than anyone. It affected her the most. It's been five years since he died. I'm not mad at that guy anymore. I'm not mad. Not as mad as my bros and sisters."

Shalah and her family have lived in that house at the end of Tract 34 since she was ten. Before that they lived at Tom's Resort, where Warren was a caretaker, fix-it man, fishing guide, and all-around help. His sister was married to the owner. After they lived at Tom's they lived in downtown Cass Lake. "At Tom's we played in the pool and went fishing and went swimming. Kids on track said, 'How come you get to do all that?' and I was like 'I don't know.' We had all sorts of friends—white friends, Indian friends. My friends were my friends, you know."

Warren had been wild in his early days. Sometimes he would take off. He would walk out the door and then, just as suddenly, walk in months later. No one knew where he went. By the time Shalah was growing up he'd largely quit those disappearing acts. Shaye's love for him is still very evident. "Other kids would say to me, 'You're so lucky. Your dad is so nice. He gives you stuff. He's around.' Stuff like that. No matter what they always stuck it out, toughed it out. They got sober after Delores was born. Before that they were still living large. My dad finally got sober when I was fifteen."

Everyone knew Warren and knew his house on the tract. It was a destination.

"People still come up to me," says Shaye. "Oh, I remember you. Maybe I cooked for them or something when they were doing ceremony with my dad."

Shaye has a measured attitude about life on track. When she hears people talk about how bad it is, how rough, she laughs. "It's rough, sure. But it can't be no rougher than how those kids have it in Africa. Or the kids in South America. It can't be any rougher than that. Or kids in Vietnam who live on top of big garbage piles. People don't put the whole world in perspective. They say, 'Oh, those poor Indians.' Don't pity me. We got it good. We got it better than most people. Don't feel bad for me. Feel bad for somebody else because, well, I don't need pity. Even my husband, he says I'm white. 'What?' I said, 'I'm not white.' 'Sure you are,' he says. 'You're from America.'"

Shaye shows me a cigarette lighter with a beaded case. Worked into the beaded pattern are the words "100% REZ GIRL."

I wish I had Shaye's equanimity. I try to imagine my father bleeding to death on my floor in front of my little sister and cousin, and that's something I can't imagine recovering from. I simply can't imagine it. But Shaye insists that life on track isn't bad—not as bad as people think.

"It's pretty rough," admits Shaye. "But people choose to live that life. Maybe they're not choosing a good life. Maybe those people haven't gotten a chance to better their life. Maybe no one was there to teach them, no one to encourage them. My dad always told me, 'Do your best. Do your best and you'll be happy.' So I've done my best and I guess I'm happy."

Warren could be convincing. Once some church people came to the house on a conversion mission. They told Warren that they thought the kids should be going to church. "'Oh, come on in here and let's talk about it,' he said. They came in and started talking to my dad and pretty soon they want to go in the sweat lodge, they want to have an Indian ceremony. There were lots of white people who came here and wanted to be Native. My dad was nice to everybody. We had lots of characters in and out of my door, I'm telling you."

So the family, making good choices, but staying on track, stayed close. The kids always had bikes and took care of one another. They'd ride all around track on their bikes, down to the convenience store, and down to the lake where they would go swimming. It was a good childhood on track—a normal one, more or less—until Warren was killed. What's life like? All the girls shrug. Life was life. Gradually they filter out of the house in their prom dresses, stepping over the threshold where Warren died, but where they still enter and exit as they go about their lives.

Tract 33, however, has captured the public imagination as the roughest, hardest, toughest, meanest, and worst of them all. The Pink Palace has a lot to do with that.

Heather Casey, the girl who died at the Pink Palace, had it rough, much rougher than Shaye, and not all of her agony was of her own construction. Her mother, Toni, a heroin addict, used regularly throughout Heather's childhood. So did her father, George Whipple Jr. When she was twelve her father shacked up with her aunt, Toni's sister, Sam. Heather went to live with her grandparents in the housing tract nicknamed Tooterville. Sam, sort of a second mother *and* aunt to Heather, sold drugs to support her habit. She sold them from the Pink Palace— the pink HUD house across the street from the tribal offices owned by Mike Newago. Sam introduced Heather to Newago's grandson Joe

Potter—a handsome, powerful boy five years older than Heather. On August 18, 2004—which was cold and windy for August—Heather put her grandmother to bed and then sneaked out of the house to meet Potter. According to Steve Hagenah, the investigator for the Minnesota State Bureau of Criminal Apprehension (BCA): "And he picked her up, and they partied. And he gave her Klonopin. I think they'd been doing some drinking and the drugs, too. They were having sex off and on. And at some point she died. She went into respiratory distress, from the drugs. He woke up with a cold, stiff, dead body next to him in bed. He dragged her in the bathroom and put her in the shower and sprayed cold water on her like that's going to revive somebody who's dead and already in rigor. He freaked out and everybody else in the house freaked out. They got her dressed and were trying to stuff her in the car and some people drove by. And remember, she was in rigor, her arms and legs were sticking out. And so then they ended up taking her to the IHS clinic and we get called. I was the first one there and got the story. The story is that this crazy girl showed up at the house and wanted to use the bathroom. Went into the bathroom and after ten or fifteen minutes we went to check on her and we found her in the bathroom, dead. But when I examined the body I saw that she was in full rigor and that this must have happened six or eight hours before. After a while I pieced it all together." Hagenah shook his head. "God she was a cute girl."

Mike Newago, Joe Potter's grandfather, was, on paper at least, the legal owner of the Pink Palace. In his sixties, suffering from diabetes and a host of other ailments, Newago had a legitimate supply of prescription drugs—scrips, as everyone in the know calls them—that he kept in a small desk safe: Oxycontin, Klonopin, Demerol. The problem was that everyone knew the combination to the safe and would dip into Newago's drugs, or so he said when he protested his innocence. In 2000 agents raided Newago's house and found prescription narcotics, both legally and illegally obtained. A few kids, teenagers, interviewed during the raid admitted that they had sold Newago's scrips. Drugs were routinely sold from and used in the Pink Palace. It had been the target of two raids. And yet until it was burned down, the Pink Palace was a destination for runaways and kids who needed some place that wasn't home. The Pink Palace became a combination drug house, brothel, and runaway shelter. Kids would go there when they had no other place to go and in exchange for sex they were given drugs and a place to crash. Reservation kids being processed at the Boys and Girls Club of Leech Lake often told workers that they were living at the Pink Palace because they couldn't go home. Other kids, like Heather Casey, simply floated into and out of the Pink Palace, tied to it through a family member—a mother, aunt, father, stepfather, boyfriend—involved in selling and using drugs. You have to wonder what home is like if the Pink Palace seems like a safe place to be.

Cass Lake, so everyone says, used to be a nice town, even if it did have a bloody start. In the late 1800s Leech Lake Reservation was closed to non-Natives; unless you were Indian you couldn't live there, and this was fine for most people. But there were two problems: there were vast timber resources still standing on the reservation and the reservation itself blocked east-west and north-south rail lines between Duluth and Grand Forks and Winnipeg and Minneapolis. Two things happened as a result. First, as the story goes, in the middle of the night, with the help of the railroads, businessmen from Bemidji, fourteen miles away, skidded half a dozen buildings from the small whistle-stop town of Rosby onto the present-day site of Cass Lake. They persuaded the president to issue an executive order that officially opened the reservation boundary. The town stayed. This was how Leech Lake Reservation was originally broken open for settlement and set up for white control.

The second thing that happened had to do with the bigger impediment to logging: the lack of rail lines through the reservation. These had been effectively blocked by Chief Zhookaa-giizhig (Dipping Sky) of the Winnibigoshish Band who had his own logging concern on the north shore of Lake Winnibigoshish. Zhookaa-giizhig was the first man to log on Leech Lake, and in 1891 he was the first to float logs down to Minneapolis, where they were milled. But white loggers wanted their share, and in 1894 Zhookaa-giizhig, who was known never to drink, was found "drunk" on the railroad tracks at Deer River, where the line ended. He had, evidently, laid his head down on the tracks and been run over by a train. After that, and with the help of the Nelson Act and the Dawes Act, the reservation opened wide.

My great-great-grandfather Charles Seelye was the direct beneficiary of Zhookaa-giizhig's death. Charles had come from Portland, Maine, a son of Scottish loggers who had cut mast timber for the king's navy going back to the 1700s. In Brainerd, Minnesota, he met and married Margaret Aspinwall, the daughter of Bill Aspinwall, the head of a family of mixed-blood traders and agents. In 1896 Charles moved to the reservation and logged Zhookaa-giizhig's allotments at Cut Foot Sioux and Pigeon lakes. But he could not get paid in advance for his timber and so could not pay his Indian workers, and he went bankrupt on March 12, 1900. His son Walter (my great-grandfather) continued the logging tradition. One outfitter said of my great-grandfather: "That Walt Seelye is all whalebone and rawhide." And up through the 1970s he was remembered for wearing a black bowler hat year-round, even in the bitter cold. According to Jim Quinn, the owner of a lumber camp, my great-grandfather defied the cold, going without ear warmers or even earflaps.

The town of Cass Lake had the same hardiness. It was a logging and rail center at one time. But after all the trees were cut down and logging slowed, it found new life as a resort town. It had a thriving main street—lined with stores such as the five-and-dime, Neises Sporting Goods, Red Owl Foods, the high school, the Big Tap Bar and Grill, the municipal liquor store, two hotels, and a few cafés. The outskirts of Cass Lake were interspersed with modest resorts. The town had everything small American towns were supposed to have: parades, festivals, a small park. The largest town on Leech Lake Reservation, it once housed a population of 1,200. That has dwindled to 860. The stores are mostly gone. A few restaurants and bars are hanging on for dear life. The streets of Cass Lake, both in the tracts and in the city itself, are dangerous these days. Trouble seems to spill out of everywhere, and nowhere. Many people, like Steve Hagenah, attribute this change to drugs. Drinking is one thing. Pot is something else. But meth, oxy, and other such drugs—"chemical fuel," as Hagenah calls them—change the game. Paranoia, violence, and pure craziness emerge. As these dangerous drugs become cheaper, life becomes cheaper.

For instance, in November 2002 (a few months after Heather Casey's boyfriend was trying to shove her body into his trunk), Louie Bisson was out walking his dog. Bisson, forty-eight, was thin and balding, part Indian but albino, and he was legally blind. He lived a few doors down from his mother's house and found work fixing decks and building sheds. He was single, and his only real hobby was walking, which he did almost every night with his dog, Little O, around the darkened streets of Cass Lake. He wore a flannel shirt and jeans and had put on long johns under his pants as a defense against the cold November night. He also carried an ax handle to scare off other dogs and kids if need be; he'd been harassed before.

That same night three teenagers—Jessie Tapio, George Boswell, and Darryl Johnson—were also walking around the streets of Cass Lake. All of them had been in trouble over the past few years. All of them had been in the foster care system, juvenile detention centers, or both. All of them had mothers who drank and did drugs. According to the reporter Larry Oakes, Jessie had fetal alcohol syndrome, George had brain damage from lead poisoning, and Darryl had been damaged somehow after falling out of a second-story window as a toddler. The boys had spent the afternoon drugging, and in the evening they sold some pot to a young woman, Ruth Bellanger, who agreed, in return, to get the boys some booze, which she did after taking a run to Safari Liquors next to the supermarket just off the highway. The evening passed with Southern Comfort and raspberry vodka in Darryl's bedroom, where the walls were covered with posters of Tupac Shakur. Eventually they headed out into the night. It was after eleven when they saw Louie Bisson.

According to testimony and eyewitness accounts the boys were jumpy, paranoid, aggressive. Earlier that evening they'd gone to the house of an acquaintance and threatened him, his father, and his sister. When they saw Louie and his dog they started running toward him. Bisson turned, tried to flee, and got as far as half a block from the police station when the boys took his ax handle and beat him with it. His skull was crushed. When the police arrived on the scene they saw the clear print of a basketball sneaker on Bisson's cheek. In the score of homicides in Cass Lake over the last ten years the most prevalent cause of death is beating. Many people, my mother included, long for the good old days. And even if it is a false nostalgia for days that were hardly good, it's easy to see why they seem better.

Steve Hagenah, the investigator with the BCA, remembers those days, too. Steve is tall, mustached, with large hands and gray eyes. He has a friendly, craggy face. After working in law enforcement on and near the reservation for thirty-five years, he has perfected a hard stare that, I imagine, isn't so nice to see across from you in an interrogation room. Steve was raised on the rez, and though he wasn't Indian by blood he came up with Indians—Gabby Headbird, my uncle Sonny. Steve was prom king in 1969 opposite my cousin Lynette, who was prom queen. Steve's family tree is complex and improbable. His mother, Beverly, was the daughter of Bessie Cooper, a white girl from Minneapolis, and Lester Young, the jazz tenor sax master. Bessie died in childbirth and Steve's mother was taken in by a Romanian Jewish family in north Minneapolis. After marrying Steve's dad and living in Fargo, North Dakota for a few years, she divorced and returned to north Minneapolis. Steve and his sister lived with their grandmother north of Cass Lake for a few years until his dad moved there and took up residence. Steve was raised in Cass Lake and roamed the town with his Indian friends, some of whom became his stepbrother and stepsisters when his father married an Indian woman. When his mother died, the minister asked Steve what kind of service he wanted for her. "Oh, you know," he said, "just your standard Jewish, Catholic, Lutheran, Baptist kind of thing. Just like you'd normally have."

The good old days, according to Steve, weren't so good. "My dad was real physical. Mean," he said. "He beat on me. He beat on my sister. I grew up raising a lot of hell." So, too, did the guys Steve was friends with into high school. Randy Headbird, Sonny Seelye, Johnny Jones. They were all into and out of trouble. But sometime during those high school years, Steve split from those friends. "The Cantys and the Stangels, and the Matthews, and all that whole crew, they all came to Cass Lake High School. So we all hung out together, palled around together, fought together. As a kid growing up—you know the 'Stand By Me' days when you go around and catch frogs and all that— we were in it together. But take Randy Headbird. And Johnny Jones. At some point someone said, 'Hey, you guys are Indian, you shouldn't be hanging around that white kid.' Their friends were giving them shit. We were the best of friends, we didn't get in trouble together, but we fished and swam and palled around together. But then someone would say, 'Why are you hanging around with that fucking white kid?' I still kind of hung out with those kids, but it became kind of an issue. What it was, was friends and family saying you should hang out with someone else. Guys were dropping out of school and going to jail. But the football team, it was one-third Native and two-thirds not. We were pals. That kind of thing brought people back together. It was never overt, just implied—you should stop hanging out. There was racism both ways. And you felt ostracized by the people you grew up with. All of a sudden I wasn't Steve Hagenah, the pal from school. I was the fucking white kid." After graduating from Cass Lake in 1969, Steve went into law enforcement. Many of his friends went the other way. In 1972 Steve came back to the reservation and worked as a city cop for the town of Cass Lake.

"Back then, every night was Saturday night. And I was busting the guys I went to high school with." There were big fights all the time. Villages were pitted against each other—Bena versus Onigum or Ball Club versus Inger. My mother remembers that every Saturday night the Bena boys would fight the Ball Club boys. "It was routine," she says, like weekly softball games. "And they still do it," she says.

These village rivalries were a part of life going back decades, if not centuries. There are at least a dozen small villages, from a few houses to a few hundred, scattered within the boundaries of Leech Lake Reservation; each has its own feel, and each is boosted by local pride. In 1920 the *Cass Lake Times* reported:

> Veterans from around Bena, Remer, Ball Club, Boy River and Federal Dam will celebrate at Federal Dam and the warriors are planning the biggest day in the history of that section. Following is the day's program: Parade of Veterans of all wars in uniform with bugle and drum corps. Patriotic Speeches. Wounded Men's Race. 100 yard dash. 3-leg race. Obstacle race. Flag race. Sack race. Egg race. Balloon ascension (via the blanket). Kangaroo Court and Belt Line (if necessary). Pup tent pitching Competition. Wall Scaling

competition. Drill Competition between squads from Federal Dam and Boy River. Football game between Federal Dam and Boy River. Minstrel and vaudeville show by Federal Dam and Boy River posts. Real Old Time Dance in the evening. (November 4, 1920).

And this from 1947: "The Battling Bena Bombadiers will play the Cass Lake Independents next week, December 17, 1947. The game of last week was one of the best ever played on the Cass Lake floor, and the game next week promises to be another spectators' game from the first to the final whistle."

But by the time Steve Hagenah started patrolling the rez in the early 1970s, these friendly rivalries had changed from ball games to fistfights. Steve remembers that when he was on patrol and a fight broke out at the municipal liquor store the officer at the station would shine a spotlight on the water tower. The tower, painted silver, glowed. "It was our bat signal." And Steve would drive down to the liquor store, leave the gun in the car, open the back door, and spray the place down with Mace. "I'd go through a quart of Mace in a month. Not everyone liked it. Once I took on your uncle Diddy and Shirley and Larry McClemek. Shirley did the most damage. After she was cuffed and stuffed I took a look at myself. I was all torn up, like I'd just walked through barbed wire."

Steve left the rez to work undercover for the BCA in 1977. ("It was easy. A monkey could do it. I bought a hundred thousand hits of LSD and all I had to do was walk up to some dealers and say 'Hey man, can I get some drugs from you guys?' and they sold it to me!") He returned to the area in 1987.

By the mid-1980s the violence—bar fights, domestics, and burglary—had changed; a different beast had emerged. Crack cocaine was making its way up from the Twin Cities, and with it came more extreme violence and gangs. Crack gave way to heroin and methamphetamine. In many states, such as Minnesota and Washington, deaths from prescription drug abuse are higher than deaths from heroin, meth, and cocaine combined. Although the rates of alcohol consumption and illicit drug use among Native American young people are not significantly higher than the national averages, the rate of binge drinking and prescription drug abuse is. According to Hagenah, most of the violence that he investigates is drug-related, perpetrated by users looking to score. And most of the deaths he's called to witness are the result of overdoses—almost always involving abuse of prescription drugs. Such was the case with Heather Casey. "Well, the number one drug of choice is stuff like oxycodone. This comes in pill form, and it's time-released when you take it that way. But these kids will smash it up and inject it, and so the drug comes as a big rush, and it suppresses the nervous system. The body can't handle it. And it's all over.

"As for meth, it really messes you up. You take some meth and then you're up, no sleep, for three, four, five days. You crash, and wake up, and all you want is meth. You get paranoid. Everyone's after you. And you need meth to make it stop. One guy, Mike Spaulding from Bemidji—you know he owned that dealership Spaulding Motors. He got hooked on meth and he lost millions. He lost the dealership. It didn't take six years or whatever. The place was gone in six months. He's got nothing now." Steve is a tough guy. He's had to see and do some tough things—lock up his friends, bury his friends, and watch a place he has a lot of affection for destroy itself. And while he talks, with a cop's verbal swagger, there is something else behind his voice, something more tender, sadder.

But is the problem just the drugs? Is it just that? If we can get the drugs out, will everything return to normal?

"The gangs keep to themselves, in a way. They mostly hurt one another, fighting for distribution. These are criminal enterprises and all the talk about safety and family and all that is crap. They're here to make money." The real problem, according to Hagenah, is the increasing acceptance of violence among the community as a whole. "It started way back. But the last generation told their stories about who did time and who beat up who. These were funny stories, rez stories. Everyone looked up to your uncle Bumsy, for instance: how he did thirty for robbing that jewelry store down in the Cities. And these kids grew up hearing that. Violence is just part of things. That's what they're taught. So you have an acceptance of violence, violence is OK, and add youth to that (and young equals stupid) and some chemical fuel, and you've got a problem." Steve seems to be right. The last three homicides in Cass Lake have been beating deaths. "Not just beating deaths. But three or four guys beating on a single guy. Stomping him in the head. Hitting him all over the body till he's totally broken."

This was true of Michael Littlewolf. He had belonged to an Indian gang in Cass Lake called the Third Avenue Killers. To outsiders the jokes come easy; it seems a little out of scale to call yourself the Third Avenue Killers in a town with only four avenues. Michael Littlewolf wanted to get out. He quit the gang and was taking steps to join the marines. But his gang friends caught up with him, beat him unconscious, and then burned and cut the tattoos off his body before leaving him by the side of the road. Michael died of his injuries. The gang members who tortured and murdered Michael told Hagenah, "You can get out, you just got to leave some of yourself behind." For many kids rez life is nasty, brutal, and short. And most people long, just long, for the good old days when a fight was a fight and you could get by. Charley Grolla, the former cop and conservation officer from Red Lake, believes that violence has always been a part of Indian life. "That's why we're here. The only reason there's any Indians at all is because we're fighters. We have a violent attitude. It's helped us, but it hurts us, too." The late Tom Stillday, who was a spiritual leader from Ponemah, saw it much the same way. "That's why we have so many

Bear Clan and Marten Clan people at Red Lake," he mused. "Those were warrior clans. And we had a lot of warriors here. This was the last frontier, the final stop before the Sioux and the Great Plains. So there were lots of warriors." That kind of violence—in defense of home and place, rather than against home and place—might be why we're here. But it's not often on display anymore.

"And you know," adds Steve, "families are all broken up. It's always been this way, sort of. Kids floating from a parent to a cousin's house, to the grandma's place. Sometimes when I've got to interview someone, a witness or whatever, I've got to go to three or four, sometimes five places before I find who I am looking for. Kids are floating all over the place and their own families don't know where they are. 'Where's little Tommy?' No one knows. These kids are like motor pool cars: no one takes care of them until they're broken. And then it's too late.

"They say it takes a village. You know the saying: 'It takes a village to raise a child.' But I think that if the village is watching the child, then no one is watching the kid. The kid doesn't have to be responsible to anyone. I think what it takes is at least one responsible parent, one parent who knows, who knows what's going on for the kid twenty-four-seven. Someone the kid has to answer to and come home to. Without that . . ." Steve shrugs, hands open. "They graduate into the exciting and dangerous. They graduate into violence and gangs and whatnot. By the time I see them, these kids fifteen, sixteen, seventeen, it's way too late. They're animals." By that time, these kids are in the system, whether the social welfare system or the criminal justice system or, increasingly, a blend of both.

❧

The number of Indian children in "the system" is staggering. Indian children in Minnesota make up 1.5 percent of the population under eighteen years of age; that is, there are roughly 20,000 Indian kids in the state. But of the 10,000 cases of child mistreatment, 7 percent involved Indian kids. That means that one in every twenty-four Indian children is in the system. These children have been assessed and treated and, in two-thirds of the cases, removed from the home. One in twenty-four doesn't sound that bad at first, but it does when you compare the figure with the prospects for white children. Only one white kid in 206 will be in the system, and fewer than half of those in the system will wind up in foster care. To look at this another way, at least one Indian kid in every classroom is not living with his or her family, whereas only one white kid in every five classrooms is eating supper with strangers. These figures don't include the vast number of Indian children who aren't living with their parents and instead bunk with aunts, uncles, or grandparents. Fifty percent of all Indian kids in Beltrami County, the ones who are not in foster care, don't live with their parents. The staff at the Boys and Girls Club in Cass Lake estimates that more than 75 percent of the kids who come to the club don't live with their parents.

Many kids have it rough; they are mistreated, abused, and neglected, and that is the main reason why they are removed from their homes. The state breaks down "child maltreatment" into five main categories: emotional abuse, medical neglect, neglect, physical abuse, and sexual abuse. Of all the children in the system, 20 percent suffered from physical abuse, 10 percent were subjected to sexual abuse, and 73 percent were victims of neglect.

Jeffrey James Weise, a sixteen-year-old boy who killed his grandfather, his grandfather's girlfriend, a security guard, a teacher, and five fellow students on Red Lake Reservation in 2005 before killing himself, wrote that he often felt neglected and abused. Weise was born August 8, 1988, and his life was hard from the start: he was a victim of neglect. After a standoff with the police in July 1997, his father, Darryl Lussier Jr. (known as Baby Dash), committed suicide by shooting himself in

the head. Two years later his mother, Joanne Weise, went out drinking, crashed her car into a tree, and suffered massive brain damage.
With a directness that was typical of how Jeff wrote, he e-mailed to an
Internet friend this account of his mother's accident: "My mom got
drunk one night and wrecked her car and had to relearn how to tie
her shoes, I was too young to fight back or too young to stick up for
myself without getting struck down when this was happening." Life
before that, during the two years when he lived with his mother after
his father's death, had hardly been ideal: "My mom used to abuse me
alot when I was little. She would hit me with anything she could get
her hands on, she used to drink excessively too. She would tell me I
was a mistake, and she would say so many things that its hard to deal
with them or think of them without crying."

Shortly after his mother's car accident Jeff moved back to Red Lake
to live with his grandfather. Weise was on Prozac. He hated school.
School, it seemed, also hated him. He wore eyeliner and teased his
hair up into devil horns. He was pulled from school and tutored at
home. On his MSN.com profile, he listed "planning, waiting, hating"
as his hobbies. He tried to commit suicide with a box cutter. A feeling of neglect oozes through his Internet postings: "So fucking naive
man, so fucking naive. Always expecting change when I know nothing
ever changes. I've seen mothers choose their man over their own flesh
and blood, I've seen others choose alcohol over friendship. I sacrifice
no more for others, part of me has fucking died, and I hate this shit.
I'm living every mans nightmare and that single fact alone is kicking
my ass, I really must be fucking worthless. This place never changes, it
never will. Fuck it all."

Jeffrey Weise tried to starve himself to death for four days in March,
2005. He ended his fast by killing his grandfather and his grandfather's girlfriend and driving to school, where he killed Derek Brun,
Neva Winnecoup Rogers, and five students and then killed himself.

*   *   *

Like Jeffrey Weise, Dustin Burnette, a Leech Lake Indian, came up hard. He and his older sister and younger brother were raised by his mother just south of Cass Lake after their father more or less left them. The father would come around once in a while, but for all intents and purposes he was gone. "That's where I grew up," Dustin says, pointing to a little house sandwiched between the Sand Trap golf course on one side and a lumber mill on the other. The house is 100 yards to the south of the city limits of Cass Lake. There are a dozen or so other houses in the neighborhood. "There were two murders on this block," says Dustin. "But that was after I left"—after his life fell apart.

Dustin grew up Indian, but it was an empty Indianness. "We didn't hear any Ojibwe language or ceremony. It was just powwow, alcohol, violence, and work." Dustin is very light-skinned, with a round friendly face and sandy brown hair. "Yeah, I got all the bad stuff about being Indian and none of the good. I got the bad teeth and the instability and the alcoholism and all that. I didn't get anything else growing up. That's what being Indian and being on the rez meant to us."

When Dustin was sixteen his mother died of an aneurysm. She had a terrible headache, and the next day she was dead. "I didn't drink much before Mom died. Maybe once. I remember she died on the ides of March. I remember because I was Caesar in our English class play of *Julius Caesar* the month before. My roommate still laughs about that. He played Brutus. I love it. Ironic, right? My mom was pissed right, because I used one of her sheets for a costume, and they marked it all up with red marker for blood. My roommate stabbed me in the back. It was great. But it was sad when she died. I mean, people die, the world turns, but I was sad because she spent her last moments scared and in a lot of pain and wondering how we were going to make it."

His grandmother did the best to take care of Dustin and his brother (his sister had been kicked out) after his mother died. "I'd seen her twice in sixteen years before that. She'd quarreled with my mom, you know. It really kicked her in the teeth—she'd been too proud to patch things up with my mom and then she died and she's trying to take care of me and brother." Dustin, who usually breaks into laughter or tries to say something shocking, gets quiet when he talks about his brother. "He's doing OK now—he's not hurting himself or anyone else. So I'm happy, completely. He's out in New Town, North Dakota. He's a night manager at a grocery store. He works and smokes himself silly and stays out of trouble. So I say: little brother, I'm happy for you. He had it worse, you know. Everyone bailed on him. He was fourteen when Mom died. I left him when he was sixteen to go to college. Grandma bailed on him. It was rough for him."

Dustin describes himself as a mama's boy. After his mother died, his stepfather left with his stepbrother. "Everything was different. Different people. Different cars. Different food. You know when you're a little baby and your folks are watching a movie late at night and you're watching with them? And now as an adult you remember watching it with them but you don't remember anything about it? That's how my old life is before my mom died. A feeling but no memory of everything. Everything was different after she died. You never deal with death before and then your mom dies in a minute. I don't know if I was manic-depressive or what. But life was surreal. Nothing mattered. School was different. My friends were different. Everyone treated me different. I'd walk up to strangers and slap them in the face and think it was OK. I didn't give a shit. No one would mess with me. I had nothing to lose. I stopped going to school. I started stealing—DVDs and stuff. If my brother and me wanted to go to a movie we'd go steal something so we could get tickets to a show. Just from retail. We never stole from people, not that that's any better."

All in all life was going down. Dustin gained weight—he ate to feel better. "I'd eat nachos. Ice cream. I mean a huge bowl of ice cream with a candy bar on top of it. Every night. It was sad, dude." He went from 165 pounds to 245 in three months. He would go to school but just to hang out, just for someplace to be. Still, he was smart. He scored twenty-nine on the ACT (in the 85th percentile). He had straight A's. He had only two classes and a lot of free time. He started to hang around the Indian education department in the high school because you could hang out there and no one expected you to be doing anything.

Then a new Indian counselor showed up at the school: Sean Fahr-lander. "I could hear him talking through those paper-thin walls. But I wouldn't talk to him or nothing. He was, and I'm serious, the ugliest, meanest Indian sonofabitch I'd ever seen in my life. He looked hor-rible, man. I was terrified. Everyone was trying to get me to talk to him. So I went into his office one day. I stood in the doorway. He said, 'It's about time.' He got up and came around and closed the door. And then he broke me down. He said: 'Who the fuck do you think you are, you little piece of shit? You're walking around here like you've got a big cock. You're nothing.'

"I'd never been talked to like that. I went home and cried in my bed. I cried forever. But I came back the next day and he said, 'Well, boy. You feel better?' The thing is, I did. I did feel better. I felt great. 'Good,' said Sean. 'That's what I call knocking you off your high horse. Now let's get started.' It's no bullshit! It was all him. I went in there to play a game of chess. I didn't expect any of that. Just that one little ear beating was all I needed. Someone to hold me accountable. It meant a lot to me. He told me that I was Indian even if I didn't look it. We hung out every day. He told me about Indian shit, beyond the stuff I knew. He talked to me about my treaty rights and stuff. My rights. I didn't know anything about those things. No one ever talked to me about this stuff. I never pursued it."

Sean went farther. Toward the end of the year he slipped Dustin a pamphlet with a picture castle on it.

"What's this?" I asked.

"It's your new home. I got you a full ride to the College of St. Scholastica in Duluth. Don't fuck it up."

It was a pivotal moment for Dustin. He had no ambition beyond finding some kind of steady job—working at the casino or at the supermarket in Cass Lake. Maybe some day he'd be a manager. That was the start. Like a lot of Indian kids, Dustin had needed help. But he didn't even know what kind of help or whom to ask. Like Weise, and like a lot of other kids, Dustin was heading in a bad direction. He credits Sean with saving his life. He graduated from Scholastica in 2009 and moved back to Leech Lake, where he teaches Ojibwe language at the tribally run Ojibwe-language immersion school. His life could have turned out very differently. "I found a family, at ceremonies, in the language. I never had that before. I never thought I would. But now I've got a ceremonial family. I've got a purpose, people who rely on me. It feels good, man. It feels great."

If the Sioux are known for being fierce warriors, the Iroquois for diplomacy, and the Cherokee for being civilized, the Ojibwe are known for being loving. In contrast to Jeffrey Weise's experience the one thing that every single explorer, missionary, anthropologist, and historian has noticed about Ojibwe culture is the closeness between parents and children. Frances Densmore, the anthropologist, noted in her book *Chippewa Customs* that Ojibwe parents were extremely permissive. "If a baby was born during the night it was customary to notify the people by firing guns. Immediately the men of the father's gens and those of one other gens went to the wigwam and attempted to gain possession of the child, the father and those of his gens defending the child against the other party. The child's relatives threw water, and sometimes a mixture of flour and water, on the attacking party, and the men fought and wrestled. It was said that 'everybody was wringing wet' when the struggle was finished. The men who secured the baby took it to the leader of the gens who carried it four times around the fire while the people sang a song with words meaning 'We have caught the little bird.' The parents gave presents to the men to secure possession of the baby. It was said, 'This was done to make the child brave from hearing so much noise as soon as it was born.'" Such was the excitement a new baby caused in the village. Densmore also noted, "Chippewa women never allowed a baby to cry if this could be avoided by any mode of pacification, and for this reason the small children were somewhat 'spoiled.' The devotion of a mother to her children was intense, and if necessary to defend them, she fought with ferocity." Parents rarely yelled at their children and never hit them. Instead, Ojibwe parents used fear as a deterrent. For instance: "An article which may be said to have represented the bear paw was called a 'ghost leg.' It consisted of an old moccasin stuffed with straw and fastened at the end of a stick. . . . If a child were persistently naughty the mother would call aloud for the bear paw [ghost leg]. The blanket hung at the end of the stick would be drawn aside and the old moccasin at the end of the stick would be slowly thrust into the wigwam by an older person on the outside.

"When the children were old enough to listen attentively it was still desired to keep them quiet in the evening. For this purpose the older people devised a game called the 'Game of Silence.' In this game a song was sung by an older person in which the most novel and interesting events were related. The song suddenly ceased at the most exciting point, and the children tried to avoid making a sound at this surprise. The song was repeated over and over with new words and new pauses, a prize being given to the child who showed the most self-control. It is said that the children were usually asleep when the game ended."

Collins Oakgrove, an elder from Red Lake, remembers that he always listened to his parents when they told him to behave because if he was naughty they'd summon his uncle. He was very scared of his uncle—whatever the uncle said to do, he'd do it. Eventually, when he was older, he asked his uncle why he'd been so scared. *Oh,* said his uncle. *That's easy. When you were about two years old, old enough to remember but not old enough to quite remember, I pretended to drown you in the lake. They picked me to be the bad uncle.*

Henry Rowe Schoolcraft—an early ethnologist of the Ojibwe who later became an Indian agent in Michigan—wrote, not without disgust, that Ojibwe children were allowed to run wild and do whatever they pleased without incurring the wrath of their parents. Ojibwe parents were, according to him, almost absurdly permissive and loving toward their children. William Warren, half Ojibwe and half white, the author of *The History of the Ojibwe People,* first published in 1885, recounts this episode during a period of intense warfare between the Ojibwe and the Fox:

> A few lodges of Ojibway hunters under the guidance of Bi-aus-wah, a leading man of the tribe, claiming the Loon Totem, [were] one spring encamped at Kah-puk-wi-e-kah, a bay on the lake shore situated forty miles west of La Pointe.
>
> Early one morning, the camp was attacked by a large war-party of Foxes, and the men, women, and children all murdered, with the exception of a lad and an old man, who, running into a swamp, and becoming fastened in the bog and mire, were captured and taken in triumph by the Foxes to their village, there to suffer death with all the barbarous tortures which a savage could invent.

Bi-aus-wah, at the time of the attack, was away on a hunt, and he did not return till towards evening. His feelings on finding his wigwams in ashes, and the lifeless scalpless remains of his beloved family and relatives strewed about on the blood-stained ground, can only be imagined. He had lost all that bound him to life, and perfectly reckless he followed the return trail of the Foxes determined to die, if necessary, in revenging the grievous wrong which they had inflicted upon him. He arrived at the village of his enemies, a day after their successful war-party had returned, and he heard men, women, and children screaming and yelling with delight, as they danced around the scalps which their warriors had taken.

Secreting himself on the outskirts of the village, the Ojibway chieftain waited for an opportunity to imbrue his hands in the blood of an enemy who might come within reach of his tomahawk. He had not remained long in his ambush when the Foxes collected a short distance from the village, for the purpose of torturing and burning their two captives. The old man was first produced, and his body being wrapped in folds of the combustible birch bark, the Foxes set fire to it and caused him to run the gauntlet amid their hellish whoops and screams; covered with a perfect blaze of fire, and receiving withal a shower of blows, the old man soon expired.

The young and tender lad was then brought forward, and his doom was to run backwards and forwards on a long pile of burning [logs], till consumed to death. None but a parent can fully imagine the feelings which wrung the heart of the ambushed Ojibway chieftain, as he now recognized his only surviving child in the young captive who was about to undergo these torments. His single arm could not rescue him, but this brave father determined to die for or with his only son, and as the cruel Foxes were on the point of setting fire to the heap of dry [wood] on which the lad had been placed, they were surprised to see the Ojibway chief step proudly and boldly into their midst and address them as follows:—

"My little son, whom you are about to burn with fire, has seen but a few winters; his tender feet have never trodden the war path—he has never injured you! But the hairs of my head are white with many winters, and over the graves of my relatives I have hung many scalps which I have taken from the heads of the Foxes; my death is worth something to you, let me therefore take the place of my child that he may return to his people."

Taken totally by surprise, the Foxes silently listened to the chief's proposal, and ever having coveted his death, and now fearing the consequence of his despairing efforts, they accepted his offer, and releasing the son, they bade him to depart, and burnt the brave father in his stead.

George Copway, another earlier chronicler of Indian history, wrote about his own parenting. Copway was Ojibwe, from Mississauga, Ontario. Born in 1818, he grew up in a traditional Ojibwe family but converted later in life to Methodism. He met and married an Englishwoman and the two moved to Minnesota Territory in 1840 to evangelize among the Minnesota Ojibwe. They had children. Eventually, Copway became good friends with the controversial Ojibwe chief Bagone-giizhig. In 1841 Copway left his wife with Bagone-giizhig while he traveled from Rabbit Lake to St. Peters in an effort to gather provisions and support for the Rabbit Lake Mission. While gathering provisions he ventured on a trip to Little Crow's Dakota village and walked into preparations for a full-scale war expedition against the Ojibwe. Little Crow told Copway, "Tell [Bagone-giizhig] I am coming for his scalp." Copway, fearing for his wife, children, and friend, ran, swam, and rode the entire distance from Little Crow's village to Bagone-giizhig's in three days, a total distance of more than 300 miles. Copway wrote in his journal, "I was so anxious . . . that I had no appetite for eating . . . having walked two hundred and forty miles, forded eight large streams and crossed the broad Mississippi twice. My coat and pantaloons were in strips." Copway warned Bagone-giizhig, who moved all of his people from the area and took precautions for the rest of the summer that probably saved hundreds of Ojibwe lives. Copway would later move to New York City after being defrocked by the Methodists for embezzlement. He wrote and published his memoirs in 1847—becoming one of the first Indians to do so.

It seems that Ojibwe parents would do almost anything for their children. John Johnson, a half-Ottawa missionary in Minnesota, panicked when Bagone-giizhig began machinations for war in the 1860s. Bagone-giizhig had threatened Johnson's life in 1857, and the Ojibwe chief was not to be ignored or dismissed: he usually carried out his threats. Johnson was convinced that his wife and two children were in danger, especially after he was held prisoner by Bagone-giizhig on August 17, 1862. That evening, after his release, Johnson fled from Gull Lake (Bagone-giizhig's stronghold) with his wife and children. He put his wife and all of his children in a canoe and dragged it by hand all night down the Gull River. He reached Fort Ripley the next day, having dragged his family 100 miles to safety. However, two of his five children died of exposure during their escape.

Indian kids have been drifting away from their families for decades. And for many years, from the late nineteenth century well into the twentieth century (and in Canada as recently as the 1970s), it was federal policy to try to separate Indian children from their parents. Indian kids were not supposed to have strong ties to their families; strong ties were considered *bad*. This was part of a larger effort to civilize the Indian and bring him into the mainstream as a productive member of society. Those who were obsessed with what was often called the "Indian problem" recognized that the bond of family, the connection between parents and their children and, sometimes even more importantly, between grandparents and grandchildren, was the most significant and strongest bond linking a person to his or her identity, tribe, and reservation. If this bond could be broken, Indians would disappear as Indians, and the "Indian problem" would be solved.

It may come as a surprise to many people that there was an "Indian problem"—the concept sounds analogous to a mold problem or an insect problem or some other pernicious infestation—but evidently there was. The term was popularized by the twenty-first president of the United States, Chester A. Arthur. The "Indian problem" was, as Arthur saw it, twofold: it was a problem of inefficient administration on the part of the government, and of failure on the part of Indians to "join the mainstream" and give up our savage ways. Arthur's efforts—which resulted in policies that were among the most disastrous and destructive to Indian people—were thinly disguised attempts to gain control of trade, minerals, lumber, and land for settlement. Arthur mournfully set out the history and problems in his State of the Union address delivered in January 1882: "For the success of the efforts now making to introduce among the Indians the customs and pursuits of civilized life and gradually to absorb them into the mass of our citizens, sharing their rights and holden to their responsibilities, there is imperative need for legislative action."

This legislative action had two components: the severing of responsibility of the federal government (as a signatory of treaties) to Indian tribes on reservations, along with an increase of state and territorial control; and the establishment of boarding schools, where Indian children would be stripped of their tribal connections. With his State of the Union address, Chester A. Arthur set the stage for legislation that still haunts many Indians today:

I advise a liberal appropriation for the support of Indian schools, because of my confident belief that such a course is consistent with the wisest economy.

Even among the most uncultivated Indian tribes there is reported to be a general and urgent desire on the part of the chiefs and older members for the education of their children. It is unfortunate, in view of this fact, that during the past year the means which have been at the command of the Interior Department for the purpose of Indian instruction have proved to be utterly inadequate.

The success of the schools which are in operation at Hampton, Carlisle, and Forest Grove should not only encourage a more generous provision for the support of those institutions, but should prompt the establishment of others of a similar character.

They are doubtless much more potent for good than the day schools upon the reservation, as the pupils are altogether separated from the surroundings of savage life and brought into constant contact with civilization.

The institution that acted as the wedge to split Indian families apart was the Indian boarding school. These schools were often run by religious orders, mostly Catholics and evangelicals, but funded by the government. Students were famously made to burn their traditional clothes upon arrival and had their hair cut. They were routinely whipped for speaking their Native languages and just as routinely sexually abused by priests and teachers alike. Boarding schools in Canada, called "residential schools," were so bad and were in place so long (until the 1970s) that Native people in Canada received an apology from Pope John Paul II for what they endured there and an apology by the Canadian government, accompanied by restitution for suffering—$10,000 for all those abused in former residential schools and an additional $3,000 for every year they spent in these schools beyond the first.

Attendance at boarding school was mandatory, and government officials, Indian agents, priests, and county workers used whatever means necessary to force families to comply. Rations guaranteed by treaty were withheld. Jobs were dangled. Military and police actions were threatened and used. Parents were faced with impossible, terroristic choices— one woman I know was told that she had to choose: voluntarily send all her kids to boarding school for most of the year or never see them again. She chose to let her kids go. The mother of a girlfriend of mine from Coochiching First Nation in Ontario was lucky. Her parents did not want to let her and her siblings go and so whenever the Indian agent came to the reserve she and her siblings were hidden—under mattresses, in flour bins, rolled in hides tucked in the rafters—until the agent was gone. He would sit in their house, with children hiding all around him like mice, drinking tea with her parents, who told him with sad faces that all the children had died. It worked. Others, like my grandmother, were not so lucky. My grandmother's mother, Izzie, had applied to the BIA for food. Her husband was gone and she couldn't feed the kids. The BIA denied her request. It wouldn't give her any flour, lard, bacon, or any other food. But the agent told her that the kids would be fed at boarding school if she consented to let them go. It wasn't much of a choice. So my grandmother, at age six, was taken to a boarding school in Tomah, Wisconsin. She traveled to the school with her siblings Tommy, Millie, Howard, and Vern, but they were all separated from one another once they arrived. She did not return until she was ten years old. When she did come home four years later she knew she should cry but she could not. Instead, she stuck her fingers in her eyes so as not to offend her mother.

Boarding schools were the first step in breaking the bond between parents and children. The second step came later, in the 1940s, in the form of the county nurse, who as many say had more power than anyone else over the destiny of Indian kids and Indian families. If a county nurse or a social worker declared that a parent was "unfit," then there was little the parent could do. The child was taken and, in almost all the cases, sent to live with a non-Native family far from the reservation. Young Indian mothers were encouraged and often forced to put their children up for adoption. There was a thriving market in Indian children. One of my mother's cousins was, in effect, given to two spinsters from Minneapolis in the early 1940s; they paid his family and took the boy. And my mother herself wound up in foster care in south-central Minnesota while my grandfather was away fighting in World War II and my grandmother was working at the Jolly Green Giant green bean factory in Austin, Minnesota. She stayed there until one summer day when, while she was playing in the yard, a black 1930s sedan drove up, the door opened, and her uncle Howard leaned over the seat and said, "Let's go." She climbed in and never went back. She did say, though, the woman who had kept her was kind and caring and sent her a card every year on her birthday with a dollar or two, and on her high school graduation and when she graduated from nursing school.

Like boarding schools, the widespread removal of Indian children from Indian homes in the middle of the twentieth century was federal policy. Administered by the Child Welfare League of America and funded by a federal contract from the Bureau of Indian Affairs (BIA) and the U.S. Children's Bureau, the Indian Adoption Project lasted from 1958 through 1967. The goal of the adoption project was to systematically remove Indian children from Indian homes and place them with non-Native families. Since enrolled Indian children belong to sovereign Indian nations, adoption and foster care in which the Indian child is placed in a white family functions as both transracial and transnational. The project director, Arnold Lyslo, thought he was doing a good thing. And he viewed the adoption project as a success. "One can no longer say that the Indian child is the 'forgotten child,'" he said at the project's completion.

Because of the boarding schools of the late nineteenth century and the early twentieth century and the ease with which Indian children were snatched from their homes by social workers and county nurses between the 1940s and the 1970s, Indian children were especially vulnerable. Many parents did not have the opportunity to save their children—unlike the chief in William Warren's account or George Copway. In Minnesota, one in four Indian children under the age of one was removed from his or her home and either placed in foster care or adopted by a non-Indian couple. Twenty-five percent of Indian children lost their tribe, their rights, and their heritage. The problem of Indian children drifting away from home and tribe was so acute that the U.S. government passed legislation in 1978 for the special protection of Indian children. The Indian Child Welfare Act (ICWA) of 1978 was the first step in recognizing the disastrous results of boarding schools and zealous foster care programs. Its main goal was to keep Indian children in Indian families. The ICWA was not based on race; it is based on the political affiliation of Indian children with a specific federally recognized tribe or reservation.

The ICWA is dry stuff, dry reading, that is. But in Indian country, it seems everyone is a lawyer; everyone has a vested interest in the exact letter of the law and nowhere else does one feel the direct pressure or pleasure of laws, statutes, Supreme Court decisions, or shifts in federal policy. The act reads:

Recognizing the special relationship between the United States and the Indian tribes and their members and the Federal responsibility to Indian people, the Congress finds:

Congress, through statutes, treaties, and the general course of dealing with Indian tribes, has assumed the responsibility for the protection and preservation of Indian tribes and their resources; that *there is no resource that is more vital to the continued existence and integrity of Indian tribes than their children* and that the United States has a direct interest, as trustee, in protecting Indian children who are members of or are eligible for membership in an Indian tribe; that an alarmingly high percentage of Indian families are broken up by the removal, often unwarranted, of their children from them by non-tribal public and private agencies and that an alarmingly high percentage of such children are placed in non-Indian foster and adoptive homes and institutions; and that the States, exercising their recognized jurisdiction over Indian child custody proceedings through administrative and judicial bodies, have often failed to recognize the essential tribal relations of Indian people and the cultural and social standards prevailing in Indian communities and families.

And with that, jurisdiction over the placement of enrolled tribal members became a federal matter and no longer a state or county matter, though all these jurisdictions overlap and feed into one another in practice.

In Beltrami County one in four children lives in poverty; this is the highest rate in the state. At Red Lake, 47 percent of children live in poverty. In 2005 the high school graduation rate was 57 percent. Only 25 percent of ninth-graders at Red Lake high school lived with both their parents. In an anonymous survey 81 percent of ninth-grade girls in Red Lake said they had thought about killing themselves. Clearly, something is out of control. Clearly, many Indians have not had control of their own lives or their own resources. But what I wonder about is the difference between someone like Jeff Weise—who seems to have had no hope at all, who had largely given up on, well, as sentimental as it sounds, love—and all the other kids who've had it rough on the rez.

❧

Even if Jeffrey Weise didn't feel that he had a reason for living, there are reasons, and they are growing each and every day, or so it seems when I stop by the Boys and Girls Club of Leech Lake. The club is located in the old high school in downtown Cass Lake, where my mother, uncles, aunt, and second cousins went. The new high school sits on the edge of town, away from the Super Fund Site that is downtown Cass Lake. The streets of Cass Lake, so dangerous for so many people, don't seem that bad with the lights blazing from the windows of the club. The old school hums with the voices of kids. About eighty kids between the ages of six and twelve show up after school and leave at five-thirty, when the teenagers take their turn. On each and every school night at least sixty Cass Lake teenagers, almost all Indian, walk through the doors to play basketball and video games, go on MySpace and Facebook, eat, joke around, and tease one another. It is loud: loud in the old classrooms, loud in the hallways, loud in the bathrooms. The kids cluster around the workers and hammer them with requests and questions. And the things they talk about—who's pregnant and who left for North Dakota and who is coming back and when can they go on the computer and so-and-so has been on longer than everyone else—suggest they are alive and excited about being alive. Well, for lack of a better phrase, they sound like kids.

Towering above them is Keenan Goodfellow, a Samoan. He grew up and lived in the tough neighborhood of north Minneapolis. Round-faced and round-headed, he has a build that the kids have to respect: broad, with arms slabbed with muscle, about as big around as my legs, a football lineman's arms. He wears a white fitted baseball cap backward, cargo pants, and flip-flops, and he makes the best ribs you'll ever eat. When I visit Keenan for the first time, he has the kids doing a writing assignment in order to earn computer time. They come up with half-filled pages. He glances at the pages and whips them back: "Get real." "Not good enough." "You've got to be kidding. This? No way." The kids groan and complain and get back to it.

Keenan estimates that 80 percent of the kids who come to the club don't live with their parents. All of them come from poverty. Vanessa Budreau is an example. Vanessa is a sharp, funny, sassy girl in the eighth grade. She has a classic Ojibwe face—round, with deep brown eyes and small level teeth. As I talked to her she kept up our conversation, teased a boy making faces through the glass door, and exchanged quips with Keenan. As part of an assignment, she wrote: "I think the reservation is an improving town. I mean around 2000–2005 it was probably one of the most ugliest, savviest, sad, poor, broke towns I have ever seen. But in 2007 the board start having meetings that actually worked and our town is looking a little better. Every day I see a bum with sad, poor kids with no education. Someone with an education wasting it with liquor and drugs. That someone is my mom she was a good mom until I turned 9 and knew what her day off from kids day was. Which were her day of drinking days. I always wondered why she would be so sick in the mornings. Everything was going good until my grandma died in 06 that was the year my dad left my mom and went all the way to North Dakota without telling anybody."

Vanessa has certainly seen a lot. I ask her what she means when she says Cass Lake is getting better. "Well," she said, "it's got lights—you know, street lights—now. And new streets. And sidewalks. Stuff like that." Her days are getting better, too. After her mother hit the skids Vanessa went to live with her grandfather, whom she clearly loves. She and her siblings and many of her cousins and their babies all landed there until there were fourteen people living in a trailer meant for three.

But they got a house on a housing tract south of Cass Lake. They have four bedrooms. Seven members of her family moved out, so there are only seven of them in a house twice the size of the one they had before. She has her own room. Her little brother doesn't eat her homework anymore. School is going well. She's decided that she doesn't want to drink or use drugs. Her friends have decided the same thing. And it's strange to hear twelve-year-olds say they've sworn off meds, pot, and booze. Stacy, one of the other workers of the Boys and Girls Club, tells me that kids as young as nine, with world-weary wisdom, have decided to "get clean" because of the club. "They can tell me what the numbers and letters on pills mean—which ones are Darvocet and which ones are Oxy. I don't know the difference. But they do." The tribal government sometimes does what it can, and often doesn't do all that it can. There are Boys and Girls Clubs in all the major communities on Leech Lake Reservation and other chapters at Red Lake and Bemidji.

Vanessa has come up hard, as hard as it gets. She's lost her parents. She's poor. She's Indian in a town full of poor, parentless Indians. It is much easier to get drugs and to sell them than it is to get into college. Before joining the club she had never been to a restaurant other than a fast-food place or a buffet. As part of SMART Girls, a program attached to the Boys and Girls Club, preteen and teenage girls who qualified because of good grades got to eat out at a restaurant of their choice. They chose Taco Bell. Stacy, the coordinator, told them to think big. They chose Wendy's. Finally, after some coaxing, she persuaded them to try a local chain, Green Mill. The girls were stunned by the stonework and the wood-paneled booths. When the server came to their table the girls reared back and looked her up and down; they thought she was "stepping." Stacy explained that the server was there to take their order, that she would bring their food to them—they didn't have to get it themselves. Just that short trip to the Green Mill in Bemidji was eye-opening for many of them.

It's March now, just a few weeks shy of the second anniversary of the shooting at the school in Red Lake. I like March. Winter is on its way out and my family is busy maple sugaring. We had a very warm spell last week and so we had to get our buckets and taps ready in a hurry. Our family has been sugaring in the same place for the last thirty years— just past the reservation boundary on Highway 12, just past the dam where I used to fish, just past the house where Reagan and Patrick used to live. Sugaring is nice work—it's not too hard, compared with ricing, netting, trapping, or hunting. The weather is usually nice. And with the fire going and tea made from Lipton's bags steeped in hot maple sap, and the smell of jack pine slab, it's a relief after the winter. In the lakes nearby the walleye are schooling and getting ready to run back up the river to thrash once again at the foot of the dam before they drop their eggs and swim back down to the lakes.

I had to set out the taps alone. My older brother is expecting another child. My younger brother and sister are busy working. My mother lost a lung to cancer and so it's hard for her to get around in the woods the way she used to. My father no longer sugars at all. He's eighty-one. So I rounded up all the pails and buckets; washed them; organized the taps and plastic tubing, my auger, and a hatchet; and set off for the sugar bush. It's only two miles from the house, and I was in a hurry, so I dumped everything into the back of the truck and took off. Right at the reservation boundary a gust came up and blew one ice-cream pail from the back of the truck, but I kept on, figuring I'd pick it up on my way home.

It was sunny, maybe fifty degrees. The snow was still deep and I slogged through it from tree to tree. The sugar bush is nice because it seems like the kind of place where nothing happens. There were no animal tracks—no deer trails, no rabbit trails, no fox, wolf, coyote,

fisher, or marten tracks at all. Just the soughing of the trees, the knack-
ering of branches. I was still working close to the road when a white
sedan with Leech Lake Reservation plates pulled up next to my truck.
The horn honked.

"Excuse me! Excuse me, sir!" someone called.

I looked up.

"This's got to be your bucket. I found it on the road."

An arm waved out the car window, holding my ice-cream pail.

I slogged over to the car and said thanks.

The man was about my age. A lot bigger. Dark. He had on fashion-
able wire-rimmed glasses and wore his hair in a loose ponytail.

"You must have to eat a ton of ice cream to get enough buckets for
this."

"We all do our part," I agreed.

We didn't have much else to say

"Thanks for finding my bucket," I said.

"No problem. No problem at all." And he drove away.

And just when he put the car in gear and pulled out into the road
I recognized him. It was Reagan Morgan. It had to be. I hadn't seen
him in twenty-five years, so I couldn't be sure. But it was the same
round, open, friendly face. The same full cheeks. The same eyes. His
hair was longer and his complexion a lot clearer. His glasses were
better, too.

It was weird. I had been writing about him just that morning. And
wondering, too. Wondering if he was doing OK. Wondering if his life
was what he wanted it to be. My sister, who gets out a lot more than I
do, says she sees him once in a while at Moose-A-Brew, a coffee shop in
Bemidji. He games there a lot, she says. I also wonder if he remembers
me and my brother, and remembers fishing with us. The man in the
white car seemed healthy and happy. Solid. And he did me a good turn
by bringing my bucket over.

I trotted back to my taps and began tapping again: drilling the holes and fitting the spigots in. The sap will start running any day now. And every morning when I go to check, my buckets will feel like Christmas, with a surprise (How much? How full?) in every bucket.

I thought about those past summers as I tapped. I thought about the afternoon after Reagan showed me his *Hustler*. We eventually landed a huge northern pike. I don't remember who did it—probably my brother Tony, who was always luckier than I was. We decided to hide the *Hustler* in our cave and to come back for it the next day—daring fate or chance or the college kids who prowled the dam drinking beer. We wrapped it in plastic we found on the riverbank and put the magazine back in the small hole as far as Reagan's longer arms could reach. And then we put the northern pike on a yellow nylon stringer, wrapped the stringer around my handlebars, and all took off for home together.

The magazine was there when we returned the next day. It was damp, wavy with moisture. The cheap magazine stock showed the text through the photos, proving that those are magazines you can read. But it was damaged, harder to enjoy somehow because the wavy paper, the leaking ink, made it impossible to pretend that we were looking at something other than a cast-off magazine, cheap, filled with cheap thrills.

But before that, as we biked home, with the northern pike banging against my bare legs all the way there, leaving slime down my thighs and grinning and turning its dead eye toward me; with Anton, Reagan, and Patrick; with the sun on our backs as we pedaled east—it felt good to be alive. We owned the whole road. Reagan and Patrick kept on toward their house. We turned right onto our road. And still we swerved and stood and pumped the pedals and swerved some more, the dead fish banging against my legs. And all the while I thought about that magazine, sleeping in its cave, and the tangled mysteries it contained, and the hope that someday it would all make sense.

Russell Bryan and Helen (Bryan) Johnson near their home in Squaw Lake, 1981

5

We saw the new Morongo Casino, Resort, and Spa rise up like a mono-
lith, like the Colossus of Rhodes, from the foothills of the Coachella
Valley north and west of Palm Springs. It was visible from fifteen miles
away, a solid, angular, basalt-colored spire jutting from the valley scree,
looking more like an ancient artifact than a new luxury destination.
It's not often that casinos can be described as beautiful or impressive
in a "not Vegas" way, but the Morongo Tower was. Even though its
architectural elements blend in with the desert, we found ourselves
wondering how it got there. Some conspiracy theorists believe that
space aliens may have built the pyramids at Giza, and the same feeling attends the spectacle of the Morongo Tower rising from the Palm
Springs desert. Casinos like this—though perhaps not quite as nice—
rise all across the American landscape. They rise from swamps, suburbs, deserts, and forests. They perch on cliffs and look out over lakes.

The presence of the Morongo Tower is even more amazing when
you remember that, historically at least, Indian reservations are a great
place to be poor if you are Indian—and a fantastic place to get rich

if you're not. It is only recently that this pattern is being reversed. For centuries, privateers, government officials, railroad barons, timber magnates, prospectors, and mining companies have made a mint exploiting Native land and resources while the Indians for whom reservations were created have gotten poorer and poorer.

After we'd checked in, and with a weird kind of pride of ownership (the Morongo Band of Mission Indians who own the Morongo casino aren't my tribe, after all), I said to the valet, as I would say to a butler in my own mansion, "The bags, please."

As the elevator gushed up toward the seventeenth floor and the desert dwindled below us, I looked at my wife, who resembles a Native American Gwen Stefani with smoky eyes and a tongue ring and tattoos, and I marveled that we (Indians, that is) actually own all this—not my wife, of course, but this casino. We own it when we are really expected to be only two things, dead or poor. But gaming has become big news—if not *the* news—about Indians in the last decade and a half: Indian gaming brought in $25 billion dollars in 2006, compared with the $12 billion generated in Las Vegas. I thought to myself as I settled into our room, which was as beautiful as the tower that encased it, "I just might win after all."

It is odd to think you can strike it rich at an Indian casino and that Indian casinos have made a few (not many) Indians rich themselves. This is especially odd because, originally, the reservations were more or less set up to be poor—and if that wasn't the intent, it surely was the effect. While the Delaware might have gotten a reservation in exchange for fighting the British, and the Dakota because they defeated the U.S. Army during the Red Cloud Wars, and the Ojibwe through negotiations in present-day Wisconsin and Minnesota, most reservations were not created with such noble principles or because of such strength in bargaining. Rather, in the nineteenth century, the

U.S. government thought reservations were a promise it would never have to keep. In most people's estimation Indians would be gone— carried away by disease or intermarriage—within a generation or two. The reservations, in other words, were promises that no one thought would need to be kept for more than a couple of decades. Few counted on Indians living and loving and making so many new Indians. And no one counted on the resources that did exist within the boundaries of some reservations and that eventually became very important to the United States. The white pine timber in Wisconsin and Minnesota was suddenly close and valuable to Chicago, which needed the pine to build itself and then rebuild itself after it burned down. No one imagined that uranium deposits in Navajo, Apache, and Pueblo coun- try would mean so much to national security. And no one knew how much oil was hidden under Osage lands.

The Osage, after more than a century of fighting, were relocated to the Indian Territories (now Oklahoma) and given what was, more or less, worthless farmland. However, in 1894 large quantities of oil were discovered beneath Osage land. Henry Foster, a petroleum speculator, was granted exclusive oil and mineral rights provided he pay to all the enrolled Osage a 10 percent royalty on all the oil sold. Within a few years, the Osage were among the richest people in the world. When royalties peaked in 1925 one family of five, all of whom were enrolled, earned about $65,000, or approximately $800,000 in today's currency. The ugliness that follows money like stink on shit found its way to Osage territory: white speculators married Osage women to get their royalty rights, and one man, Ernest Burkhart, married an Osage woman and conspired to kill her and her family so he would receive her royalties.

But these were accidental grants of wealth. Reservations in general —far from urban centers, lacking infrastructure, without strong gov- ernment, with no strong representation to speak of, with little abil- ity to protect or exploit natural resources, and far from shipping and transportation networks—were poor. Poverty kills. Indians were supposed to be dead.

The Harvard Project on American Indian Economic Development, begun in 1987 and designed to address economic inequality and development, identified about a dozen reasons why life on the rez was virtually synonymous with a life of poverty. Lack of access to capital was a significant roadblock. "Unfair lending practices, the difficulty of collateralizing assets held in trust by the U.S. government, and low penetration of banking facilities continue to limit the supply of capital in Indian country." This is a polite way of saying that, for at least three reasons, no one wants to lend to Indians. (1) They are Indian. (2) Since most Indian land, what there is left of it, is held in common and in trust, it is not generally possible to use this land as collateral for loans; thus Indian individuals and communities are deprived of the number one asset with which most Americans strive toward the middle class— the houses they live in. (3) There simply weren't many banks on the rez until casinos were established. The nearest banks were off-reservation and owned, operated, or staffed by non-Indians who were not always keen on acquiring Indian accounts.

The Harvard Project also suggested that the lack of human capital (education, skills, technical expertise) and the means to develop it was also a problem. "The need for skilled employees in all aspects of economic activity is critical," the report says. "Because of high rates of unemployment, 'work until the grant runs out' experience, and common incidences of political nepotism, a large segment of the reservation workforce typically has been unable to develop consistent workplace experience and a career path. For years, the U.S. government has underwritten job training skills and education programs for adults and children. But without related economic opportunities, these efforts have either been wasted or led to 'brain drains,' in which new or newly trained talent flows off-reservation."

The Harvard Project went on to list other impediments to economic development: lack of infrastructure, of effective planning, of access to natural resources, or of control over the available resources; distance from markets; the high cost of transportation; corruption; factionalism; the instability of reservation government; and a lack of entrepreneurial skill.

This is nowhere more true than on Pine Ridge Reservation in South Dakota. Pine Ridge is the eighth largest reservation in the United States—larger than Rhode Island and Delaware combined—and has an Indian population of about 15,000, as of the 2000 census. Unemployment is at about 80 percent, so only one in five people has steady employment, though this is not for lack of trying. The result? Half of all the Indians on Pine Ridge live below the poverty level. While there are a few small businesses owned by individuals and also a few owned by the tribe, there is little else. The tribe began a moccasin factory, a meatpacking plant, and a fishing tackle business. All of them failed. In contrast, it opened the Prairie Wind Casino in 1994 in three double-wide trailers, and by 2007 this casino was successful enough that the tribe opened a $20 million upgrade with hotel and restaurant. It provides hundreds of jobs, mostly to Indians from Pine Ridge. Despite the casino, which is far away from any urban center and doesn't generate the kind of revenues one sees at Foxwoods or Morongo Casino and Spa, Pine Ridge is still crushingly poor, like most reservations.

Like Pine Ridge, the Cabazon Mission Band of Indians, the owners of the Morongo Resort and Casino, were desperately poor in the early 1980s. The Cabazon Mission Band has a tiny reservation along with eight other bands of Cahuilla Indians in Southern California. Located in the arid Coachella Valley, bounded by the San Bernardino, San Jacinto, Santa Rosa, and Little San Bernardino Mountain ranges, the homeland of the Cahuilla Indians is dry, nearly unfarmable if not for the Coachella Canal, which was completed in 1948 and brings the troubled waters of the Colorado River into the valley to support fruit farming. As of 2006, 100,000 acres of the valley were irrigated and farmed, bringing in revenues of $576 million, or almost $12,000 per acre. Ninety-five percent of all the dates grown in the United States are grown in the Coachella Valley, but aside from the date trees, which are almost all owned by whites, there was little to recommend the valley or the reservation except for Palm Springs.

In the 1950s the Cahuilla Indians of the Coachella Valley weren't doing well. Not that you would know it by looking at the non-Natives who lived in the valley. Nearby, in Palm Springs, located at the northern end of the valley, Frank Sinatra was entertaining his brat pack friends in bungalows named after his hits. (You could stay in "New York, New York" or "My Way" or, if you came with a lover, the "Tender Trap" was open to you.) Albert Frey and John Lautner were designing houses for Bob Hope, Robert Mitchum, Mary Pickford, Shirley Temple, and Charlie Chaplin. Meanwhile the Agua Caliente Indians, half of whose reservation is within the city limits of Palm Springs, were living in huts and shacks. Joseph Benito, a Chemehuevi tribal member who grew up near Indio and who served for many years as the spokesperson for the Cabazon Band, remembers: "Life was pretty primitive in those days. There wasn't much on the reservation except sagebrush and rabbits. We didn't even have electricity until the 1950s. Housing was limited to makeshift quarters. . . . There was no running water. We walked two miles to school every day, even in the summer heat, and thought nothing about it. . . . A highlight of our lives was the monthly trip to Torres-Martinez Reservation where the Indian Agency handed out rations for our food allotment. We always could count on a good meal after that."

The total number of members of the Cahuilla Tribe was around 800 as of the 1990 census, and the Cabazon Band of the Cahuilla is tiny. In the last fifty years the number of enrolled Cabazon Indians has fluctuated between thirty and forty. By comparison, the Cherokee have more than 100,000 enrolled members. There are also Cahuilla Indians living in the Coachella Valley—the Augustine Band of Mission Indians. The Augustine Band is the nation's smallest federally recognized tribe, with an enrollment of eight. From the 1950s through the early 1980s, such low enrollment numbers were a drawback for a tribe that wanted to make its lot better. Some populations were smaller than many family Thanksgiving parties. The first Thanksgiving, celebrated in 1621 in Plymouth, Massachusetts, was actually three times larger than the entire population of the Cabazon Mission Band.

With such a small population the Cabazon Band had tremendous difficulty in obtaining basic social services, let alone coercing an unwilling government into honoring treaty obligations, such as providing housing, education, roads, and annuities. It sometimes paid to be a big tribe, either warlike (such as the Dakota) or more conciliatory (such as the Cherokee). In 1852 and again in 1877 both the state of California and the federal government unilaterally refused to ratify existing treaties or simply rewrote the treaties without the input of the Cabazon. The government was more interested in courting prospectors and railroad developers. Both groups wanted something from the valley—the railroads wanted to go through it and the miners wanted to go under it. There was nothing to compel the government to act; nothing about the geographic position or political insignificance of the Cabazon encouraged the government to even remember them.

For instance, in 1967 the Cabazon Mission Band submitted a budget for the fiscal year to the Bureau of Indian Affairs (BIA). The budget totaled $350: $200 for committee expenses, $100 for telephone charges, and $50 for miscellaneous expenses. The band then realized that actual expenses exceeded those reported and submitted a revised budget for $1,500. The budget resolution was returned to the Cabazon Band on July 3, 1967. The accompanying letter from the

BIA stated: "The resolution is not in good form, because the Resolved clause does not state who is to be paid. However, if you have telephone bills which are marked Paid, and if you can determine the bills were paid by Mr. Joseph Benitez, Chairman, you could accept the resolution as authority to reimburse the Chairman. If you do not obligate FY 1967 tribal funds by submitting MOR document to OS in Albuquerque, it appears that you will have to delay payment until FY 1968 budget has been approved, and until funds have been allotted. The original resolution is returned herewith."

This is a classic example of the "death by bureaucracy" that plagued Indian reservations across the country; uneducated and unsavvy tribal officials who were trying simply to have the needs of their communities met were stonewalled by a corrupt, clumsy, inept, and uncaring BIA.

The late 1960s—filled with the furor and success of the civil rights movement, Johnson's War on Poverty, and the rise of the American Indian Movement (AIM)—gave way to the 1970s. And while tribal councils watched as grassroots organizations fought for justice and as a cadre of educated Indians took positions and gained experience in Johnson's Great Society (in the BIA; in the Office of Economic Opportunity; in the Department of Health, Education, and Welfare; and as administrators for CAP), the 1970s turned out to be pretty good years for Indian tribes. Nixon's administration turned out to be a good one for Indians—millions of dollars were appropriated for the Indian Financing Act of 1974 and the money went into insurance, loan, land, and business projects.

The Cabazon Band capitalized on the experience of its members and on the increased availability of funds. Band members opened a smoke shop and sold tax-free cigarettes. When the state tried to collect taxes on the proceeds of the smoke shop, they fought it. Other tribes around the country were doing the same thing—the Seminole,

Oneida, Seneca, and others were reaching out and exercising what strength they had. Many of them, having cut their teeth on small businesses like smoke shops and trading posts, began venturing into the realm of gambling—mostly bingo or small card halls. And this is where two significant, jagged pieces of history going back, once again, to the dawn of Indian-Anglo relations came into play. Both pieces of history, one involving the Trail of Tears, the other the taxes on a trailer amounting to $147, spoke to the issue of sovereignty. Both moments were not merely a struggle between the United States and the Indians, but actually a three-way struggle between states, the federal government, and Indian tribes. The outcome of these two struggles between three powers, in turn, paved the way for Indian gaming as we know it.

One question people always ask is: why do Indians get to have casinos and we don't? Fortunately, the question is easy to answer: because of the Cherokee and because of a mobile home in Squaw Lake, Minnesota.

In the first part of the nineteenth century the Cherokee were doing very well. They had alternately befriended and fought the British, the Americans, and various other Indian tribes and somehow always managed to come out on top. The Cherokee had fought the Shawnee and forced them north of the Ohio River. In 1711 the Tuscarora began attacking colonists in North Carolina, as a last resort after treaty negotiations continued to whittle away their rights. The colony of South Carolina, short of troops, sent two armies against the Tuscarora. Each army was made up of just a few white colonists and both armies were dwarfed by the numbers of their Indian allies—Yamassee, Catawba, and Cherokee. The Tuscarora were soundly defeated and fled north, eventually settling in upstate New York and becoming part of the Iroquois Confederacy. The Cherokee, having thus secured the friendship of the English, watched as the Yamassee were defeated by the colonists. And then the Cherokee themselves drove out the Yuchi and then the Creeks. This made them the dominant power in the region. By the mid-1700s the Cherokee and their allies were powerful enough to treat on a nation-to-nation basis with England. Trade increased. The Cherokee started farming on the southern plantation model, and many Cherokee bought and worked black slaves—a signal of their economic and social status in the region. (In fact, a lot of African Americans with Indian blood have Cherokee blood—and not because the Cherokee and African Americans were good friends, but because Cherokee masters slept with their black slaves.) Then, in 1828, gold was discovered on Cherokee land in Georgia, and the Cherokee, the state of Georgia, and the U.S. government all came into conflict with one other over the pleached issues of control and power.

The federal government, the state of Georgia, and the Cherokee all fought over and for their respective sovereignty. The federal government believed that the states fell within its power as a sovereign nation—it and only it could make treaties, raise an army, negotiate trade relations, etc. The state of Georgia (like North Carolina and South Carolina) believed it could ignore and dismiss any laws it considered "unconstitutional." The Cherokee—with their own army, representative government, laws, courts, customs, language, writing system, and mode of dress, and the might to enforce their desires, thought they should be in charge of their own destiny. And so began a tripartite dispute. In the same year that gold was discovered, the state legislature of Georgia passed an act that made Cherokee territories part of and subject to the laws of Georgia. As a way of proving its power, Georgia created a test case. In 1830 a Cherokee man, George Tassels, killed another Cherokee man on Cherokee territory. This case was clearly within the physical and legal bounds of the Cherokee to prosecute in their own courts. But Georgia took Tassels into custody and planned to try him. The Cherokee, led by Chief John Ross, prepared to petition the U.S. government because they wanted to deal with Tassels according to their own laws. Georgia ignored them. What began as a legal wrangle became much more melodramatic. Messages were rushed to the Georgia legislature, which ignored them. The government did not intervene. The Supreme Court ruled that sovereignty was not affected by states, but Georgia ignored the ruling (even though today it remains the basis for tribal sovereignty and gaming). The dispute ended with Tassels hanging from a tree on Christmas eve in a barren field. Georgia had stood its ground and hanged Tassels above it.

With Tassels hanging from a tree, Chief John Ross, with the support of many people in the national Republican Party, including Henry Clay, Daniel Webster, Ambrose Spencer, and Davy Crockett, continued his efforts to uphold the sovereignty of his people by filing a case against Georgia with the U.S. Supreme Court. The Cherokee had tried this before, in 1829. At that time the secretary of war, John H. Eaton, informed the Cherokee delegation that Andrew Jackson would support Georgia's right to remove the Cherokee and other tribes to territories west of the Mississippi. Cheered by the verdict, in 1832 Georgia began offering lotteries to settlers who wanted Cherokee land. Ross, representing more than 20,000 Cherokee and armed with a Cherokee constitution and the will of the people, brought his case before the Supreme Court. *Worcester v. Georgia* ended in a semivictory for the Cherokee; they were a "dependent nation" in the eyes of the court. Chief Justice John Marshall ruled that neither Georgia nor the U.S. federal government had jurisdiction over the matter, because the Cherokee nation and other Indian tribes who had treated with the U.S. government were "denominated domestic dependent nations," a phrase that haunts the legal wrangling between tribes and the government to this day. Justice Marshall's narrative was compelling and poetic: "A case better calculated to excite them can scarcely be imagined. A people once numerous, powerful, and truly independent, found by our ancestors in the quiet and uncontrolled possession of an ample domain, gradually sinking beneath our superior policy, our arts and our arms, have yielded their lands by successive treaties, each of which contains a solemn guarantee of the residue, until they retain no more of their formerly extensive territory than is deemed necessary to their comfortable subsistence. To preserve this remnant, the present application is made." It wasn't until *Worcester v. Georgia* that the court recognized the complete independence and sovereignty of the Cherokee.

Despite Marshall's poetry, or because of it, Georgia ignored the ruling. Andrew Jackson lent his support to Georgia. Jackson is probably the least-liked president in Indian country. Born three weeks after his father died in an accident, Andrew Jackson grew up fast. He enlisted as a courier during the Revolutionary War at age thirteen. An incident that testifies to his toughness occurred when he was a prisoner during the war. A British officer commanded the fourteen-year-old Jackson to shine his boots; Jackson refused; the officer attacked him with a sword, cutting his hand and head badly, and instilling in Jackson a violent hatred of the British. After an early career in politics and in business as a landowner (and slaveholder) he found success in the military. He was instrumental in putting down Tecumseh's rebellion during 1812 and 1813, when the Red Stick Creeks rose up and killed 400 settlers. During the ensuing battles more than 800 Red Sticks were killed by Jackson and the Tennessee militia. Cherokee, Southern Creek, and Choctaw soldiers were under his command—the very Indians he would remove to the Oklahoma Territories twenty years later. The war effectively ended at the Battle of Horseshoe Bend in 1814. Jackson went on to fight more British (at the Battle of New Orleans) and more Indians (during the Seminole Wars). While engaged in fighting the Seminole he succeeded by dint of his ruthlessness in getting Spain to relinquish its title to Florida. While Seminole warriors were fighting, Jackson attacked Seminole villages, burned them to the ground, and destroyed the crops. He executed British traders who were supplying the Indians. Spain could not afford to battle against such a ruthless adversary. It was largely as a result of military service and military victories that Jackson became president.

This was the man, the president, against whom the Cherokee were fighting, but this time with briefs rather than bows. The Cherokee went back to court in 1832 with their third appeal, in *Worcester v. Georgia*. John Marshall, dismayed by a bully for a president and a brat for the state of Georgia, ruled in favor of the Cherokee. He declared that the Cherokee tribe constituted a nation. But instead of claiming that neither Georgia nor the United States had jurisdiction over other sovereign nations, he softened his tone. In *Worcester* he ruled that "domestic dependent nations" such as the Cherokee were entitled to federal protection against the actions of individual states. This did not deter the Indian-fighter and Indian-hater Andrew Jackson or soften his support of states' rights. Jackson is alleged to have said after the ruling in favor of the Cherokee: "John Marshall has made his decision; now let him try and enforce it!"

On May 26, 1838, General Winfield Scott in command of 7,000 troops began rounding up Cherokee at gunpoint. Ten days later Cherokee and other members of the Civilized Tribes were forced into camps in Tennessee, North Carolina, and Alabama; 17,000 Cherokee and 2,000 of their black slaves were herded together and sent to departure points at Ross's Landing and Fort Cass in Tennessee and Gunter's Landing in Alabama. From there they variously walked, rowed, and rode wagons out to Indian Territory over a total distance of 1,200 miles. More than 4,000 Cherokee died on the way.

But even though the Cherokee (most, but not all) and their allies were removed to Indian Territory, the legal precedent, the language, and the sense of the three cases decided by the U.S. Supreme Court remained: these concerned domestic dependent nations, sovereignty, and the notion that tribes need not negotiate with the state but exist on a government-to-government relationship with the federal government.

It was this tension—between tribal rights, federal law, and state law—that created both the *possibility* and the *difficulty* of Indian gaming. This was the political and legal landscape in which small tribes began to open gaming operations in the deserts, swamps, and cornfields of America in the mid-twentieth century—that they were sovereign (sort of) and that as domestic dependent nations they could not, say, raise an army, issue passports, invade, secede, or have representation at the United Nations. The Iroquois Confederacy (made up of the Mohawk, Seneca, Onondaga, Oneida, Cayuga, and Tuscarora), never a tribe to accept what limits others might impose on it, declared war on Germany in 1917. The Iroquois Confederacy was joined by the Dakota and Ojibwe in declarations of war against the Axis Powers during World War II. Members of the Iroquois Confederacy still travel on their own passports, much to the chagrin of the U.S. government. So while there are limits imposed on sovereignty, the courts ruled that Indians could sell cigarettes and operate gaming halls without interference from the state.

The Cabazon Mission Band near Palm Springs did just that. The band members made a lot of money selling tax-free cigarettes on their reservation during the 1970s. Sometimes they netted more than $4,000 a day. Annual gross receipts came in at just under $500,000. But the state of California and other states as well were getting envious. Cigarette taxes typically benefit the states in which the cigarettes are sold, and that wasn't happening. A cover story appeared in the *National Enquirer* (the same tabloid where the Cabazon advertised their mail-order cigarette business)—Indians making $10,000 a day! As this was going on, another legal wrangle ensued: the Colville tribe in

Washington state had a case at the state supreme court. The Colville, too, had a cigarette business, and the state supreme court ruled against them: they could sell tax-free cigarettes but not to non–tribal members, and not through the mail. The tribe lost when the court decided that cigarettes sold to non–band members were subject to state tax. This became a precedent nationwide. When the ruling came down in 1980, the cigarette boom seemed to be over, although some tribes still operate tax-free cigarette businesses.

The Cabazon Band had been wise to take its profits from cigarette sales while these still lasted and invest the money in embryonic forms of gaming: high-stakes bingo and a card hall in particular. The Cabazon opened a poker room on the reservation in 1980. Two weeks after it opened the Indio police raided it and arrested the tribal employees, the managers, and all the gamblers. The case went to state court, then a federal court, and finally the U.S. Supreme Court. A similar case from Seminole country in Florida also reached the U.S. Supreme Court. The Cabazon case wouldn't be resolved until 1987, at which point the final legal roadblocks to Indian gaming crumbled. The Cabazon (along with other tribes from California to Washington to Florida) claimed the right to own and operate casinos on Indian land.

On our first day at Morongo, I lost sixty dollars at Lobstermania. Somehow, I didn't feel very bad. And maybe that old Indian chestnut is true: we are all related. What I felt on the floor and later when I played poker (sandwiched between a pale man with a goatee who looked like a mortician and spoke in funereal tones about "the river" and an African-American cement contractor) was that Indian gaming has brought together a lot of people from different classes, ethnicities, and walks of life. And all of us together keep on giving and giving and giving, even though not all of us win. As I reveled in the luxury and noticed the tan cocktail waitresses and the other happy gamblers and the angular tower seventeen stories high, it was strange to remember that Indian gaming began far away from the sun, palm trees, and luxury of places like Morongo. Gaming began with the Cherokee in the nineteenth century, formalizing the relationship between sovereign tribes and the federal government. And it began again in 1971 with a $147 tax bill on a trailer.

⤚

In late 1971 Helen and Russell Bryan made an $800 down payment on a small, two-bedroom trailer in the small frozen village of Squaw Lake on Leech Lake Reservation, Minnesota. Helen's younger brother had been killed just after he got out of the armed forces, and Helen's mother gave Helen some of the money they received from her brother's GI insurance to make the down payment. The Bryans put the trailer on Helen's ancestral land in the village of Squaw Lake, on the north side of Leech Lake Reservation, where she had spent her entire life. Russell was also Ojibwe, from White Earth Reservation, fifty miles to the southwest. Their mortgage payment for the trailer was ninety-seven dollars a month. These were tough times for Helen. She was thirty-one years old. She had a job with the Leech Lake Head Start Program, but Russell was unemployed. Together they were raising six kids in their new trailer—eight people in two bedrooms. "It was a little crowded," remembers Helen. "The girls slept in the bedroom and the boys slept in the living room." But they had running water, electricity, and heat.

Early in the spring of 1972 Helen and Russell were drinking coffee at their kitchen table when they saw a pickup truck pull into their yard. "This guy from the county came. Parked his truck on the road there and walked up and measured the trailer house. He didn't come in. He didn't knock on the door or nothing. He just come out there and measured the trailer house and we were sitting there wondering what he'd say. He didn't say anything about what he was doing. We didn't know what he was up to. We didn't think it would be tax." A short while later the Bryans received a bill for $29.85 for the last two months of 1971. "It wasn't very much," says Helen. "But I told my husband: this is wrong. But it seemed like he didn't care. His attitude was like, so what? He wasn't mad like I was. I said it was wrong, it's got to be wrong. And how was I going to pay for taxes and feed my kids and make house payments? Good thing electricity was low. It was a big deal to me because I was the one working. He wasn't." She ignored the tax notice for a while. The first bill was followed by a second in July 1972. The entire tax bill for 1972 was $118.10. "And then I remembered they had a legal services department, it was new. Legal services for Indians. So I called them up and talked to someone."

The staff of Anishinaabe Legal Services told her that it sounded like a good case. They got all of Helen's information, and then she didn't hear anything. "We didn't know what they were doing. I mailed them the tax notice and they said they'd handle it." Once in a while the lawyers at legal services would call. "But I was busy working. It didn't really mean anything to me. I just thought they'd take care of it. I didn't know what I thought." So the case was in the back of Helen's mind. Jerry Seck, the lead lawyer, called her and said they were going to court with her case. "I told him if we win I'll buy you a beer."

Helen Bryan's case could be argued in one of two ways. First, since tribal land, held in trust, cannot be taxed, the lawyers could have made an easy argument: the trailer was annexed to the tribal land; was therefore, like a house, to be considered tribal property; and was thereby exempt from tax (just as county and state buildings are not taxed by the feds). Second, they could make a harder argument: that the state could not assess a personal property tax on Indians living on Indian lands. The young go-getting attorneys for the Bryans chose the hard way.

The U.S. Constitution grants the nation, not the states, plenary power over Indian tribes. Without express congressional assent written into law, states have no power over tribes. But Public Law (PL) 280, enacted in 1953, transferred criminal and limited civil law enforcement authority from the federal government to state governments. The problem was that the federal government's law enforcement programs were "neither well financed [nor] vigorous, and that tribal courts often lacked the resources and skills to be effective." The result was, largely, "the absence of law enforcement on reservations." PL 280 was enacted to deal with a public problem: "the complete breakdown of law and order on many Indian reservations."

Even though PL 280 was passed to combat "lawlessness" it was, as laws go, fairly vague. It was vague because in the 1950s, when it was passed, the federal government was less interested in the ins and outs of jurisdiction than in washing its hands of the Indian problem once and for all. Rather than try to terminate Indian bands, an effort that cost a lot in litigation and time, the government wanted to pass the buck. It was getting out of the Indian business. This was not because it wanted Indians dead—by that time, it just didn't care. What it did want was cheaper federal administration. The first section, which addressed criminal jurisdiction, was clear: "Each of the States or Territories listed in the following table shall have jurisdiction over offenses committed by or against Indians in the areas of Indian country listed opposite the name of the State or Territory to the same extent that such State or Territory has jurisdiction over offenses committed elsewhere within the State or Territory, and the criminal laws of such State or Territory shall have the same force and effect within such Indian country as they have elsewhere within the State or Territory." But the section pertaining to civil offenses was not clear: "Each of the States listed in the following table shall have jurisdiction over civil causes of action between Indians or to which Indians are parties which arise in the areas of Indian country listed opposite the name of the State to the same extent that such State has jurisdiction over other civil causes of action, and those civil laws of such State that are of general application to private persons or private property shall have the same force and effect within such Indian country as they have elsewhere within the State." What was intended as a remedy for "lawlessness" was taken by most states and counties as a mandate that gave them power over all civil and criminal offenses on reservations. In effect, tribal sovereignty, as outlined and strengthened by John Marshall and strengthened again by the Indian Reorganization Act of 1934, was being done away with. Reservations were in danger of becoming nothing more than vast neighborhoods controlled by tribal councils with no more power than chambers of commerce or the Rotary Club.

The Bryans lost in Itasca County Court. Their lawyers appealed to the Minnesota state supreme court, but they lost there, too. Finally the case went to the U.S. Supreme Court. By this time the underpaid legal services lawyers who had begun working on the case had moved on—some to other states, one as far away as Micronesia. The case was now in the hands of a lawyer from New York, Bernie Becker. Huge, articulate, personable, Becker masterfully guided the Supreme Court through the ins and outs of PL 280. He was far more expert than the justices on this relatively obscure and poorly worded law, which had, since its passage, been amended more than thirty times.

The heart of Becker's argument was that PL 280 had been passed to combat lawlessness, not to regulate or tax Indians. Dan Israel, one of the lawyers working for Leech Lake and the Bryans, wrote, "Congress intended the civil portion [the part that could be construed to speak to the issue of taxation] of Public Law 280 to govern the where and how of disputes and not to grant general regulatory power." A lot hinged on the distinction that Becker made in his oral argument: if PL 280 were conceived of as regulatory, imposing state and federal law across the affected reservations, it could be seen as a "termination law"—a law designed to terminate the special standing that sovereign

231

Indian nations enjoyed, a standing that went back to treaty times and had been affirmed in case law and the U.S. Constitution. However, if, as Becker argued, PL 280 was a measure to fix the problem of lawlessness on Indian reservations, the civil section of PL 280 was simply a forum for addressing civil disputes where there was no forum before. Rather than terminating Indian rights, PL 280 was supposed to give Indians better access to justice.

Just before the lunch break during the oral argument, Becker claimed that Indian tribes had asked for PL 280, that they had lobbied for and consented to the law precisely because they wanted, and needed, to retain their rights and also to fix the problem of lawlessness on the reservation. "This statute was not imposed upon the Indians. The Indians came looking for the statute." Becker's logic was simple: if the law had been designed to do away with tribal sovereignty and self-determination, the Indians would never have consented to it, much less asked for it. But that logic was potentially flawed: if Indians had consented to the law, then they had no real standing if the law wasn't applied in a manner to their liking. With that, the court broke for lunch.

A thirty-three-year-old, almond-eyed Indian woman had been watching the oral arguments from the gallery. She was living in Washington, D.C., and attending Catholic University Law School. On that day in April 1976—100 years since the Battle of the Little Bighorn, 200 years since the founding of the United States—she had gotten up early, ushered her two children out the door and off to school, and made her way to the Supreme Court, where she waited in line for over an hour so she could watch the oral arguments. She was a Leech Lake Indian who had grown up less than fifteen miles from Squaw Lake in a village where trailers like the Bryans' were an unknown luxury. She had grown up in a ramshackle cabin with no plumbing and no heat except for a barrel stove. To get water she had to fill buckets from a hand pump in the yard and carry them inside. She was my mother, Margaret Seelye Treuer.

She made her way to the cafeteria, ordered a sandwich, and saw Bernie Becker sitting by himself eating his lunch and preparing for the afternoon session. With the combination of steely nerve and nervousness that always compelled her to do not just *a* thing but the *hardest* thing, she approached Becker, introduced herself, thanked him for his work, and asked if she could sit down. He said yes. And then he asked her what she thought of the case so far.

She had been listening all morning with half her mind on her childhood and upbringing and half on case law and legislative history. The idea of "lawlessness" did not have the same meaning for her and her family that it might have had for the legislators. For her and her family and the other Indians from villages on reservations around the county, lawlessness was often more a problem with the law enforcers than with the Indians. Being poor, being from a community where everyone was poor, was different from being broke in a community that was not. Game wardens took their rice. They were denied loans. Their houses were searched for game such as venison and ducks. Whatever the sheriff, the social worker, and the cops wanted, they got.

So she told him what she thought: that Indian tribes had not "consented" to, much less asked for, PL 280. Rather, PL 280 had been imposed on them. She reminded Becker that tribes had long complained that PL 280 had been passed without their consent or input. The only reason Red Lake was exempt from PL 280 was that Roger Jourdain had fought it tooth and nail with every means at his disposal. If the federal government had wanted to terminate Indian rights, as it had in the past, going so far as to terminate the legal standing of whole tribes—such as the Menominee in Wisconsin—it would have done so. PL 280 was not meant to terminate rights, but it had been used to further erode Indian autonomy.

When oral arguments resumed after lunch Becker corrected himself on record. He said that tribes did not consent to PL 280. And if tribes had consented, and if PL 280 was meant to give regulatory powers to state governments, then Congress would have "slipped one by the Indians." Becker continued to push a narrow argument confined to taxes and personal property. Though his argument was narrow, it is a marvel that the Bryans' lawyers didn't take the easy road and simply argue that the trailer was affixed to the land sufficiently to make it real estate (held in trust) rather than personal property. The justices continued to question widely.

After Becker concluded, the attorney for the state attorney general's office argued on behalf of Itasca County. His main argument was that PL 280 was, in fact, a termination act—that it was regulatory in nature and aimed at terminating the special status of Indian tribes.

In the history of federal policy it is hard to find anyplace where the effect of policy itself is more noticeable than in Indian affairs. For most Americans policy has a limited immediate effect, except in extreme cases such as civil rights and the New Deal. Not so for Indians. And for Indians, Winston Churchill's quip that "Americans always do the right thing after they've tried everything else" couldn't be more true. There have been five major policies and five major shifts in those policies that have shaped the lives of Indians on reservations around the country.

During the treaty period in the mid-nineteenth century many Indian tribes—including the Cherokee, Creek, Choctaw, Chickasaw, Seminole, Winnebago, Sac and Fox, Delaware, Dakota, Ojibwe, and dozens of others—were either coerced into moving or moved by force to areas that were less important or had fewer natural resources than their homelands. Sometimes the tribe moved a matter of a few miles. In other instances whole tribes were force-marched under cruel conditions to lands and landscapes alien to their culture and history.

The disaster of allotment was somewhat ameliorated by the "Indian New Deal." Passed in 1934, the Wheeler-Howard Act (also known as the Indian Reorganization Act, or IRA) reversed the policy of assimilation and allotment. Rather, tribes were encouraged to form representative governments with their own elected officials and to strengthen their own governments. Two million acres of Indian land were returned to Indian control. Various economic initiatives were launched and a new era seemed to dawn—in which Indians were encouraged to be in control. It didn't last.

The U.S. government—buoyed by its economic superiority during the 1950s, and convinced that suburbs, the nine-to-five workday, and industrial production were the way to go—initiated a new policy beginning in Truman's administration: termination. This policy was dedicated to ending the U.S. government's responsibility to and for Indian tribes. Money dried up. Programs set up under the IRA went unfunded. Indians were actively encouraged to leave the reservation through the Voluntary Relocation Program, which promised work and education, but only in cities far from reservations. Few of the promises made were kept, and hundreds of thousands of Indians ended up in San Diego, Los Angeles, Chicago, New York, and Minneapolis with no housing, no education, no job training, no jobs, and no money with which to return home. Five reservations were wiped off the map and 112 Indian tribes in California lost their federal recognition. This was the policy in place when PL 280 was passed in 1953.

So it made sense for C. H. Luther, arguing the state's case before the Supreme Court in 1976, to suggest that PL 280 was a termination act. But his strategy played right into Becker's hand. When Becker was called on to rebut he said that the U.S. Congress knew very well how to pass laws that were explicitly designed to terminate tribal rights. It had passed many termination laws that were quite clear on the rights they no longer recognized. But since PL 280 had no such clear language, it was surely not a termination act, meant to destroy tribes. Rather, it had been passed to help them. Furthermore, he argued, if PL 280 was meant to destroy tribes, to assimilate them and terminate them, then it would have been aimed at tribes with strong governments that resisted assimilation, such as Red Lake, and not at tribes already close to capitulation, such as Leech Lake. With that, Becker rested. The court adjourned and everyone waited.

The climate was good for a win. Termination policy had been reversed, again. With Johnson's Great Society still in the works, lots of money had been poured into tribes, making them stronger. Anti-poverty measures had been enacted in America's poorest places. Self-determination was the new policy, the new watchword. Tribes were encouraged to make life better for their members, to think creatively about how to solve the dire problems they faced. And on the heels of the civil rights movement and with a liberal court, things just might go our way.

They did.

On June 14, 1976, the Supreme Court ruled unanimously in favor of the Bryans. Jerry Seck called Helen Bryan with the news. "I was really happy," says Helen with a laugh. "That was $147 off my mind. And I didn't get no more tax notices." My mother was home on Leech Lake and interning at the same offices where the case began—the Leech Lake Reservation Legal Services Project—when the call came. The director, Michael Hagedorn (normally quiet-mannered), answered the phone and began jumping up and down shouting, "We won! We won! We won! We won!" The next day a headline in the *Minneapolis Tribune* shouted, "States Forbidden to Tax on Reservations," although the *New York Times* was more subdued and more accurate: "Justices Bar State's Taxation of Reservation Indians."

Helen had endured abject poverty and disenfranchisement— she remembers having had a phone before either running water or electricity. Her current husband, Bob Johnson (Russell died in 1994)—shy, dark, self-effacing—remembers clearly the way Indians were treated back then. "I joined the 82nd Airborne during Korea. I lied about my age and joined when I was fifteen. I did nineteen months in Korea. Two tours. I fought over there. I went all over the world. And I came back to Cass Lake—and I saw the racism for the first time. I saw what everyone did to us. I'd been around but when I came home I was just another Indian. All the business guys down the street here [he waves down Third Avenue in Cass Lake] were John Birchers, were racists. And they got rich off of us." Helen pipes up, in her quiet way: "I never got nothing from nobody. I never got a penny from the tribe for housing or anything like that. I supported all eight of us my whole life. But when Russell died the tribe offered to pay for his funeral and for his headstone, but only if they could choose the wording for it. I said sure. So they put RUSSELL BRYAN VS. ITASCA COUNTY— VICTORY, right on his headstone. That's all I got from them."

The ruling was more than a victory for Helen Bryan and for Leech Lake. It was a victory for Indians across the entire country. The Supreme Court made a sweeping ruling about the limits of PL 280: "The same Congress that enacted PL 280 also enacted several termination Acts—legislation which is cogent proof that Congress knew well how to express its intent directly when that intent was to subject reservation Indians to the full sweep of state laws and state taxation." And the court found nothing "remotely resembling an intention to confer general state regulatory control over Indian reservations." It was a huge victory. But no one—not Indians across the country, not the Bryans who would not be taxed, and not the court—knew just how huge.

No one knew how huge because no one imagined gambling. It was simply something no one had in mind. People thought immediately about taxes on income and property. Some thought about tribal courts and civil cases. But almost no one thought about gambling until the Cabazon Band and the Seminole started up their card rooms four years later. Reservations were largely seen as poor places with little to no economy. Helen herself didn't know, but she knows now. "I don't want anything. I just want a little recognition. I want people to know that I fought when it was hard to fight. Another guy from Ball Club had a similar case. I think his name was Joseph Whitebird. He dropped it. Life hasn't changed for me much," she says. "I'm still poor!" But because Helen Bryan stuck up for herself and her family, a lot of Indians and a lot of tribes aren't. "The papers picked up the story and said that the ruling affected ten thousand Indians in Minnesota. I told Russell at the time," says Helen, "if we did so much maybe if every Indian in Minnesota sent us a dollar, we'd be rich!" In my opinion, everyone should. Send your dollars to Helen (Bryan) Johnson, 60876 County Road 149, Squaw Lake, MN, 56681.

⋙

We decided to pull up stakes, head out of the broiling desert, and get closer to the coast: Temecula. The Pechanga Resort and Casino. I have to say I was impressed. There is a huge, fake (but very nicely faked) coast live oak in the lobby and a stained-glass window showing another oak tree. I learned later that one of the oldest coast live oaks is on the Pechanga reservation, near the eleventh hole of the golf course. When I checked in and went to our room, I noticed a lot more Native motifs in the carpet and in the artwork on the walls. It was a beautiful casino. The rooms were tasteful. The whole place was elegant, especially the clubhouse and restaurant at the golf course.

Casinos have an interesting aesthetic, and Indian casinos even more so. In the eighteenth century in Europe, casinos were playgrounds for the rich, and they were built to resemble aristocratic chateaux and mansions. Think of *Casino Royale*. In fact, the word "casino" is derived from the Italian *casino,* a small house, summerhouse, or pavilion built for pleasure. It is interesting to note that in Italian *casino* can now mean "whorehouse," and the gambling establishment is spelled the same way but with an accent: *casinò.* This is interesting because American casinos, as reinvented in Las Vegas, worked to combine the excitement of a carnival or circus (the big top, marquee entertainment, the "big show") with the intimate naughtiness of a bordello. Then the 1980s came, and those of us who've watched *Casino* know that the honest dirt of mob-controlled Vegas was replaced with dishonest, Disney corporate dirt. Under new leadership, casinos became "family destinations" with water parks, boats, gondolas, and so on.

None of this evolution was able to erase completely the species of the past, so casinos are a weird aesthetic jumble with blackjack dealers in tuxedos, circuslike dings and whistles coming from the slot machines, big shows (many a has-been rock and country band has Indians to thank for its continuing career—Whitesnake, Styx, and Air Supply are all regular performers at Indian casinos), theme parks, a whiff of prostitution, and now Indian images and motifs.

I opted to play in the poker tournament offered nightly in the Pechanga card room. Small poker tournaments are hilarious. I don't know why, but the white guys (almost always between the ages of eighteen and twenty-eight) wear caps and sunglasses and fiddle with the headphones of their iPods as though they were being filmed in the World Series of Poker. These guys are almost always the ones who lose first. I lost, too. I made it just short of the final cut and decided to play poker at the three- to six-dollar table instead. (Three dollars is the minimum bet, six dollars the maximum.)

Poker, in particular Texas Hold 'Em, has become a huge phenomenon. Partly because of cameras that allow TV viewers to see the players' cards, and partly because Indian casinos have allowed backroom players to play in public with strangers all across the country, Texas Hold

'Em has entered millions of American households. It's a brutal sport. Each player is dealt two cards. Betting ensues. The dealer then deals the "flop"—three cards faceup. More betting. Another card is dealt faceup—the "turn." More betting. Then the last card is dealt—"the river." More betting. At each stage, there is intense mental warfare, as well as frustration, hope, and a chance that the last card will make your hand. Even at a three-to-six table it can get expensive. The problem is that it isn't expensive enough, so people will play just to play, regardless of their hand or their position. Hands that most sensible people would fold are kept until the river. And good hands lose—they've been "rivered." The house makes its money on the rake—a small amount taken from each pot at regular intervals—and on drinks, too.

My table was a weird mix. To my left a Vietnam vet there with his son. To my right a marine vet of Gulf War I now working in army intelligence. And to his right a young racially vague kid, age twenty-one, who had just enlisted and was supposed to ship out two days hence. It felt comfortable to a certain extent. I heard the usual tomahawk jokes one hears from non-Natives when they think that Indians aren't listening. But I couldn't really get mad. The more they lost, the richer some Indians (without tomahawks) got. Across from us were some Asian men—Laotian, Cambodian, Vietnamese.

I was winning. The kid kept betting against me and kept losing. I felt bad. But poker's poker. Just before I was about to cash in, the table won the "bad beat jackpot." The bad beat is a great hand that loses to a slightly better hand. The bad beat jackpot is an institution that casinos have set up to create excitement and to keep gamblers at the table. Basically, a pot of money grows and grows until a very rare combination of cards comes up. In our case, Pechanga's bad beat jackpot was winnable only if one player had a full house with jacks or better, beaten by a better hand. Jackpot amount: $25,000. The table, which had been a mix of forced joviality, genuine joke telling, and snide comments ("Hey,

Heineken, thanks for playing, your money feels better than mine"), erupted in a moment of unabashed togetherness. The Vietnam vet high-fived the sour-faced Cambodian. The army kid smiled and then frowned when he realized he would have only two days to spend his winnings. The bad beat got $8,000, the winning hand $4,000, and the rest of the table split the remaining $12,000. I walked away with $1,423.

And if casinos play on illusion, the illusion at Pechanga was enchanting—a beautiful casino where one can find brotherhood, equality, and wealth. A place that rose from poverty to strike it rich and where you can, too. In short and ironically, inside a casino (that manages to suggest aristocracy, bordello, Indians and nature, the big top, and a theme park) on Indian land, one feels, well, American.

Within a few years of the Bryan case the Cabazon Mission Band of Indians and the Seminole would be in court defending their fledgling gambling operations. Indian gaming around the country was under way and was already a $100 million annual industry. Finally, an industry had appeared that seemed to fit reservations: one that required little start-up capital, little infrastructure, little land, and no wrangling about natural resources. Finally development could occur without depletion. The Cabazon case, which relied heavily on the precedent set by *Bryan v. Itasca County,* opened the gates to Indian gaming as we know it. The Cabazon won. The Seminole won. Everyone seemed to win.

The federal government, seeing the influx of casino money to reservations, has been happy with the arrangement: it has to pay less for and worry less about that pesky "Indian problem." The states, on the other hand, weren't always so happy. More cases followed, and so did more legislation, culminating in the Indian Gaming Regulatory Act (IGRA). This was a compromise between tribal sovereignty affirmed by the Bryan and Cabazon and Seminole cases and state rights. The three spokes of the wheel came together again. The IGRA affirmed that states do not have control over Indian issues, but it demanded that tribes wanting to start gaming operations could do so only in states where gaming was already legal, where the state wanted it to be legal, and in consultation with the states, which couldn't regulate or prevent gambling but could negotiate some terms. Moreover, IGRA clarified that the Cabazon ruling would apply to all tribes, even those where PL 280 was in effect. Those gaming compacts between tribes and states are like minor treaties or agreements that lay out where, when, how, and how much. Some states demanded a cut in the form of taxes. Connecticut has received more than $20 billion from the Pequots since Foxwoods opened in 1992. Other states weren't so lucky. Minnesota gets no direct revenue from its casinos (though real estate and corporate and payroll taxes bring in plenty).

No one could have foreseen a $20 billion-per-year industry springing out of the Bryans' $147 tax bill. No one could have foreseen that tribes such as the Pequots, the Seminole, the Cabazon, and the Mille Lacs Ojibwe would become the largest employers in their respective regions. The gaming industry at Mille Lacs has made Mille Lacs and Grand Casino Inc. the largest employer in the area. No one could have foreseen that the Seminole would buy the Hard Rock Café franchise. If people had been asked in 1980 whether Indians would someday own Paul McCartney's guitar or, say, Elvis Presley's glitter suit, it's safe to say most would have answered, Probably not. No one could have foreseen that in 2004–2005 Governor Tim Pawlenty of Minnesota, facing a budget shortfall and trying to honor his campaign promise of "no new taxes," would try to extort taxes from Minnesota's poorest communities by threatening to open up gambling statewide unless casino tribes forked over money to the state. No one could have foreseen that tribes would use casino profits and branch out into banking, hedge funds, real estate, and even tech industries. No one could have foreseen the number of disputes over membership and federal recognition. Tribes made up of fractional descendants (1/64 or 1/128 Indian blood) with no culture, land, community, or language but with plenty of lawyers have been springing up across the county. No one could have foreseen so many people wanting to *be* Indian after 500 years of trying to kill us and 200 years of trying not to be Indian. No one could have foreseen that being Indian means, for a precious few, being rich rather than being poor. No one could have foreseen a new set of Indian wars—fought between tribes for market share and membership, and fought between tribes and states—springing up across the country.

Still at Pechanga, we went for dinner at the Great Oak Steakhouse, one of the nine restaurants inside the casino. We were told it was good. We were told that the steakhouse raises its own cattle. We were told that the cattle eat organic feed and are kept on the lot twice as long as most prime cattle are. We were told we'd never taste anything like the steaks we ordered. We were told right—I had the best steak of my life.

There are all sorts of unintended effects of Indian gaming. Great steak is only one of them. Casino profits have helped fund a dramatic renaissance in Indian culture and language. Powwows like the ones held at Foxwoods, Oneida nation, Lac Courte Oreilles, and Gathering of Nations in New Mexico offer such large purses for singing and dancing contests that a whole generation of Indian performers has made a living on the contest circuit. The result—a growing richness and complexity of Indian pop culture. Several tribes—such as the Blackfeet, the Leech Lake Ojibwe, and the Cherokee—started language immersion schools without tribal funding, but have begun to support these schools with their newfound wealth. Others, like Mille Lacs, have the best elder care in the state, funded almost entirely with casino profits.

The area director for the Indian Health Service in Bemidji told me that 80 percent of new hospitals and clinics are tribally funded. This is astounding, considering the dearth of health care on reservations fifty years ago.

One popular conception about Indian life and Indian tribes is that we would be nothing without help from the federal government. That is sometimes true. About one-third of the 500 tribes in the United States have casinos, and only a very small fraction of those turn any kind of useful, sustained profit. But communities such as Pechanga and Morongo, the Seminole in Florida, and the Mashantucket Pequots in Connecticut make a lot of money and do not depend on the government; rather, the government often depends on them. The Pechanga Band of Luiseño Indians employs 5,162 people directly and 24,422 indirectly. It has given $82 million in funding for local government and nongaming tribes and has paid $60 million in payroll taxes since 2004. In Florida, the Seminole are regularly called on to bail out the state when it experiences a budget crisis. In 2009 the state of Florida began negotiating new gaming compacts with the Seminole—in exchange for expanded gaming operations, the Seminole would contribute millions in revenue that would be tagged for education and thereby save the Florida school system.

The Seminole are interesting. They have long had an entrepreneurial spirit. To put it another way, they've been ass kickers and name takers for a long time. One Seminole I interviewed told me: "We fought the Spanish and won. We fought the British and won. We fought the Americans three times and won. We are the fightingest, winningest tribe in American history." He was right. The Seminole have held on to their land and their ways under enormous pressure, the like of which few of us will ever experience. They're also cowboys (and cowgirls—both men and women ride and tend herds) and have been raising and killing cattle and eating steak for a lot longer than the Pechanga Band.

During the time of the dust bowl, when pasture was drying up and blowing away, the U.S. cattle industry shipped its remaining herds east to Florida and inadvertently brought ranching to the Seminole. The Seminole began raising their own herds, riding horses, and joining rodeos. With the advent of gaming, they expanded their cattle business. According to Seminole cowboy and elder Willie Johns, the Seminole are the third largest beef producer in the entire United States.

As we strolled back to our room at Pechanga, it was clear that rather than living uninspected lives at the margins of American society, Indians have become part of the American fabric in ways no one could have guessed when gaming as we know it emerged in the 1980s. I was feeling proud of the Pechanga Band, the Morongo Band, the Seminole, and the others—proud of what they made against all odds. No one is untouched by Indian lives. I thought of what the tribal member told me about the golf course: it is good to look back at where you've been; you get some beautiful views.

You also get some strange ones.

In late August the drive from Minneapolis to Shakopee, Minnesota, takes you past the kind of humdrum success that marked much of the 1990s and early 2000s in America. Strip malls, Subways, Starbucks, Caribou Coffee, Mail Boxes Etc., Holiday Station, QuikTrip, Kum & Go, interspersed with big-box retailers such as Best Buy and Home Depot. As Highway 13 twists and turns these stores disappear behind cornfields where the corn is already brown and rattles against itself. The road reappears in small towns transformed into suburbs and studded with whorled concentrations of spec homes, housing developments, and golf courses. These settlements resemble each other so much that it is hard to say where you are when you're there. The developments—sometimes half-finished, with many of the homes empty these days—resemble the corn. The houses are planted in rows that twist and turn around the rising and falling land; there are acres and acres of suburban sprawl, identical, evenly spaced, and placid. This is wealth of the usual variety. And this is America of the usual variety. It changes as soon as you pull into Mystic Lake Casino Resort just outside Shakopee.

The casino complex is visible for miles. It is really the only thing, other than the Mall of America, fifteen miles to the northeast, that you can see and identify by shape and scale. It's huge. The hotel has 600 rooms, seven restaurants, and a spa, all looking out over a premier golf course tamped into the wetlands that once defined the landscape. (As I was sitting outside drinking an espresso I got from the espresso bar in the lobby, an Indian man with a bag of golf clubs bigger than his grandson, who sat down next to him, told me: *It's the best golf course in the world, I tell you. The best. And cheap. Only a hundred dollars for a full round including the cart. You've got to use a cart. Mandatory*.) The casino—with more than 4,000 slot machines and ninety-six blackjack tables—is equally visible: though the building is low to the ground, floodlights set around the perimeter come together in a laser-show tepee. All in all, the casino is as visible, as powerful, and as delightfully menacing as the Mdewakanton Sioux were ignored, pushed aside, and disenfranchised in the 200 years before gaming became recognized in 1988 as a legal enterprise (it had always been an unrecognized right of Indian tribes). The drive curves around under a massive timbered portico lined with limestone quarried from the Mississippi basin near Little Falls. A waterfall and a gurgling brook surround a statue of an elk. Indian kids are throwing change into the water and making wishes. Two of them, having used up all their change, are sending bits of torn Styrofoam down the water chase. It is late August, time for the Shakopee powwow. The place is alive with activity. Cars line up, unload, pull ahead. The bellhops hand out chits for parking, get in, and zoom off. Luggage carts fill up with suitcases, pillows, duffel bags, and golf clubs. The revolving doors spin at a dizzying rate.

Everything is pleasantly backward. The cars that pull up spit out three, four, five, six Indians and hail from Saskatchewan, South Dakota, North Dakota, Nebraska, Montana, Wisconsin, Michigan, and Alaska. The white bellhops load the luggage carts with Indian luggage and bring it to a reception area staffed by white people. It is truly a strange sight to see rubbed brass and chrome wheeled luggage racks loaded with suitcases, garment bags, beaded buckskin, and velvet, and, balanced on the top, enormous bustles made with the feathers of bald eagles. A long line of Indians waits to check in; each Indian is given a magnetic key; and up they go into one of the rooms at the Mystic Lake hotel. Almost every room in the hotel was filled with Indians, so there were more Indians in the hotel than were enrolled members of the Mdewakanton Dakota Tribe: actually twice as many, since that tribe has fewer than 300 enrollees. Indians are giving white people money; from brown hands to white it goes. Most of the time the Indians don't tip. Or if they do it is usually one or two dollars.

The impression, the strange impression of Indian wealth, is heightened when you go to the powwow itself: the parking lot reserved for tribal members was filled with (I counted) twelve Lincoln Navigators, seven Hummers, three 2008 Mustangs, and four Dodge Chargers with "HEMI" stenciled on the side. A few minivans, sadly out of place, decorated the lot as well as six Harley-Davidson motorcycles and one Indian motorcycle. All in all, most of the cars cost double the average household income for most Indians in the United States. Navigators and Hummers cost upwards of $50,000 apiece while the median household income for Indian families is $17,000. The Mdewakanton Band, which used to be a small band of Dakota Indians with little land and no money, is growing. The number of households has grown from 229 in 1990 to more than 360 today. Of those households, the proportion making more than $200,000 a year went from zero to over 50 percent in ten years. The houses are growing, too. Thirty-eight percent of the houses on the rez are in the supersize category: that is, they contain nine bedrooms or more. The only figures not growing rapidly are high school graduation rates (still below 50 percent) and Indians with college degrees (a terrible 5 percent).

But then the strangeness recedes. Except for frybread burgers and Indian tacos priced at $7.50 and fresh-squeezed lemonade at $5, everything about the powwow is the same as most other large contest powwows. The emcee, having exhausted or seeming to have exhausted his store of jokes, announces the grand entry, the host drum starts the song, and the dancers dance into the arbor between the bleachers. Only minutes before, many were taking last-minute puffs on Marlboros, joking with friends, flirting, or telling dirty jokes, but now they bend to the music, duck into the arbor, straighten with the song, and begin dancing in styles both old and new. First the color guard carrying the American flag, the POW/MIA staff, the flag of the Mdewakanton Dakota Nation, and an Eagle staff dance in. They are followed by the rest of the dancers, by category. The regalia is beautiful, some of the best. Huge bustles. Silky, fantastically colored grass-dance outfits. Head roaches with the eagle feathers supported on springs so they spin, dip, and shake with each step the dancer takes. Beaded yokes on the traditional women dancers that must weigh at least twenty-five pounds. All of the dancers, from the youngest to oldest, no matter the category, have numbers taped or pinned to their outfits, like the kind worn by runners in a race. Judges and powwow officials with clipboards begin scoring the contests. They judge the dancers by category—the dancers get points for the completeness and aesthetics of their regalia, their bearing, their energy, and their moves. (Do the fringes of the traditional women dancers swing evenly in time with the drumbeat? Do the grass-dancers complete clockwise and counterclockwise movements? Etc.) And then the flag song. And then the invocation, delivered in Dakota. And then the crow hop. And after that a sneak-up. And then intertribal dancing.

By the time the dancers are all in and the first intertribal is ratcheted up by "The Boys"—with singers drawn from Minnesota, Utah, Wyoming, Wisconsin, and elsewhere—with the most amazing and inspiring intensity, the lead wavering, floating, high over the crowd, and the rest jumping in on the tail, all of them hammering it down at the end of the first push-up, pausing, and the lead emerging from the silence to once again coast above, beyond, somehow out of reach but then reached by the rest of the singers—by this time the sun is beginning to set.

From the top of the metal bleachers crowded with spectators (most of them Indian) sitting on fleece and colorful geometric Pendleton blankets, the dancers lose their individuality. Instead of single people, among whom you might recognize a lot of friends, what you see is a snake. A mass of color snakes around the arbor. The speakers amplify the singing and the jingling of ankle bells. Outside the arbor, down on the grass already collecting dew, people walk back and forth with baby strollers and children race each other through the crowds. Some people carry paper cartons of french fries to wooden picnic tables. Above and beyond the dancers, lit now by floodlights, and the spectators, and the scores of RVs, minivans, and campers, across a small valley hidden from sight, rises the reservation itself, or part of it. On a tall hill rising from the opposite side of the valley the houses of the Mdewakanton are circled like tepees of old. This is their housing tract, their "track." Rez housing like nothing you've ever seen before. Each house glares back across the valley defiantly, fronted with Low-E antiglare windows (windows that cost about $3,000 to $4,000 each) behind which lurk houses many of which boast more than 5,000 square feet of living space (twenty times bigger than the sixteen-by-twenty shack my mother grew up in). Housing is provided for all the members of the tribe, with each house, even at an average of $120 per square foot, costing about $600,000. The tribal members themselves receive about $84,000 per month in per capita payments—payments made to them because they are Indian and because they are enrolled at the Mdewakanton Sioux Community. One million dollars a year for each and every tribal member over the age of eighteen. They pay federal income tax, but if they are living on the rez they are exempt from state income tax. There is no local income tax in Minnesota. This money is considered a marital asset in divorce court. Most Mdewakanton Dakota live on the reservation. Unemployment at Shakopee is very high. I think the divorce rate is high, too. They possess a kind of wealth that no Indian could have imagined twenty-five years ago at the dawn of Indian gaming and that few Indians can still get their minds around. They possess a kind of wealth most Americans can't grasp.

Staring out over the dancers, proud in their regalia and proud to be dancing at this powwow, and over the Navigators and Hummers and Harley-Davidsons, over to the mansions of the Indians where stood, just 100 years ago, nothing at all, it is easy to see that Indian casinos are the single biggest change on the reservation—even on reservations where there are no casinos or where casinos just barely exist—since the reservations were themselves established in the nineteenth century.

Life changed dramatically for many Indians, such as the Mdewakanton Dakota, living near large urban centers. The Cabazon Band, with only twenty-eight members, is beyond rich. It's been said that every band member has his or her own private golf course, but I couldn't verify this. And neither they nor the Mdewakanton were too keen on being interviewed about their wealth. In an ironic twist, celebrities go to Palm Springs to detox at treatment centers on the reservation. White people going to a reservation to dry out—no one saw that coming. The Choctaw, Chickasaw, Seminole, Pequots, and Mdewakanton Dakota are rich. But they are the exceptions. Many reservations have no gambling at all, and many that do have gambling, such as mine, barely break even. As of 2006, 12 percent of Indian casinos generated 65 percent of all casino revenue.

Of those that do have casinos, only a small fraction see much profit, and a small fraction of those make enough to give per capita payments to their members as the Mdewakanton Dakota do. Red Cliff Reservation, on the shores of Lake Superior in northern Wisconsin, has a casino. It has never really produced much profit. It struggled on, but when tribes to the south at Flambeau, LCO, Fond du Lac, and St. Croix opened casinos much closer to Minneapolis and Duluth, there was no reason to go to Red Cliff. Now the tribe—one of the poorest in the state—is wrestling with a new decision: expand casino operations by building one on the site of their campground and marina (cherished by many band members) or stay poor? Casinos are something that tribes do not just gamble in but also gamble on. This is especially true since the recession of 2008; Indian gaming revenues are down 40 percent. The tribes who branched out—like Mille Lacs— are doing OK. They discussed suspending per capita payments but are now offering these at a slightly lower level—about $8,000 per year. Tribes like Leech Lake, which did not branch out much, are dangerously close to losing what they have. Some cynics think casino money hasn't changed anything. "Yeah," one told me, "Mille Lacs is the richest slum in the country. And everyone still crashes their cars into trees, the only difference is that they crash newer cars." There is some truth to this. Mille Lacs might have a clinic built with casino money, but Indians are still going there for drug overdoses, car wrecks, diabetes, and overall poor health.

Some say this isn't fair—some Indians get rich while others still don't have a pot to piss in. But in this, Indian country mirrors America nicely: a shrinking middle class, a large underclass, and an elite that controls most of the wealth. So while they may be eating Kobe beef in Mdewakanton and Palm Springs, on most Indian reservations, even those with casinos, they are not. Some reservations have made just enough to provide some employment, pave some roads, build new government offices and new schools—enough to edge toward the middle class. This in itself is a huge accomplishment.

The ramifications of Indian gambling are only now unfolding. Tribes have discovered that they can control their lives more than at any other period in the last 300 years. It is only a matter of time before tribes realize that the logic and precedent that enable Indian gaming might also enable other enterprises. Tribes could begin a banking industry to rival offshore banking. They needn't be bound by U.S. banking laws. Tribes might very well begin data farming. They might offer corporate tax shelters. There might be no reason for pharmaceutical companies to plant themselves in far-off Puerto Rico. Much is possible. It is not clear what role the state would play in operations such as banking. The tribes might have to enter compacts to run banks, just as they have to sign compacts for gaming. But whatever states regulate is open for negotiation on reservations.

So the next time you're asked how come Indians get to have casinos, or if you're asked why Indians own Paul McCartney's guitar, the answer is: because of *Worcester v. Georgia,* because of a $147 tax bill on a trailer at Squaw Lake, and because a few tribes and a few people did the hard thing and fought and won.

Our last day. We decided to eat brunch at the Pechanga clubhouse before driving back to the airport. I saw a guy who looked awfully familiar. He was wearing a T-shirt that read "Ojibwe Veterans' Powwow, Red Lake, 2005." I looked hard, and I said, "Rocky, is that you?" It was. Rocky Cook, from Red Lake Reservation, just up the road from me. He was with his wife, Lorena, also from Red Lake. They have both known my parents since the 1960s, and both knew my siblings. I had gone to high school and graduated with their daughter Holly. I wasn't totally surprised: I knew that Holly had married Mark Macarro, the Pechanga chairman. I knew also that Holly was expecting a baby, so it must have come.

We talked about Holly and my siblings and parents. The usual home stuff. They asked me what I was doing out there, and I said I was researching a piece on Indian casinos.

"Yeah," said Lorena (a quick wit). "They get mad at us for being poor, and then when some folks do all right, they get mad at us for being rich." Not that Red Lake, where she and Rocky are from, is a well-off place. But what Lorena expressed is something many Indians ponder: the complicated disdain many people have for Indian poverty and the rare instances of Indian wealth.

Indians are famous for a few things—for a kind of off-brand environmentalism, Sitting Bull, and broken English, and most of all for being poor. Poverty is, for many, synonymous with the very idea of Indians and Indian reservations. This thought stuck with me as we loaded up the BMW, drove back to LAX, flew back to Minneapolis, and drove north in my pickup back to Leech Lake.

Leech Lake is a big reservation—forty miles by forty miles, peppered with lakes large and small, and broken in half by the slow, shallow course of the northern Mississippi River. We passed two of our casinos (we have three) on the drive to my house on the northwestern edge of the reservation. We don't have good steak. We don't raise our own cattle. We don't own any famous person's shoes. Many people on Leech Lake don't even own their own shoes. My reservation will be poor for a long time, maybe forever.

Indian gaming has changed very little on my reservation—it has generated some money for infrastructure and jobs, but not much. Whereas twenty years ago we had little in the way of business, now we have a tribally owned gas station–convenience store, a mill, and three casinos. Unemployment at Leech Lake has gone from 50 percent to 22 percent after the casino, though this change certainly isn't solely because of casino employment. Gaming at Leech Lake has generated a lot more fighting and squabbling and severe politics than it has opportunity. The median household income at Leech Lake is $21,000, less than half of the median U.S. household income. More than half our kids do not live with their parents. At Leech Lake, we're poor—but we've worked very hard at it and come by our poverty honestly.

And even though Indian gaming began at Leech Lake with a $147 tax bill, perhaps we contribute something a little harder to measure. When I asked people in Florida and Pechanga and Morongo what they wanted most, what they worried most about not having, they all responded: culture and language; our ways. And at Leech Lake at least we have that. Other folks from other reservations might laugh at this next comment, but when I tell people where I am from, they often raise their eyebrows in both surprise and appreciation—surprise that I come from a place so rough, and appreciation because they are sometimes awed or humbled and even a little envious that I come from a place where our language is still spoken, a place that doesn't feel like the rest of America, even though it is, only more so. So, while I am proud of what other tribes have accomplished, I wonder whether (and hope that) they are proud of us, too.

When I drew near my house, I passed our first casino, the Palace Casino and Hotel. I decided, just for comparison's sake, to stop in. It was now 2 a.m. The place was mostly deserted. The Memorial Day crowd had left. Fishing opener was a few weeks behind us. Some regulars sat at keno machines smoking and hoping their numbers would come up. Half a dozen or so blackjack players tapped the baize table and shook their heads. The air was smoky and heavy. Everyone seemed depressed and I got a little depressed. There was no spa. No steak. No golf. No bad beat jackpot. The Palace isn't the loneliest casino in America (that honor,

I think, goes to Isle Vista at Red Cliff Reservation), but it's pretty damn close. Our problems—unemployment, drug and alcohol abuse, lack of access to education and employment—are as they've always been. But the riches at Mdewakanton and Mille Lacs have done little to change those problems on their reservations. Even though I heard that some people at Shakopee wear their shoes only once and then just throw them away, they are poor in many things—overall health being one of them. Their poverty might be a new kind but ours is old.

Even so, the Palace is homey. Built in 1988, it's an ancestor of the larger, happier places in California, Connecticut, and Florida. And it's home.

I used to spend a lot of time at the Palace. I won my first hand of blackjack there. It was where my uncle Sonny (now deceased) scored $4,000 on a keno machine. Where my aunt Barb (now deceased) used to work. Where a medicine man sitting next to my mother said, "Give me the eight of hearts," and the dealer did, and my mother said, "Adam, that's not fair!" Where I met, way back when, a wonderful, wonderful girlfriend. Behind the casino is the veterans' center, built with casino profits, where we held the funeral ceremonies for not a few good friends. And behind that are the powwow grounds, also built with casino profits, where I sang for the first time.

The Palace Casino and Hotel was built while I was away at college (back then, it was the Palace Bingo and Casino, sans hotel). In the fall of my freshman year, in a fit of loneliness, I once called home (never mind the long-distance charges that ate up a few hours of work).

"You OK?" asked my mother.

"Yeah. Homesick. Wish I were back there."

"I thought you said you were never coming back to the rez."

"I was wrong."

"Hey, this is exciting," she said, trying to cheer me up. "We're getting a casino."

"A what?"

"You know. Bingo. Blackjack. Slots. A casino. For gambling."

"I wonder if that'll change anything."

And then, the understatement of the decade: "Who the hell knows, Dave. But at least we'll finally get good prime rib on the rez."

Dan and Dennis Jones bass fishing on Rainy Lake, August 2008

6

I am not supposed to be alive. Native Americans were supposed to die off, as endangered species do, a century ago. Our reservations aren't supposed to exist either; they were supposed to be temporary in many ways, and, under assault by the Dawes Act in the nineteenth century and by termination policy during the Eisenhower era in the twentieth century, they were supposed to disappear, too.

But I am not dead after all, and neither is rez life despite the coldest wishes of a republic since two centuries before I was born. We stubbornly continue to exist. There were just over 200,000 Native Americans alive at the dawn of the twentieth century; as of the 2000 census, we number more than 2 million. If you discount population growth by immigration, we are the fastest-growing segment of the U.S. population. But even as our populations are growing, something else, I fear, is dying: our cultures.

Among my fellow Indians, this is not a popular thing to say. Most of us immediately sneer at warnings of cultural death, calling the very idea further proof that "the man" is still trying to kill us, but now with attitudes and arguments rather than discrimination and guns. Any Indian caught worrying that we might indeed vanish can expect to be grouped with the self-haters. While many things go into making a culture—kinship, history, religion, place—the disappearance of our languages suggests that our cultures, in total, may not be here for much longer.

For now, many Native American languages still exist, but most of them just barely, with only a very few living speakers, all of them old. On January 21, 2008, Marie Smith Jones, the last living fluent speaker of Eyak, one of about twenty remaining Native Alaskan languages, died at the age of eighty-nine. Linguists estimate that when Europeans first came to North America, more than 300 Native American languages were spoken here. Today, there are only about 150. Of those languages, only twenty are spoken by children. Only three languages—Dakota, Dene, and Ojibwe—have a vibrant community of speakers. Within a century, if nothing is done, hardly any Native languages will remain, though the surviving ones will include my language, Ojibwe.

Cultures change, of course. Sometimes they change slowly, in response to such factors as warming temperatures, differences in food sources, or new migration patterns. At other times, cultural changes are swift—the result of colonialism, famine, migration, or war. But at some point (which no one is anxious to identify exactly), a culture ceases to be a culture and becomes an ethnicity—that is, it changes from a life system that develops its own terms into one that borrows, almost completely, someone else's.

To claim that Indian cultures can continue without Indian languages only hastens our end, even if it makes us feel better about ourselves. Our cultures and our languages—as unique, identifiable, and particular entities—are linked to our sovereignty. If we allow our own wishful thinking and complacency to finish what George Armstrong Custer began, we will lose what we've managed to retain:

our languages, land, laws, institutions, ceremonies, and, finally, ourselves. Cultural death matters because if the culture dies, we will have lost the chance not only to live on our own terms (something for which our ancestors fought long and hard) but also to live in our own terms.

If my language dies, our word for bear, "makwa," will disappear, and with it the understanding that "makwa" is derived from the word for box, "makak" (because black bears box themselves up, sleeping, for the winter). So too will the word for namesake, "niiyawen'enh." Every child who gets an Ojibwe name has namesakes, sometimes as many as six or eight of them. Throughout a child's life, his or her namesakes function somewhat like godparents, giving advice and help, good for a dollar to buy an Indian taco at a powwow. But they offer something more too. The term for "my body," "niiyaw" (a possessive noun: ni- = "I/mine"; -iiyaw = "body/soul"), is incorporated into the word for a namesake because the idea (contained by the word and vice versa) is that when you take part in a naming, you are giving a part of your soul, your body, to the person being named. So, to say "my namesake," niiyawen'enh, is to say "my fellow body, myself." If these words are lost, much will happen, but also very little will happen. We will be able to go to Starbucks, GameStop, Walmart, and Home Depot. We will still use Crest Whitestrips. Some of us will still do our taxes. Some of us still won't. The mechanics of life as it is lived by modern Ojibwes will remain, for the most part, unchanged. The languages we lose, when we lose them, are always replaced by other languages. And all languages can get the job of life done. But something else might be lost and there might be more to the job of life than simply living it.

⁂

At Waadookodaading Ojibwe Language Immersion School at Lac Courte Oreilles (LCO) Reservation in Wisconsin, people are doing something about this. You drive past a lot of natural beauty between Hayward and the school—a lot of maple and pine; deep, clear lakes—most of it owned by whites. At the school, in two yellow modular buildings built with tribal funds in what used to be the corner of the school parking lot, a cultural revival is occurring. On the hot day in May when I visited the school I saw silhouettes of students drawn in chalk on the wooden decking that connects the buildings. The third and fourth grades were studying solar movement as part of their science curriculum, all done in Ojibwe, and done only here. Inside, the classroom walls are covered with signs in the Ojibwe language. A smartboard, linked to the teacher's laptop, provides state-of-the-art learning opportunities.

One of the teachers who helped start the immersion program is a lanky, tall, excitable man named Keller Paap. When these teachers started the school in 2000 they had only a few students in kindergarten. Now, there are about twenty students in the program between kindergarten and fourth grade. After greeting the fourth-grade students in the classroom, Keller brings them to the music room in the main school building, where they all sing along with Keller's guitar playing to welcome the new day. They speak, sing, argue, and flirt with each other in Ojibwe at a level that eludes most adults at LCO and every other Ojibwe reservation across the United States. After the morning singing they head back to the classroom and begin working on their science unit. "Ahaw," asks Keller. "Awegonesh ge-ayaayambam da-agawaateyaag?" [So. What do all you need to make a shadow?]

One girl says, shyly, "Andaatewin."

"Mii gwayak," says Keller. "Awegonesh gaye? Giizis ina?"

"Ahaw," says a playful boy, without a hint of shame or bashfulness.

"Mii go gaye apiichaawin," says another kid, in a spurt of intuition.

This classroom is light-years ahead of most tribal language programs, which are still stuck on "bezhig, niizh, niswi," and "makwa, waabooz, waagosh" ("one, two, three" and "bear, rabbit, fox"). They aren't listing things in Ojibwe at Waadookodaading; they are thinking in Ojibwe.

Keller; his wife, Lisa LaRonge; Alex Decoteau; and the other teachers at Waadookodaading are, together, saving Ojibwe culture. Keller Paap is one of a few activists who have devoted their lives to saving the Ojibwe language. He is an unlikely hero. Raised in a suburb of Minneapolis, college-educated, a recovering rock star (he is an accomplished guitarist), he has given up all financial security, all his other possible prospects, everything, in order to move to LCO to open an Ojibwe-language immersion school. He is a new kind of activist for a new kind of reservation community.

Indian activism used to be a tough guy's game. In the late 1960s and early 1970s the American Indian Movement (AIM) rose from urban Indian populations across the country. Cleveland, Minneapolis, Chicago, Oakland, and Los Angeles had been destinations for Indians relocated during the 1950s, and they became the seed plots for a surge of Indian activism. Relocation, a government-sponsored program, yet another switchback in the U.S. government's long road toward freeing itself of Indians and of all responsibility toward us, was a policy that sought to integrate Indians into the mainstream workforce by severing their relationship to their reservation communities. The relocation program promised jobs, education, and housing in up-and-coming American cities. Very little of this was forthcoming. Instead, Indians were crowded into ghettos, fought for work, fought for education, and suffered. It should be said that many Indians flourished in cities in the 1950s and many still flourish there today; more than half of all Indians live in urban areas. Still, the common notion that reservations are prisons should be revised; it was the city that became a prison for many Indians. They were stuck in a city and could not get out. They hadn't the money to move back to the reservation and yet they had little reason to stay. Franklin Avenue, Gowanus Canal, Chicago's South Side—these became signifiers of rough life as important as the reservations the Indians had come from. Out of this situation, which was supposed to gradually make Indians as Indians "disappear," came AIM.

Clyde Bellecourt, Dennis Banks, George Mitchell, and Herb Powless, among others, founded AIM in 1968. Its rationale and goals were: the U.S. government has never had the interests of American Indians in mind or at heart, and any attempt to work within the system or with the system is bound to fail. Unlike the black civil rights movement, AIM had no great strength of numbers, economic capital, or visibility to use in getting its point across. The answer: bold, graphic takeovers and marches. Within seven years AIM had marched on and taken over Alcatraz Island (more accurately, a group of Bay Area Indians took over Alcatraz and some of the high-profile AIM leadership came toward the end of the takeover); the Bureau of Indian Affairs (BIA) headquarters in Washington, D.C.; Mount Rushmore; and a replica of the *Mayflower*. At each event the AIMsters dressed in cowboy boots, tight jeans, buckskin jackets, and headbands and issued passionate, even poetic, statements about the continued mistreatment of American Indians. Often, light-skinned Indians were told they couldn't belong to AIM or had to march in the back. AIM was always concerned with its image. Its activism was a kind of art—street theater that was visual and often violent and that conveyed clear messages about the mistreatment of Indians.

The most shocking and visible moment for AIM, and the moment that marked its decline, was its standoff with the federal government at the Jumping Bull Compound on the Pine Ridge Reservation in South Dakota, which left two federal agents dead. Leonard Peltier was charged with and convicted of murder and is still serving a sentence at Leavenworth. Afterward, marked by vicious infighting and infiltrated by the FBI, AIM became, in the opinion of many, aimless. And not everyone had approved of AIM in the first place. During the 1970s anger at the Red Lake Reservation chairman, Roger Jourdain, at his policies, and at embezzlement by other employees fueled riots at Red Lake. Jourdain's house was burned down and cars were shot through with bullets. AIM tried to muscle in on the unrest and was rebuffed. The traditional community of Ponemah took a stand against AIM. As Eugene Stillday recounts, a number of veterans (of World War II, Korea, and Vietnam) from Ponemah gathered at The Cut—a narrow place in the road, bordered by the lake on one side and a large swamp on the other. They barricaded the road, built sandbag bunkers, and kept constant guard, armed with deer rifles and shotguns. Carloads of AIMsters drove up the road, were stopped, and after looking at the faces of the Ponemah veterans chose to turn around and go elsewhere.

This was what passed for activism in the late 1960s and 1970s. Keller Paap, on the other hand, is an unlikely activist. He was raised in a comfortable suburb: White Bear Lake, on the north side of St. Paul. His mother is from Red Cliff Reservation in Wisconsin; his father is of German ancestry. After graduating from high school in White Bear Lake he started college, stopped, and devoted himself to becoming a rock and roller. Keller *looks* like a rock star. He's tallish (six feet and change), thin, and bony, with long black hair, wide cheekbones and lips, and long tapered fingers that were made to hold a guitar and to play it well. When someone is talking to him about the Ojibwe language, the glazed look that comes over his eyes must be the same look he had during a guitar solo. It is not difficult to imagine him wearing a bandanna, like Steven Van Zandt, or the same purse-lipped expression when he is focused on his guitar. During the day the kids sometimes start spacing out during their lessons and Keller jumps up, thumbs his iPod while gushing at the kids in Ojibwe, finds Herbie Hancock's "Rockit," and gets his kids to kick off their shoes and try to do the "robot," the "scarecrow," and "the moon walk." During the early 1980s Keller spent a lot of time practicing his break-dancing moves. Later, he and his friends followed the Grateful Dead.

I first met Paap in 1994 at the University of Minnesota, where he was finishing his undergraduate degree. He was a student in the Ojibwe-language class offered through the department of American Indian Studies. At the time he didn't seem all that interested in the language.

"Back then I thought it was sort of cool," he says. "I was Ojibwe, my people were from Red Cliff, and this was our language, and it felt good to study it."

That good feeling quickly became a passion.

"It all started with hanging out with Dennis Jones, the Ojibwe-language instructor at the U. I traveled around with him and recorded his mom and worked on translating her stories. And, man! The intricacy! The crazy complexity of the language totally got me. I mean, hanging out with Nancy, and Rose Tainter, and Delores Wakefield—all those elders, sitting around the kitchen table drinking Red Rose tea and talking—it felt comfortable, like it was with my uncles and cousins and relatives up at Red Cliff when I was a kid. Even more than music, even more than the guitar, the complexity and music of the language and the feeling of belonging to something totally caught me."

Catch him it did. Soon after graduating he worked as a teaching assistant for the language program. He met his wife there. Lisa LaRonge is from LCO Reservation, due south of Red Cliff. Like Keller she is tall, with long brown hair. Like Keller, she has gone through many incarnations before devoting herself to the language.

They moved to Lisa's reservation in 1998 and, with a few others, opened an Ojibwe-language immersion school—Waadookodaading ("we help each other"). Waadookodaading has been in operation for ten years now, as one of only a few schools generating fluent speakers of the Ojibwe language. Strangely, many other Ojibwe-language activists have some kind of artistic pedigree. Leslie Harper—who along with her sister Laurie, Adrian Liberty, and elders like Johnny Mitchell founded the Niigaane Immersion program at Leech Lake—is a writer and a former Miss Indian Minneapolis. Liberty is a drummer—his band Powermad was featured in David Lynch's *Wild at Heart*.

The goal of these activists seems odd to many: in communities rife with drugs, violence, gangs, domestic abuse, suicide, and high dropout rates, Ojibwe-language immersion seems like a perverse luxury.

Odd or not, what these fighters are after is something very different from what AIM was after in the 1960s and 1970s. AIM wanted the world to stand up and take notice of the injustices we suffered and continue to suffer. By taking notice public opinion might actually sway policy. Language activists look in the other direction—instead of looking out at the government and the mainstream and trying to convince them of something, they are looking in and are trying to convince their fellow Indians of something else. As my brother has put it on a number of occasions, "The U.S. government has spent millions of dollars trying to take our language away from us. Why would we expect the government to give it back? It's up to us to give it back to ourselves."

The U.S. government did indeed spend millions of dollars and many years trying to stamp out indigenous languages, mostly through subtle discriminatory practices (such as hiring and education) but the government also used unsubtle means, the most destructive of which was the institution of Indian boarding schools. As Native American languages endured a sustained assault, Indian identity—those elusive bonds that wed self and society and that make a people—took the greatest number of hits. Many Indians see this as proof of the spiteful, harmful attitude the feds have always had toward Indians. But governments really aren't spiteful just to be spiteful. They are like animals—they do what they do out of self-interest. And for many years, Indians were a threat—a constant, powerful, very real, very physical threat—to American imperial expansion. We were, quite simply, either in the way or powerful enough to pose a threat if provoked. The process by which Indians were dealt with only sometimes took the form of war. In many other instances Indians were subjected to a process of "Americanization." In place from colonial days, Americanization was aimed at creating a uniform public body, one that shared the same values and lifestyles and put the same premium on work, saving, expansion, and accumulation of capital. However, for Indians, the late nineteenth century and the early twentieth century was a dark time, in many ways because of the boarding schools.

In 1878–1879, the U.S. government built and funded the first of twenty-six federally controlled Indian boarding schools. Carlisle Indian Industrial School, in Carlisle, Pennsylvania, came to epitomize the boarding school era, which for many Indians was one of the darkest times in our history. The idea of the boarding schools was to forcibly break the family bonds that, in the opinion of many, kept Indians from becoming civilized and part of the American public. Carlisle drew students from more than 140 different tribes. The students had their hair cut short. Their names were changed. They were forbidden to speak their Native languages. No Indian religions were allowed at the school—attendance at Christian services was compulsory. Students were beaten for speaking their languages. Many were abused. By 1902, with twenty-six schools in operation, more than 6,000 Indian children had been removed from their homes and sent hundreds of miles away from their communities. When boarding schools and the policies that supported them were finally abolished in the 1970s, hundreds of thousands of Indians had been sent there. Carlisle alone admitted more than 12,000 students by the time of its closing in 1918.

Attendance at boarding schools was not compulsory. Parents had to agree to let their children go. But their permission was often effected through coercion. Indian agents, who got bonuses for collecting children for school, threatened to withhold annuities or supplies. They blacklisted Indian families who refused to send their children along. Some parents, like my great-grandmother, could not afford to feed their children, and while their Indianness was under assault at these boarding schools at least their children would have something to eat. After the schools had been in existence for a few decades the pressure to send children away became a norm. If you wanted your children to have a chance at a job or an education you sent them away. It simply was what was done. Agents from the BIA were extremely effective at coercing families into letting their children go. But it didn't always work.

In 1887 the U.S. government established a boarding school at Keams Canyon. It was a terrible place, so much so that the Indian agent at Fort Defiance wrote to the commissioner of Indian affairs to say: "If deaths occur a strong prejudice will be aroused against the school, to say nothing of the policy of conducting a boarding school for any human pupils with such conditions of accommodations." Nonetheless, agents tried their best to get the children into school. Hopi parents promised to send them and then did nothing. Frustrated, the commissioner withheld annuities and halted the construction of all houses and buildings at Second Mesa. When that didn't work he ordered that wells being dug for precious groundwater be left unfinished. This was a cruel act: there was two feet of snow on the ground and the temperature was minus seventeen degrees Fahrenheit. Nonetheless, the Hopi held on to their children. In 1890, with nothing to show for the commissioner's efforts, the army marched onto Hopi land. In Orayvi it captured 104 children and sent them to Keams Canyon Boarding School. The Indian agent Plummer thought this wasn't such a good idea—it would make people angry, and each and every action would necessitate the use of force. Instead, he suggested arresting the chiefs and headmen of the Hopi. If they were taken, that would send a strong message. Eventually, because of the school issue and for "hostile behavior" the U.S. Army captured nineteen Hopi leaders and sent them to Alcatraz, where they served a year before they could return home. (This is the only instance I know of in which people who took back land that was stolen from them and planted with wheat could be considered "hostile." In 1832, however, the starving Sac, led by Chief Black Hawk, sneaked across the Mississippi River to harvest their corn from fields that had been fenced and trampled by settlers, and they were met by the Illinois militia, which considered this harvesting mission an act of war. The Sac were attacked by the Illinois militia, federal troops, and their Dakota allies and an army gunboat killed Sac women and children who were attempting to swim across the Bad Axe and Mississippi rivers. The seventy Sac warriors who made it across were butchered by their longtime Dakota enemies once they reached shore.)

As destructive as boarding schools might have been, many Indians actually enjoyed their time there and had no unpleasant experiences. The schools were the brainchild of a fairly well-meaning man. Known best for stating that his purpose at Carlisle was "to kill the Indian in him to save the man," Captain Richard Henry Pratt was something of a do-gooder. He had served in the Civil War. After the war he was put in charge of the 10th Cavalry Regiment, famously known as "buffalo soldiers"—freed blacks who joined the Union army. After there were no more southerners to fight they were sent west to kill Indians. In the aftermath of the Red River War—between the United States and a coalition of Indian tribes made up of Comanche, Kiowa, Cheyenne, and Arapaho (which had to be one of the strangest and most ignored ironies of plains warfare, since the Indians were largely objecting to the extermination of buffalo herds by white buffalo hunters and then found themselves at war with black buffalo soldiers)—Captain Pratt and his buffalo soldiers were tasked with escorting seventy-eight Indians from the Southwest to prison in St. Augustine.

Pratt was very concerned with the welfare of these Indian prisoners. He improved living conditions and diet and eventually set up a kind of "self-guarding" system whereby the Indians policed themselves. He did this largely as a way to help the Indians preserve their own dignity in captivity. Eventually white vacationers, many with missionary backgrounds, became interested in Pratt and his endeavors at Fort Marion. They encouraged him to continue his efforts to "civilize" the Indians in captivity. They volunteered to teach the Indians English, how to read and write, basic math, and history. About twenty of the Indian captives went to college at Hampton after their release. Others settled in New York. Buoyed by this "success," Pratt took his idea of "cultural immersion" to political friends of his and he secured funding for Carlisle. Basically Pratt saw the civilizing of Indians as being not dissimilar to his domestication of wild turkeys (he had stolen a nest of wild turkey eggs and hatched them, and they were raised by a barnyard hen). Comparing Indian students to his turkeys, he said that all the Indians needed was "the environment and kind treatment of domestic civilized life to become a very part of it."

In order to effect the "kind treatment of domestic civilized life" Pratt and his fellow teachers at Carlisle tried to erase as much of the

Indian from the Indian as they could. They succeeded in that aim, but they also turned generations of children and their parents against education. The boarding school system persisted in the United States only until the late 1930s and early 1940s, but by then the damage was done. In Canada, a similar system lasted much longer, well into the 1960s and 1970s.

Dan Jones was a child in the Canadian residential school system and endured some of the worst assaults on his sense of self, not to mention his body, that anyone should have to endure. "My earliest memory," he says. "Trees. You know how, when the light is going, it's almost night, and the sky is black but the trees are even blacker. The very first thing I can remember is that jagged line of the treetops, spruce trees. I was in the rabbit-fur sleeping bag my mom made for me and my brother Dennis, sleeping on the rocks next to the fire on a portage trail someplace. That's the very first thing I remember."

Dan and his twin brother, Dennis, were born on their family's trapline just north of the Minnesota border, in northwest Ontario. His father's Ojibwe name was Pawanjigwaneyaash ("He is Soaring Up"), but the Indian agent couldn't say it, so he substituted the English name Johnny Jones. The children were raised in the traditional Ojibwe manner, and although the family was only a few miles from the American border as the crow flies, it might as well have been living in a different century altogether. At the time, the 1950s, this region of boreal forest and lakes was accessible only by canoe or floatplane. There were no roads, no stores, no cars or TVs. There was not much of anything except water and trees. Their village, situated at the mouth of the Otter Tail River on Redgut Bay of Rainy Lake, is a beautiful place, with pines, poplars, lowlands, rocky shores, and cliffs. Work was seasonal. In the summer the men guided tourists who wanted to fish in Rainy Lake. In the fall the Indians harvested wild rice. In the winter they trapped furs, in the spring they netted fish. Nancy Jones and her husband Johnny raised eight children in "the bush."

During one long winter Nancy went into labor while on the family's trapline. Johnny was two days away by snowshoe. She delivered her baby herself, cut the umbilical cord with her skinning knife, strapped the baby to her back, and walked out of the bush back to the village. Johnny helped with the delivery of Dennis and Dan. Nancy gave birth to Dennis and neither she nor Johnny could figure out why she was still in labor. After another forty-five minutes she gave birth to Dan. When they traveled Nancy would change diapers (packed with moss) on portages while Johnny carried the canoe and gear around. It is a different way to be connected to a place. Once, while I was trapping with Dan, he pointed to a flat rock on the portage trail: "My mom used to change our diapers there." It was hard to believe. But then, I know Nancy and she is so knowledgeable, so impressive, that you have no choice but to believe. She once shot and killed a moose, and since she had forgotten her knife, she skinned the animal using the lid of a snuff can.

In recent testimony before a Canadian commission convened to assess damages caused by residential schools in Canada, Dan Jones said, "We lived off the land. The Anishinaabemowin [Ojibwe] language was the only one spoken. We put tobacco out as an offering for our first kill ceremonies, ceremonies for wild rice, and blueberries. My father was always strong in that way. It was all done in the language, being thankful and giving thanks for everything that was given to us. The only thing I thought was traumatic before boarding school, was once I thought I was left on a portage. My father went ahead to start the motor and I thought we were being left behind and I started crying. He came back and comforted me. They were nurturing and gentle. Firm when they had to be."

The Joneses slept outside when they were traveling on their trapline or moving between camps. "My parents would make a little lean-to, and my mother had made a rabbit-skin blanket which was the warmest thing I ever had. When we were sleeping outside we'd tease her. I'd say, 'Look at me, look at me, I got a rabbit-skin blanket and you don't have anything. I'm a lot warmer than you are.' So a lot of those memories are fond memories."

Dan was four years old when he saw a white man for the first time. "We were swimming off the dock in front of the village and a float-plane landed in the bay and came over to the dock. I was scared. I'd seen planes in the sky, but never up close. It was so loud. A man got out and he looked strange to me. I told my mom that something was wrong with his skin. That a man was here and he must be sick. She told me he was fine. He was white. He just wasn't like us." The plane was there to pick up winter furs.

Within a year Dan was taken from this idyllic childhood and sent to boarding school in Kenora, two and a half hours by car from Dan's community. His mother was told that if she didn't send him voluntarily the kids would be taken anyway, and instead of seeing them on holidays and over the summer, she wouldn't see them at all for years. So she let them go. The school wasn't all that far from Redgut Bay. The boarding school Dennis and Dan Jones attended was a unique model—they were housed in dorms as part of the residential school system but bused to a public school they attended along with white children. It was supposed to be a good place for Indian kids; a lot of the staff and teachers were Indian, too. But this only made it worse. The betrayals more severe. "I remember watching the white kids get off the bus (we rode the same bus) and their parents were standing there and watching and waving. I looked at that just forlornly. Later my kindergarten teacher asked us what we wanted to be when we grew up. Everybody said fireman, lawyer, stuff like that. I said I wanted to be white when I grew up, because, to me, being white meant you had privilege, you got to go home to your parents, you had all these things."

Within a few months Dan, who knew no life other than his Indian life, began to think of his Indian life as a shameful impediment, and looked on with longing at the lives the white kids around him were encouraged to lead.

Dan and his brother Dennis were kept together, so at least they had that, but they were separated from their older brothers and sister who were already there.

While still in kindergarten Dan, who had never been hit in his life, started getting beaten, as a matter of school policy. "He'd come up with a strap or a paddle, and he'd call our names. The teacher would say, are you Dan? Yes, I am. Did you—and he'd read something off a piece of paper. I couldn't really understand him so I'd say, 'Yes, yes I did.' 'Well, you're going to get the strap.' And they showed me the paddle and the belt and asked me which one I wanted. I didn't even know what the paddle was for, but I knew a belt could be useful, you could keep your pants up with one of those, so I said, 'The belt, please.' And they pulled my pants down and had me bend over and they started to hit me with that. I don't know what I was doing wrong. I think it was because I was using Ojibwe, Anishinaabemowin."

Even some of the older boys would torture Dan and Dennis. One boy from the reserve near theirs told Dan and Dennis that their parents had died and they would never get to go home. Dan and Dennis had no way to know if this was true or not.

"The loneliness was overwhelming," says Dan. "Not just a month at a time. But two, three, months. I quit counting days. It was unbearable. I remember shaking and thinking to myself that I got no resources, no one to turn to, and all those feelings stayed with me a long time. I didn't realize how deep those feelings ran until I started having kids of my own."

In the second year that Dan and Dennis were there, things got worse. Around that time the school administration changed. The school hired Indian administrators, trying to make residential boarding school more culturally sensitive. It also hired a "boys' keeper" who oversaw the boys' dorm on the weekends. "His name was Gerry Red Sky," says Dan, "and I was glad that he was there. A Native role model. Someone I could look up to who would understand me. He was from Kenora, near Kenora." Dan's joy soured quickly.

"Gerry Red Sky would visit me in bed. The first time I woke up and he was penetrating me. I was scared. I didn't understand. I said I had to go to the bathroom and I hid in there. A few times I fell asleep in the bathroom because I was so scared to come out. He kept trying. He got me once and I went to the bathroom and sat on the toilet and blood came out. I couldn't understand why I was bleeding. I was spilling blood all over the place. I was six years old. In talking to my sister Shirley, my older sister, later in life, I never knew that she knew. But she did. She'd gone and offered herself to Gerry so that he would leave me and Dennis alone. And so he was violating her, and not honoring his agreement with her to leave us alone." Gerry Red Sky anally raped Dan and most likely many others until he stopped working there after six months. Evidently Dennis, as an adult, went looking for him, to settle the score. Gerry Red Sky was homeless on the streets of Kenora.

Dan and Dennis emerged from boarding school in awful shape. They drank, smoked dope, and fought. They have a typical Ojibwe build: short, stocky, wide-shouldered, thick-waisted, with strong legs and hands. They have dark skin and black hair that is now turning gray. They are cheerful, funny, and hardworking. It is hard for me to imagine them back in their wild days. But once I was walking down the road at Seine River Indian Reserve with Dennis and his wife. A man was walking toward us. When he recognized Dennis he walked across the road and passed us on the other side and then switched back. I asked what that was all about. Dennis said he didn't know. His wife, Lorraine, said, *Oh, Bouncy* [Dennis's nickname] *beat him up once.*

He did? *We were at a party up the road and he insulted me, called me names. Bouncy beat him up in the kitchen and then threw him down the front steps.* Lorraine laughed and stroked Dennis's neck. I could tell Dennis was embarrassed. *You were just sticking up for me, you tough guy, you.* And she laughed. I would think twice about fighting either one of them.

But both Dennis and Dan turned their lives around. By age nineteen Dan quit drinking. Dennis quit soon thereafter. They went to college and got their teaching degrees. Both have children and both teach children and college students the Ojibwe language they grew up with, the language the Canadian government couldn't quite beat out of them. Both brothers credit the language, their culture, and the time spent with their parents trapping, fishing, and living Indian lives as the forces that helped them endure and eventually overcome the residential school experience. Both men happily live lives of meaning, helping others recover from trauma.

Forced assimilation in the form of allotment and boarding schools had terrible effects on reservation life and Indian lives. But as bad as the U.S. government has been in its treatment of Indians, sometimes Indians are as bad or even worse to one another. One really fucked-up aspect of Indian life is that, unlike any other minority, Indians have rules, based on genetics and "blood quantum," that determine whether or not someone is *officially* an Indian. Brooke Mosay Ammann is one of the people on the wrong side of that determination. She is, as far as her tribe and the BIA and the U.S. government are concerned, not really an Indian.

Born in 1975 to Dora Mosay and Tony Ammann, Brooke is about as Indian as they come. Brooke's father, Tony, is a broad-shouldered, balding, white man of Swiss descent, a marine (once a marine, always a marine) who has been a union sheet-metal worker for his entire adult life since he got out of the service. Tony fell in love with and married Dora Mosay, the daughter of the spiritual chief Archie Mosay. Archie (who was given that name by an employer who found his Ojibwe name, Nibaa-giizhig, unpronounceable) was born in 1901 near Balsam Lake, Wisconsin, in a small village of wigwams. This village was one of the few that had resisted removal to Lac Courte Oreilles Reservation. "There were Indians all over, living on nothing," says Brooke. "When they came around with the IRA boilerplate constitutions, the plan was that all the St. Croix people would move to Hertel. And all these Indians around these little towns like Luck, Balsam Lake, Milltown, Round Lake. My grandfather was part of making sure people didn't move. He didn't want to leave his old village at Balsam Lake. That was his life's work—to stay there." As a result they got nothing from the government: no housing, no annuities, no food. Their poverty forced them to live as their ancestors had lived for generations: in bark-covered wigwams made of bent maple and ironwood saplings. They hauled their water from a natural spring; slept on bulrush mats; killed deer, ducks, and fish; and harvested wild rice. Archie's father, Mike Mosay, was a spiritual leader for the entire region and ran the much-protected and secret Grand Medicine Lodge until he was well over 100. Archie and his brothers served as messengers, or oshkaabewisag, for their father, a coveted and important ceremonial position. Archie, since he was the second-born, was the second or number two messenger. His brother was niigane-oshkaabewis, number one. The only change in this order occurred when Archie's brother went away to fight in World War I, during which time Archie assumed his duties. When the war was over and his brother came back, Archie was bumped back down to number two.

Archie grew up and worked for the county road crew (a job he held for life). He never went to school and never lived anywhere other than the village where he was born. He had his own children, nine of them. His first wife and one son died during the flu epidemic of 1918.

All his children were born in wigwams or tar paper shacks and lived in the village of their father's birth. When Archie's father, Mike, died in the 1970s Archie waited seven years, then took over his duties as the chief of the Grand Medicine Lodge. His daughter Dora held the ceremonial position of boss lady, equal to the boss or chief, a position she still holds.

Dora, a full-blooded Ojibwe, with a wrinkled face and carefully cut and set salt-and-pepper hair, could illustrate an encyclopedia entry for "Ojibwe woman." She, in her late sixties, still scrubs her floors on hands and knees. She can't abide a mess. She sometimes sneaks cigarettes. She always wears a bandanna or kerchief tied over her hair when she goes out in the woods. She is rigid but soft-spoken. When she decides to be funny she can be devastating. Her voice is a dead ringer for that of Marge Simpson.

Since Brooke's father is white and her mother is a full-blood, Brooke is, technically, half Indian by blood (though you can't measure culture by percentages of blood). The fractions, in her case, are straightforward. But there is some dispute at the tribal level; for some reason Archie Mosay's wife is listed as having a white grandfather, and so Archie's children are considered slightly less than full-blood and Brooke is considered slightly less than half-blood.

"There are old animosities," says Brooke. "He fought removal to Hertel during the 1930s. People were jealous of his ceremonial position. Jealousy—that's a big symptom of rez life, let me tell you." As a result of this animosity, Brooke, on paper at least, has slightly less than one-half Indian blood.

"We didn't live on 'the rez.' I mean, I didn't grow up in the village of Round Lake or Maple Plain or Danbury or wherever. I grew up in New Richmond. I spent every weekend when I was a kid with my grandfather and my extended family. We were connected, you know? He didn't, technically, live on the rez either. He lived in a place that predated the reservation." Connected to her Indian family, and encouraged by the educational director of the St. Croix Band of Ojibwe, Brooke applied to and was accepted at Dartmouth. After Dartmouth she moved to New Mexico and then eventually back to St. Croix, where she worked as the education director from 2002 to 2004. She took a leave to attend Harvard and got her MA at the Harvard Graduate School of Education. She came back and held her job at St. Croix until 2010. "I lost my uncle Wayne and my aunt Betsy. I wanted to be home. Everyone, all those old people, were passing, and I wanted to be home. I wanted to help people."

But even though she is the granddaughter of the most important Ojibwe ceremonial chief of the twentieth century, even though she has spent the better part of her life living her Indian ways and participating in ceremony, even though she is now the educational director for the tribe—despite all that, Brooke is, as far as the tribe and the federal government are concerned, not Indian. The St. Croix tribe requires at least one-half Indian blood and descent from the St. Croix Band for membership. This means that Brooke can't run for tribal office. She doesn't receive per capita payments. (The tribe is very small and has a large casino; until recently per capita payments were $1,000 a month.) She doesn't qualify for health care from the Indian Health Service (IHS, one of the many provisions of treaties signed by Ojibwe bands and the U.S. government). She cannot live in tribal housing. She didn't get federal financial aid for college, available to most enrolled Indians as part of their treaty rights. She cannot get anything from her tribe or the government; nor—and this is more alarming for her people—can she give as much as she could.

"It factors. Enrollment matters," says Brooke. In her years working for her tribe Brooke focused on how to create supportive policy for incorporating Ojibwe language and culture into school culture; on second-language teaching and learning; and on, in her words, "decolonizing school policy." She applied for and received an Administration for Native American Native Language Revitalization grant. But, as Brooke says ruefully, "This work was my downfall. Doing language work in a Native community opens you up to all sorts of criticism. Add that I was Ivy League–educated, a Mosay, and not enrolled in the tribe, practiced our ceremonies, and I dared ask questions of the tribal council and questioned their actions as I would question the supposed leaders of any nation. Add all that up and you have a threatening woman on your hands." So much so that Brooke was fired in the winter of 2010.

"We're breeding ourselves out of existence. And that's what the government wants. It's used to divide people—those who are in and those who aren't. At the bottom of it, I think it's chauvinism. I really do. We've adopted those harmful attitudes because of colonialism. We've bought in to all that us-them stuff. It's symptomatic. And when there's power to be had, who suffers most? Women. If you want to gauge the health of a community, of a nation, look to the women. If they are suffering from threats of violence, fear, poor health in any form—physical, mental, spiritual—lack access to education—both traditional and academic—then there is something wrong with your nation. There is something wrong with ours and there is something wrong with America. I am an underemployed feminist super Indian. But I can't get enrolled and I can't keep my job because of all that tribal jealousy and fighting and dysfunction. Let me tell you this, since I don't have to worry about my job any more: tribal council is where good ideas go to die. And that's the truth. The other truth is that we need to enlist the aid of all the people for success. We need the help of others, even non-Natives, even the marginalized. We have to work together. Sometimes I think—ah, the hell with you Indians. I tried, I did my time. I worked for the tribe for eight years, a good run. But then I remember my grandfather. He never gave up."

Sure, it would be nice if Brooke were officially Indian. It means something to Indians to be enrolled and it means something else not to be. Since Brooke is not enrolled, she enjoys none of the treaty rights her family fought so hard to maintain. She gets no per capita payments from the casino, no health care from the tribe or IHS, no housing. She can't hunt, gather, or fish on the reserved lands. "I had to suffer through the treaty wars," she says, "I was threatened and abused along with my fellow Indians but share in none of the bounty. I have to buy a permit like any white person to harvest my sacred food, the wild rice. And I can't do it on my reservation because that is reserved for enrollees." But Brooke will be OK. She is educated, ambitious, and hardworking and remains committed to her Indian life. Having managed all this, she is, by any standard, a success. She is an Indian success and she is also an American success—proof that you can rise up; you can go from humble origins to success with humility; you can go from having a tenuous hold on the American fabric to being wrapped up in it in just a generation. The greater loss is to her tribe. It could use her. It would, I think, benefit from her inclusion. She knows this, even if the tribe doesn't. Proof: her two sons are named Tecumseh and Osceola. The historical Tecumseh led a pan-Indian effort to overthrow the U.S. government in the early 1800s. Osceola was the Seminole war chief who fought the Americans to a standstill during the Second Seminole War. He was captured through deceit—lured out of hiding with promises that the Americans would capitulate.

"Blood quantum" is a strange way to determine who is and who is not officially Indian. And whatever impact this might have on how one feels about one's identity, such exclusions have direct and sometimes dire consequences for people much poorer than Brooke. There have been blood quantum laws on the books since the eighteenth century, most notably in Virginia, where it was illegal to mix with Indians and blacks. Ironically, "one drop" laws (one drop of black blood made you black) were reversed for Indians: they had to prove they had a certain fraction of Indian blood in order to qualify for enrollment and membership and to receive their treaty rights. But it wasn't until the 1930s that blood quantum became a widespread marker for racial descent, on which hung the issue of an Indian's nationality. Until then, for hundreds of years, Indian tribes had various means of including or excluding someone. Many tribes, mine among them, practiced widespread "adoptions." Indian children (and often white children) were captured or kidnapped and formally adopted into Ojibwe families to replace children and men lost in war or lost to disease. That's what happened to John Tanner in the mid-eighteenth century. He was abducted by Shawnee in the Ohio River valley when he was about ten years old, was marched into northern Ohio and Michigan, and later was sold to an Ojibwe family. He grew up among the Ojibwe, spoke our language, married an Ojibwe woman, and made his life with us. Not that it was always a happy life for him—his Shawnee captors beat him, left him for dead, smeared feces on his face, and piled other humiliations on him during his captivity. His Ojibwe family was only marginally more loving, until he proved he could hunt and provide for them. Indians from other tribes were adopted or married in and they enjoyed not only an Indian identity but the rights secured by the tribes and bands they joined.

Such fluid cultural boundaries became more rigid in the twentieth century. As part of the IRA, which brought constitutional government to many tribes, the tribes could set their own blood quantum requirements for enrollment (half, one-fourth, one-sixteenth, or whatever), but only in consultation with, and with the approval of, the BIA. Since its inception, even though Indians are the fastest-growing segment of the U.S. population, official Indians in some tribes are declining. That is, many tribes are getting smaller.

Now many tribes are shrinking by their own efforts. The Mde-wakanton Sioux Community has roughly 250 enrolled members. This number has remained quite static for the last twenty years—interestingly, the period when the tribe has run multibillion-dollar Mystic Lake Casino. The Mdewakanton is supposed to be a community reserved for the descendants of Dakota Indians who sided with the U.S. government during the Dakota Conflict of 1862. In payment for their support and their reluctance to join their tribesmen they were given land near present-day Shakopee, Minnesota. However, a lawsuit working its way through the courts alleges that there are more than 20,000 eligible enrollees (according to blood quantum rules on the books) living in the United States and Canada who meet the tribal enrollment criteria and can prove membership to the band at Shako-pee. These descendants have appealed to the tribe and been rejected. The tribe doesn't want them and doesn't want to enroll them. In their case this is not a matter of "identity" but a matter of resources. If enrolled they would be entitled, along with the 250 officially enrolled members, to per capita payments, which would drop from $80,000 a month down to $1,000 a month. It is easy to see why the Indians in power and enrolled at Shakopee don't want to open their arms to their tribal brothers. They are as greedy as any other Americans; I can't think of many people who after a lifetime of struggle would gladly give up $1.2 million a year in exchange for the moral high ground.

Who gets to be an official Indian and who is an unofficial Indian is sometimes a matter of identity and insecurity about that identity. Sometimes it is a matter of economics and greed. In both instances tribal enrollment confuses race (descent) and culture (environment). Being enrolled won't necessarily make you more culturally Indian. And not being enrolled won't make you less so. But enrollment and nonenrollment can make you more or less poor and can determine where and how you live.

* * *

One of the strangest and most fascinating instances of the question "Who is and who isn't Indian?" is the case of the Cherokee Freedmen.

The forced removal of Cherokee and the other four members of the Five Civilized Tribes from their lands in Georgia, Florida, Tennessee, Kentucky, and South Carolina in the 1820s and 1830s to the Indian Territories on what was known as the Trail of Tears has become a symbolic moment in American history. The Trail of Tears has come to signify American injustice, Indian-hating presidents, paternalistic Supreme Court justices, and the Indians' plight in general. It has been written about, sung about, painted, reenacted. The Trail of Tears was brutal. Of the 15,000 Indians who were forced to march to Indian Territory in the dead of winter, 4,000 died along the way—from starvation, hypothermia, typhus, or pneumonia. One can envision the long line of the downtrodden and disposed staggering through blizzards and fording icy rivers. The Cherokee and allied tribes were forced to march because they had been dispossessed. Their 5,000 black slaves were forced to march because they were the personal property of the Indians. Once they reached Oklahoma, the black slaves continued to be slaves until emancipation. During the Civil War the Cherokee Nation was divided. Some Cherokee sided with the Union, others with the Confederacy. After the Union victory the Cherokee Nation was forced to the negotiating table, largely as punishment for supporting the Confederacy, and forced to sign a treaty. One stipulation of the treaty of 1866 was that former Cherokee slaves, known as Freedmen, were to be given full citizenship in the Cherokee Nation. As members of the Cherokee Nation, the Freedmen would be entitled to all the rights and benefits of Cherokee citizens, such as allotments, the right to vote in tribal elections, the right to stand for office, and receipt of annuities.

A little over 100 years later the Cherokee Nation wanted to remove the descendants of the Freedmen from the rolls and deprive them of tribal membership. This meant that these descendants—who considered themselves culturally (if not completely racially) Cherokee, who had lived and worked on Cherokee lands, who had the same values and language as the Cherokee—would no longer be eligible to vote, hold office, receive federal housing assistance, or receive whatever casino profits might come their way. One can smell divisive greed in the air again, though one senses something else, too: the Cherokee in Oklahoma have long had one of the most welcoming, inclusive, and progressive enrollment policies. Unlike the St. Croix Band of Ojibwe in Wisconsin, the Cherokee Nation requires only proof of descent from the "Dawes rolls," a list of Cherokee and other Civilized Tribe members compiled in 1893 and closed in 1907 for the purpose of allotment. The Dawes rolls had included a few categories of tribal membership: by blood; by marriage; and, specifically, Freedmen or descendants of Freedmen, and Delaware Indians adopted into the Cherokee Nation. There is no minimum blood quantum requirement. Such a policy has been a blessing and a curse to the Cherokee. With more than 250,000 enrolled members living in almost every state in the Union, they have remarkable power of presence and numbers and a much more flexible understanding than any other tribe of what it might mean to be Indian. They also suffer from encroachment and the constant threat of cultural dissolution through acculturation—many who want to be Indian claim to be Cherokee, not because they are but because it's easy. Hence the popular refrain we all hear at parties: my grandmother was a Cherokee princess. (No one seriously claims to be descended from a Hopi princess, a Dakota princess, or an Inuit princess.)

In the late 1980s the Cherokee Nation tried to disenroll the descendants of the Freedmen. The case went to federal court, which ruled in *Nero v. Cherokee Nation* that tribes had the right to determine the criteria of their own tribal membership. This ran counter to a century of policy that said tribes could determine the criteria for membership but only in "consultation" with the BIA. Many members of the Cherokee Nation were (and are) divided over the issue, and in 2006 the Cherokee Nation Judicial Appeals Tribunal maintained that the Freedmen were potentially eligible for enrollment. The Cherokee Nation put the issue to a referendum, and as a result a constitutional amendment was passed in 2007 that limited membership in the Cherokee Nation to those who were Cherokee, Shawnee, or Delaware by blood, listed on the Dawes rolls.

The wheels on the bus go round and round. The Black Congressional Caucus got involved. It saw the exclusion of the Cherokee Freedmen as an instance of exclusion based on race. As the case worked its way through the courts, Representative Diane Watson of California introduced legislation that would block $300 million in federal funding and annul all gaming compacts between the Cherokee and the state of Oklahoma until the Cherokee Nation reinstated the Freedmen. The basis for the legislation is about as potent an irony as exists in the history of Indian-white relations: the Cherokee were being punished for breaking a treaty they made in "good faith" with the United States!

The U.S. government and the state government of Oklahoma don't want to be too hasty or too autocratic in dealing with the Cherokee Nation—if only because the Cherokee suffered so much, before, during, and after the Trail of Tears. But haven't the Cherokee Freedmen—not just disposed, but the dehumanized *property* of the dispossessed—suffered more? In 1828, leading up to the Trail of Tears, the Cherokee had standing in U.S. courts. Their slaves did not. Tribal enrollment has been, from the beginning, a way of determining who can claim economic benefits that devolve from treaties. From the start, enrollment and Indian citizenship have been institutions created by the U.S. government as a way of limiting its responsibility toward Indians and eventually getting out of the "Indian business." But it couldn't always control the ways in which tribes sought to define themselves. Blood quantum was supposed to be a way out for the government. But this has been tricky. The Dawes rolls (and this fact seems to have been lost) were created as a means of fractionalizing collective Cherokee landholdings and opening up the Indian Territories for white settlement. When the white bureaucrats made the rolls, they listed people who looked Cherokee as Cherokee, and those who looked black (even if these were mixed black and Cherokee) as black. The Dawes rolls were based on blood, but only on how blood "looked" (and here we remember the anthropologists scratching the chests of White Earth Indians and measuring their skulls). From the beginning, the rolls were flawed and were designed to cheat Indians. One wonders: why rely on them now for any purpose? Enrollment has become a kind of signifier for Indians that says (or is believed to say) what someone's degree of Indianness is. But this is a relatively recent development. One wonders: by fighting about enrollment at all, aren't we just adopting a system of exclusion that helps the U.S. government but doesn't help us? And couldn't the Cherokee have won a little something from everyone had they thought of the problems of race, identity, and enrollment differently? After all, very few nations in the world base citizenship on race. It can be based on many things—such as language, a naturalization process, an oath, residency, or all of the above. Couldn't the Cherokee Nation say: since we were slaveholders, we have a moral debt to the descendants of the people we wrongly enslaved? Couldn't the Cherokee say: in order to pay that debt we will allow the Freedmen to remain on the rolls as citizens of the Cherokee Nation (or even limited citizens, nonvoting citizens, or whatever), though they are not racially Cherokee? This way the Cherokee would have sacrificed some autonomy and spread some resources a little thinner but would have made right a historical wrong and emerged as the moral victors in the enrollment issue.

Many Indian tribes, many reservations, are stronger than they have ever been before. Gaming has something to do with that. So do numbers. But we are not so strong that we can afford to waste our people. We are not so strong that we can keep excluding one another. But that's exactly what tribes often do. At Leech Lake, for example, we are undoing, in exchange for very little, a lot of the hard work done by those who have come before.

Being enrolled at Leech Lake gives you a few advantages—treaty rights, health care, housing, education assistance, and access to a host of social service networks. But even being enrolled might not be enough. In 2007 Leech Lake Reservation signed a new compact with the Minnesota Department of Human Services regarding the care of enrolled children at Leech Lake. The compact clearly protects the sovereign *right* of Leech Lake to maintain jurisdiction over its kids on and off the rez but makes counties responsible for funding court orders regarding child welfare. This was an apparent win for the tribes, plus the financial bonus of direct funding for their own social security programs. But the compact also absolves the tribes of any financial responsibilities for paying the costs of Relative Care Assistance, MFIP, TANF, and other related social security programs. So the tribe can and now customarily does decide not to pay for anything other than its own court costs. Thus, the request to have the tribe provide a chemical dependency evaluation of the son of a friend of mine would have cost the tribe $150 and an hour of someone's time. But, since the tribe is empowered by the compact to require counties to be financially responsible, it said: we can't help you. That doesn't matter in any real way, except that the Leech Lake Band of Ojibwe recently made a deal with the state of Minnesota and the counties that overlap the reservation. The deal (as part of the Indian Child Welfare Act and other agreements with the state) was that Leech Lake would release the counties (Hubbard, Cass, Itasca, and Beltrami) and the state from the responsibility of providing social services to Indian young people (fought for and won by the passing of the Indian Child Welfare Act) in exchange for $1 million a year. The counties and the state were thrilled. The $1 million was a small price to pay. They were spending much more than that serving the hundreds, if not thousands, of Leech Lake children who live off the reservation. Most Leech Lakers don't live on the rez. Only about one-fourth of the enrolled population lives there. So three-fourths of the tribe (even if they live within sight of the reservation boundary) don't get the benefits that are theirs by treaty and congressional act.

Meanwhile my friend's son was drinking and drugging. He got the clap at age sixteen. He said he is suicidal. The boy is an enrolled member of the Minnesota Chippewa Tribe at Leech Lake. However, father and son live 500 yards outside the reservation boundary. They get no chemical dependency counseling, no foster care, no psychological or CD assessment. This is much less sexy than the fate of freed slaves or per capita payments or rich Indians. It's less sexy, less interesting, but more important—what little safety is provided by social services is desperately needed by the most vulnerable, the poorest, the most disenfranchised Indians. Interestingly, as part of the tribal constitution all the elected officials must live on the reservation to hold office. So those making decisions (such as the decision to deal with the counties) aren't making choices that could hurt them directly. They've sold out hard-earned ICWA rights. To put it another way, they've sold out our children. My friend's son will be emancipated in a year and a half. He figures he's got one last chance to turn his son's life around before he's lost. He feels that the tribe doesn't care about him or his children.

Less final but perhaps as damning is the identity war that plagues Indian communities on and off the reservation. Being "from the rez" has become a kind of marker of authenticity for many Indians—more important and more telling than being enrolled or being full-blood, quarter-blood, or whatever else. You'll hear it said of someone, "Oh, yeah, he's Indian, I guess, but he's not from the rez." In that is a kind of commentary on the authenticity, the degree of Indianness, that someone does or doesn't possess. Unlike the criterion applied to Brooke, this degree of Indianness can't be measured, but it is as final as the kinds of comments made about someone who is African American by blood but lacks the social credentials that make him or her "really black." Such is the thinking, anyway. But the problem of Indian identity is far more complicated than the terms of such identity wars would suggest.

For instance, Ryan Haasch could be considered about as "rezzy" as the next guy. He was born in Stevens Point, Wisconsin, and moved with his parents at age two to a modest split-level on the Leech Lake Reservation. That is where he grew up, in the small enclave (you can't really call it a village anymore) of Mission, just north of Cass Lake. Ryan's father worked for the Leech Lake Reservation vocational training program and his mother is a teacher at the Alternative Learning Center (ALC), a school within the Cass Lake Schools for at-risk or troubled kids. Most of her students are Indian. Ryan is a good man: thirty years old, of medium height, a teacher like his mother. He plays in softball leagues and is a drummer and songwriter for a punk band he started with friends in Minneapolis. But Ryan has no Indian blood to speak of: he is white. Because of the Dawes Act and the Nelson Act and the economic superiority of non-Indians for the last 100 years, Ryan's family is one of many non-Indian families that live on reservations like Leech Lake. The stunning fact of life for many reservations is that there are more white people living there than Indian people.

Even though he was raised on a reservation, he never really gave it much thought while growing up. "I mean, I just lived there. Grew up there. I didn't go around thinking: 'I live on a reservation.' When I told people in college where I was from, where I lived, they were baffled."

Most people are. Most people assume that only Indians live on reservations, or that if white people live there it is only by special permission. As good a guy as Ryan is, he grew up on land that was taken from Indians around the turn of the century by way of the Dawes Act, either illegally or immorally or both. The land inside the external boundaries of the reservation that passed from Indian control to private, state, or county ownership creates some strange problems and even stranger jurisdictional complications. Much of the land inside the reservation boundary is not reservation land

As for Ryan, the only really noticeable effect of living on the reservation was that he was one of just three white kids on the school bus that brought them back and forth to school off the reservation in Bemidji. "The rest were Indian. It was a rough bus. These big kids sat in back. Corey Kingbird was one of them. He died in a police chase on Mission road. Gordon Fineday was another. I think he's still around. Corey would tell us these stories. He showed me his pinkie finger which was all bent and broken and he told us that he had to break his own pinkie as a gang initiation. I don't know if it was true, but when he told us that it *seemed* true. Anyway, these other kids would shoot spitballs at the back of my head and call me 'fucking white boy.'"

The other two white kids on the bus—Tommy Erickson (who was Indian by blood but blond and didn't himself identify as Indian) and Chris Rutledge—are dead. Chris overdosed on morphine patches and Tommy died when he fell asleep at the wheel of the car he was driving on his way back to school in North Dakota.

"Yeah, my school friends were scared to ride the bus with me. Chris Claypool and Mike Blodgett. Those were the names of my friends.

They were too scared to ride the bus to my house. Mike's mom would drive them out so they could sleep over."

Living on the reservation didn't really affect Ryan one way or the other, except for having to endure a bus ride with bullies.

"We'd bike all over the place. We'd bike to Cass Lake. Once or twice we got chased around Cass Lake by a bunch of Indian kids who wanted to beat us up. But that was about it."

Ryan and his buddies, however, were scared to go into the Plantation, a notoriously rough housing tract near the old village site, the Mission, about four miles from Ryan's house.

"When we'd go stay at Tommy Erickson's house—you know he lived in that place just off the highway near the Plantation—well, we'd just stick close to his house, in his yard. One time we saw some kids a ways away and they were yelling stuff at us, looking to fight. But we didn't go over there."

What Ryan described was a kind of continuum. He felt like a member of a minority on the bus, but not around his neighborhood (if the scattered houses set back from the highway in the woods can be described as a "neighborhood"). Most of his near neighbors were white, but many were not. There were the kids on the bus and Kevin Northbird, whom Ryan and his friends called "Guitar Man." However, just three miles down the road were the housing tracts called Plantation, Mission, and Macaroni Flats, where Ryan felt uncomfortable going. These tracts were coded as "Indian" zones.

There was a store just around the corner from Ryan's house called Midway Store (since it was midway between Bemidji and Cass Lake). It was owned by Guitar Man's father, Ron Northbird. Ryan and his friends called the Midway Store the Niij Store. "Niijii" is Ojibwe for "friend."

"We tried to shoplift at the Niij Store, but never could pull it off. Ron Northbird was too sharp. He had this way of watching us. It was very casual, but you could feel his eyes on you. We called him Eagle Eyes." It is a strange irony that white kids were trying to shoplift in an Indian-owned store on a reservation. But these were the contours of Ryan's life.

Maybe Ryan felt comfortable on the reservation because his parents worked there and because they were good people, like their son. They were respectful of Indians and Indian ways and didn't tolerate racism in their house.

"My dad was working on the rez for the vocational program. They'd be in the woods or something and he'd pull something off a tree to show his students, just rip it off the tree, and one of the guys in the program would say: 'You might want to put down some tobacco when you take something from a tree or from nature.' And my dad listened and he shared that stuff with us, the things he learned from his Indian students. I got a lot of credit for being my parents' son. One more story: when I was in high school, working at Wendy's in Bemidji, my coworker Z-Mark was a little older. He'd buy us beer and stuff. He was going out with a girl from Bena. Anyway, I was at a party at Z-Mark's little apartment in Bemidji and Darryl Stangel was there. He was from Bena, too. 'You're Patty's son,' he said. 'You should party with us. We're heading to Bena. Don't worry. No one will mess with you. Everyone'll be cool with you because you're Patty's son.'"

When asked what he sees when he thinks of "the reservation," Ryan says, "I think of Guitar Man. One time we heard this really loud guitar sound coming through the woods. I mean it was this loud, awesome, feedbacked guitar solo. We got on our bikes and rode around and we went by the Northbirds' house and there was Kevin on the deck. Guitar Man. This was the 1980s. And he had on some black concert T-shirt, AC/DC or something. And short bright orange running shorts and white high-top sneakers, the ones they had in the 1980s with big tongues and laces. And Guitar Man had all this hair, loads of it, and it was curly and wavy. And he's on the deck with his guitar and amp just jamming, letting it rip out in the middle of the woods. It was awesome." But Ryan, even though he was "rez-raised" and grew up with many of the same markers of authentic Indianness as his neighbors like Guitar Man, such as brushes with the law, the violent deaths of close friends, and even violence in his own life, he lacks Indian blood—and so, despite everything, no one considers him Indian.

In part, impatience with the sometimes self-serving identity politics is what motivates language-immersion activists such as Keller Paap. They feel that if they are able to bring language back to the center of our sense of ourselves, all the other complicated politics of self, all the other markers of authenticity, will fall away. They feel that the government's attempt at assimilation created the destructive, diseased social fabric in which we are wrapped today. And so the work that Keller Paap, Lisa LaRonge, David Bisonette, Adrian Liberty, Leslie Harper, and others are doing to bring the Ojibwe language back is, essentially, an antiassimilationist movement. In many ways it turns around what AIM started. (One of AIM's cries was "Indian pride"—and AIMsters didn't style themselves as BIA bureaucrats with short hair and bolo ties.) The renewed interest in tribal cultures and tribal language runs against hundreds of years of government policy. It also runs directly against the thoughts of many Indians.

In the late nineteenth century many powerful Indians—Dr. Charles Eastman, William Warren, George Copway, and others—were pro-assimilation. They had witnessed the gradual encroachment of whites, the power of the U.S. government, the advantages of technology, and even the advantages of Western medicine and agrarianism and made up their own minds: assimilation was the only way Indians would live. It was assimilate or die. Assimilation wasn't always a grand ideological choice—it was a physical one. In contrast, traditionals (in places such as Montana, Nebraska, and South Dakota) couldn't live the way they had lived but didn't know how to live on their newly created reservations. One could either watch one's children die from disease or warfare or see them survive—with short hair, speaking English, and practicing Catholicism. Many of the graduates of boarding schools found themselves with an education, skills, social networks, clothes, food, and employment. Many of them did just fine in boarding school and they couldn't help seeing assimilation as the best course. In contrast to suffering, starving, and dying, assimilation was a logical, realist, practical choice.

There were a few Indian activists who took assimilation to its fullest in the early twentieth century. One of these was the "fiery Apache," Carlos Montezuma. A Yavapai Indian (it is unclear why he became known as the "fiery Apache") from Arizona, named Wassaja in the Pima language, he was captured by Pima Indians in 1871 when he was five years old and sold to Carlo Gentile, a traveling photographer, for thirty dollars. Shortly before his death, Gentile said to an interviewer from a Chicago paper (with Montezuma listening in) that this purchase was "the best investment I ever made in my life." Carlo Gentile named the boy Carlos Montezuma and raised him in the East. Gentile speculated in various businesses, lost everything, and, upon their return to Chicago, committed suicide. The young Montezuma was placed in the American Baptist Home Mission where he got a good education—good enough so that the young Yavapai was admitted to the University of Illinois. He graduated in 1884 and soon afterward received his medical degree from Chicago Medical College. Montezuma opened a private practice and became an Indian activist after meeting and befriending Captain Pratt at Carlisle Indian Boarding School in Pennsylvania. His work as a doctor brought him to North Dakota, Montana, and the Colville Agency in Washington. He saw, firsthand, reservation conditions and the brutal war between traditional life and "modern life." Not only did

Montezuma believe in assimilation, as did Pratt; he came to believe that in order to save Indians, every vestige of tribal life should be wiped away. Reservations, dance, language, customs, religion—all of it should be stamped out. He felt that other assimilationists, such as Pratt and Charles Eastman, were soft. The incremental approach they advocated was not enough. Half measures were not measures at all. He helped found the Society of American Indians, an exclusive Indian organization devoted to the idea of assimilation, in 1911. Montezuma began publishing a journal. He needed a forum for his extremist views and, since there wasn't one, he made one.

However, when Montezuma reached middle age he traveled back to the land of his people and a switch occurred. He came to believe in tribal life. Instead of fighting to abolish reservations and rez life he sought to protect them and it. When the U.S. government tried to relocate the Yavapai he fought their removal from their reservation with all his considerable power. He tried to become an enrolled member of the tribe. In 1922, dying of tuberculosis, he moved to Fort McDowell Reservation. He lived there in a traditional Yavapai grass hut until he died in 1923. He is buried on the reservation.

Keller Paap and the others working for language preservation believe in antiassimilation as strongly as the "fiery Apache" believed in assimilation, and for the same reasons—they are trying to save a people, and to have lives that are full of meaning. David Bisonette has been a part of Waadookodaading since the beginning and shares many of Keller's and Lisa's beliefs.

"We're headed down a dark road," he tells me. We're in Hayward, just off LCO reservation, sitting at a picnic table by Shue's Pond. Hayward is a notoriously racist town, a center of the anti-treaty protests that occurred during the walleye wars of the 1980s. David is a man of mystery. He is short and powerfully built. He laughs a lot and loudly and seems pretty much unafraid of anything. Sometimes he disappears into the American Southwest for weeks at a time. I've never seen him without a baseball cap on. He is a gifted visual artist, and an expert with a walleye spear. When I asked to see his driver's license, just for grins, he said, "Fuck you." And then he laughed. When he talks his narrative bounces all over the place. But there is real thought behind all of it. "We're headed down a dark road. People are unwilling to talk about the most important stuff that affects us. No one talks about acculturation. No one, I mean no one, wants to talk about that. Of course, if we do talk about it and write about it, then the dominant society can use that against us. But it's like the emperor's new clothes. I think that like ninety-eight percent of Indian people think powwow and having an enrollment card make them Indian."

He added, "Even at Navajo and Hopi. They think they're safe. They think they're not becoming acculturated. But they're close. It's a dangerous time."

David's been around, and he's been around a lot of different Indian communities.

"I'd been living out east. I'd done that. Lived in Rhode Island. I was almost killed on my bike. Hit by a car. I've done this. I want to go home. I was always interested in language and history. All my grandparents were church people. Because, well, my dad's parents, my one grandpa belonged to three Big Drum societies. But something happened. It was a time, in the 1950s. It was hard. I had two uncles killed within months of one another. One died of a war injury. The other was murdered in Chicago. It must have been in the fall, before they died. They were hunting—my grandfather and my father were hunting and saw some deer. My grandfather was a great shot and these deer ran in front of him and he missed. He never missed. He turned and told my dad, 'Something's going to happen.' Sure enough—two of his sons died. So they left LCO, they closed up shop. Maybe we'll do what everyone else is doing. It was impossible, an impossible situation they found themselves in. So maybe that's why they left.

"People don't remember how Indians were treated. People don't remember how hard it was. No one remembers how they had to go in the back door, never the front. My grandpa never went in the front door of a store. He always went in the back. It was OK if he spent his money there but no one wanted to see him. When you're dealing with that kind of thing, maybe leaving is the best option. Maybe letting your Indianness go is the answer. Trying to pass was about trying to make your life a little easier. Talking about that kind of thing hits a nerve."

David has strong opinions. One of them is that as hard as times are now, they aren't as hard now as they were back in the day. "It's easier now. Not easy, but easier. But people still want to blame the white man. They don't want to think about the choices they make. Like enrollment. If I got to decide how people would be enrolled, I'd say there'd have to be a language requirement. I mean, they did it in Estonia. They did it in Moldovia. Why can't we do that? Blood quantum doesn't tell you anything about a person's culture."

Brian Bisonette—David's older brother, the secretary-treasurer of the LCO Tribe—backs this up, to an extent: "You won't believe this, but two of the worst anti-treaty hecklers, the worst racists there ever were at those boat landings in the 1980s . . . they are enrolled members now. They checked out their history, found out they are Indian from here, and got enrolled. Now they spear! They spear fish—just because it's fun, not because they care about treaty rights or the community."

"Boarding schools," muses David, "changed us into Americans. But schools and blood quantum and all that stuff turned us into the worst kind of Americans. The worst thing that happened to us was that we became Americans. They trained us to become the worst kind of Americans and then blamed us for it. That's why language and culture are so important. By stressing those things we can stop being what they want us to be, bad Americans. But it took one hundred years to get to this point. It will take one hundred years to get us back."

David Bisonette, Keller Paap, Lisa LaRonge, and Alex Decoteau all believe in language and culture for the same reasons the "fiery Apache" changed his name back to his tribal name, Wassaja, and lived with his people—that reservations are a homeland, a community, islands of Indian majorities in a vast America that doesn't care about Indians.

For language activists, the language is the key to everything else—identity, life and lifestyle, home and homeland. Most language activists are also traditional Indians, but very modern traditional Indians, as likely to attend a ceremony as they are to have smartphones on which they record language material and Indian ceremonial music they are trying to learn. This new traditionalism is not a turning back of the clock, but a response to it; modernism (and modern, global capitalism) is a great obliterator of cultural difference and a great infuser of a new kind of class difference, and language activism is one way Indians are not only protecting themselves and their rights but also creating meaning in their lives. For Keller Paap and his family, this means tapping maple trees, ricing, hunting, collecting wild leeks, blasting Hendrix and Chris Whitley from the tinny speakers of their VW Westy van, and competing every year in the Birkebeiner cross-country ski race held in Hayward, Wisconsin. It means choosing to live their modern lives, with all those modern contradictions, in the Ojibwe language—to choose Ojibwe over English, whether for ceremony or for karaoke.

My older brother Anton and I, among many others, have for the last two years been working on a grant to record, transcribe, and translate Ojibwe speech in order to compile what will be the first (and only) practical Ojibwe-language grammar. During that time, we have traveled once, sometimes twice, a week from our homes on the western edge of Leech Lake to the east, to small communities such as Inger,

Onigum, Bena, and Ball Club, where we record Ojibwe-speakers. We've also taken longer trips, north to Red Lake Reservation and south to Mille Lacs. Recording Ojibwe speech in Minnesota, where the average age of fluent Ojibwe-speakers is fifty-five, means recording old people. My brother, at thirty-eight, is very good at this, much better than I am. For starters, he is much more fluent. And he looks like a handsomer version of Tonto: lean, of medium height, with clear eyes, a smooth face, very black shiny braids, and very white shiny teeth. This helps. He has made this kind of activity his life work; it is what he does.

Right after college, he apprenticed himself to Archie Mosay. When my brother met Archie in 1991, Archie was ninety-one years old. He had been born in a wigwam, apprenticed under his father to be a ceremonial chief, and earned an eagle feather when he was only fourteen by saving a woman who was being attacked by her husband (Archie was stabbed six times). Archie and my brother were friends. During the time of high ceremonies my brother worked for him, sang for him, helped him into and out of his wheelchair, translated for him, and listened to him—every day for at least fourteen hours a day, for weeks on end. Deep affection, respect, and tenderness ran in both directions. And it changed my brother's life. He had direct access to and deep involvement with a man out of our time and the satisfaction of friendship and affection and the deeper satisfaction that he was helping people, that his life had meaning.

It does something to a person. Arguably, Anton's best friend, all through the 1990s, was a man who had come of age in 1914 and who had spent most of his time with his own father (Mike Mosay, born in 1869) and grandfather (born when the Cherokee were being removed from Georgia to Oklahoma). While AIM might have made a name for itself standing in roads and occupying buildings, Anton, Keller, Adrian, Leslie, Lisa, and scores of others are making names for themselves standing next to old people, cooking for them, driving them to the store, and joking with them. It not only does something to a person but does something to a community as well. Fifty years ago many Indians believed what they were told—that they were best off learning how to nail two-by-fours together, perfecting their penmanship, and acquiring skills like tilling or accounting. The great shift is that on reservations around the country (many of them controlled by tribal councils that still believe in penmanship, accounting, the IRA, the BIA, and school-bonding bills more than anything else), Indians like Keller, Lisa, and David believe in the practical as well as the traditional. (Actually, the traditional is proving to be much more practical than anything the BIA and the U.S. government tried to shove down our throats. The students at the Waadookodaading Immersion School not only speak Ojibwe but test higher than the children their age in reservation and public schools around the state.)

All this activity around "old ways" and "old language" could be seen as an outgrowth of modernity more than a throwback to the past. Casinos have brought a lot of things to a lot of reservations— much more than good roast beef, poker tournaments, per capita payments, and personal wealth. Powwows such as Schemitzun at Foxwoods and the Shakopee powwow in Minnesota, and others largely funded by casino profits, have turned what were previously small social gatherings into a magnet for Indian talent. Dancing and singing competitions aren't just opportunities to display talent. Now you can win big money. At Schemitzun in 2007 the purse for the winning drum group was more than $20,000. The winning group, the Battle River Singers from Red Lake Reservation, split the purse ten ways among themselves, sold hundreds if not thousands of their CDs, and guaranteed themselves a place as a host drum (an honor and a financial boon) at powwows around the country. Drum groups and dancers can now make a living singing and dancing, or they can at least supplement their income. That is exactly what Tito (one of the Battle River Singers) did after Schemitzun. When I saw him at the car wash in Bemidji washing his almost new Buick, I asked, New car? *That there's my Schemitzun car,* he said. *Hoka hey.* There has been more talent and innovation in Indian singing, beadwork and visual arts, and dancing in the last twenty years than ever before, largely due to casino-sponsored powwows.

At Red Lake, after the fishery crashed and the tribal members brought it back, they found a way to blend their need to create industry and hold on to traditions by launching Red Lake Food Industries. Instead of robbing themselves of their own resources they turned themselves into a retailer of natural foods. The tribe pays members to pick berries (blueberries, cranberries, and the like), rice, and fish. And they create their own jelly and package their own rice, retail them over the Internet, and sell them in grocery stores across the country. Instead of fishing their lake and wholesaling the fish to distributors they have, since 2006, become a distributor in their own right—selling the fish netted on a few reservations in Minnesota and Canada. In doing so they are feeding their people, and their people are feeding a resurgence in tradition.

Last spring, I went spearing with Keller Paap and Dave Bisonette on a lake in their treaty area. Band members fought for and won the right to continue exercising their treaty rights on ceded land, and so they do. One of those rights is to spear and net walleye pike during the spring spawning. It is cold on the water in April, and it was that night. We took the boat across Round Lake to the northeastern shore and into the shallow waters where the fish spawn. One person ran the motor; the other stood in front wearing a headlamp and speared the fish with a long pole. With a few modern modifications, this is something we have done for centuries.

The night was very foggy. Mist skated over the water and billowed up, disturbed, over the gunwales of the boat. We kept close to shore. Round Lake is a resort lake and many of its bays and inlets are packed with houses. (It is rumored that Oprah Winfrey has a house there.) Most of these places were closed up, shuttered, waiting for the tourists to come in for the summer. The docks reached down into the lake as if testing the water but, finding it too cold, drew up halfway on the banks. Yet here and there, lights shone from living room windows. And when a house was perched especially close to the lake, we could see a television glowing ghostly and blue.

It was past ten o'clock. Dave, Keller, and I spoke Ojibwe over the puttering motor and the watery stab of the spear going down into the water and the clang as it came out with a walleye wiggling against the barbs. The pile of fish grew on the bottom of the boat, and they flapped dully, trying to fly against the unforgiving aluminum sky of the boat. A dog barked from shore. I could hear, clearly, Letterman's "Top Ten List" coming from an open window. Fish scales, knocked loose by the tines of the spear, were plastered all over the inside of the boat, and they sparkled like jewels when swept by the lamplight.

If we lose our language and the culture that goes with it, I think, something more will be lost than simply a bouquet of discrete understandings about bears or namesakes, more than an opportunity to speak to my children and friends in public without anyone eavesdropping. If the language dies, we will lose something personal, a degree of understanding that resides, for most fluent speakers, on an unconscious level. We will lose our sense of ourselves and our culture. There are many aspects of culture that are extralinguistic—that is, they exist outside or in spite of language: kinship, legal systems, governance, history, personal identity. But there is very little that is extralinguistic about a story, about language itself. I think what I am trying to say is that we will lose beauty—the beauty of the particular, the beauty of the past and the intricacies of a language tailored for our space in the world. That Native American cultures are imperiled is important and not just to Indians. It is important to everyone, or should be. When we lose cultures, we lose American plurality—the productive and lovely discomfort that true difference brings.

While spearing walleye on Round Lake that April I felt this way of life and the language that goes with it felt suddenly, almost painfully, too beautiful to lose, unique and too impossibly beautiful to be drowned out by the voice of a talk show host or by any other kind of linguistic static. And I thought then, with a growing confidence I don't always have: we might just make it.

Eugene Seelye and son Lance (Lanny) Seelye at Bena Cemetery, 1969

Eugene Seelye with grandsons Micah and David Treuer, Cass Lake, 2003

EULOGIES

A few weeks after my grandfather's funeral in August 2007, my mother called me and asked if I wanted to take over the payments on his new truck. My grandfather was a hard-ass and a skinflint. And he was sentimental, too. He never bought clothes or books. He never went to the movies. The furniture in his house was older than he was, and only occasionally could my grandmother sneak in something new to replace something that was falling apart. The only things he ever bought new were vehicles. He bought a new truck every two years and many used ones in between. You never really knew what he was driving because just when you got used to the Buick Century or the white Ford F150 he'd come rolling up in something else. By the time you visualized him in the new truck—the black Maxi-Cab GMC Sierra, say, or the tan Silverado with silver pinstripes—he'd have moved on to something newer. This was one of the strange exceptions to the usual stasis of his life. He wouldn't even let my grandmother change the curtains in the house, because his mother had sewn them fifty years earlier: since "Ma Seelye" had put them up, only she could take them down. I asked him once why he bought so many cars (after all, he had only his pension from the VA to live on). *I was supposed to drive a truck in the army, boy. But my truck didn't make it past Normandy.* So what did you do? *I didn't have nothing to drive in Belgium during the Bulge.* So what did you do? *I shot people instead.*

The day after my mother called, my uncle Davey came over to her house with the truck. It was a maroon 2006 Chevy Silverado with gray and silver decals, a tonneau cover, chrome running boards, tan leather seats, XM radio, OnStar, an off-road package, and a tow system. One hell of a truck. He'd barely driven it before he killed himself. There were only 14,000 miles on it. Davey took out some chains and some #120 body-grip traps from the back, and a battery charger (which Davey pronounced "bat tree," just like my grandfather) from the rear seat. There was a large piece of tagboard in the backseat. *You can have that,* said my uncle. The tagboard was hot pink and someone had taken a lot of care writing out and coloring in the phrase GRAND MARSHAL—BENA DAYS' PARADE. A few half-deflated balloons eddied on the floor. *What the hell is this?* I asked. *Oh,* said Davey. *We had Bena Days last week. The one hundredth anniversary of the town of Bena. Ma was the grand marshal.*

Davey's getting older. But he is still a tough guy. He possesses a toughness matched with a sense of humor and a sweetness not found in most people (a combination that always made him my favorite uncle). He was the first person to give me a drink, the first to take me deer hunting, the first (and only) person to catch a snowshoe hare with his bare hands because he thought I might want it as a pet. Once when I was feuding with a well-known Indian writer and Davey caught wind of what the other writer was saying, he slapped me on the back and said, *If he comes up here I'll be waiting and I'll stick him in the neck. With this,* and he lifted his shirt to reveal his skinning knife stuck in his belt. Once he came over and his glasses were held together with tape. I asked him what had happened. *Some guy cold-clocks me at the bar and breaks my damn glasses. So I get up and beat him down and then his dad comes to help him and I beat him up, too.* He's tough like that. But he's loving, too. Good to family. Good to me. That toughness is still there along with the tattoos acquired in North Carolina when he was with the 82nd Airborne at Fort Bragg. *Best time of my life,* he said about his time in the All American (AA) 82nd Airborne, an airborne infantry regiment that had included, among others, Sergeant York (who single-handedly took thirty-two German machine guns, killed twenty-eight German soldiers, and captured 132 others during the Meuse-Argonne offensive in World War I), Strom Thurmond, and Chief Dave Bald Eagle, the grandson of Sitting Bull. *I jumped out of planes all over the world—Africa, Scotland, Asia. Night jumps, blind jumps, high altitude, low altitude.*

Once when my grandfather was alive and we had taken out his World War II infantry uniform just to look at it, Davey had said, *Second Division! Second to none. First to run!* as only a member of the 82nd Airborne could say (even to his father, who had fought in Normandy, Belgium, and Germany and had been attached to the 101st Airborne Division). Even my grandfather laughed.

You should have seen it, Dave, he said, speaking of the Bena Days parade. *I drove the truck and Ma sat in the back on a lawn chair like a prom queen, waving all the way down the street.*

I could imagine it. My grandmother—still beautiful; still elegant; still, even in the worst instances, so poised—sitting on a lawn chair in the back of the truck, the other trucks and four wheelers and tractors and skidders snaking up from the old gravel pit past the empty Catholic church, the rectory, the empty Bena Grocery, the full Bena Bar, past the community center and new post office, and down to the ball field. She's almost blind, my grandmother, but I could imagine her riding in the back of her dead husband's truck. They had been together for more than sixty years but now were suddenly separated. I could imagine her waving to all the people, all the town, all that she could not see, while the truck (so plush, so stable) crunched along the gravelly asphalt and the people cheered. I could imagine her smiling at the hazy lines of people—whites and Indians, loggers and ex-cons, pipe fitters and guides, heavy-equipment operators and derelicts, maybe waving at the ghost of her husband in the ground for not even two weeks. Good for her, I thought. Though I also heard that she didn't ride in the Silverado at all. I heard that she was in a silver Mustang convertible.

There was a lot of paperwork we had to get through to put the truck in my name. I went to the Cass County Department of Motor Vehicles. But since the truck was registered through the tribe, I had to go across Cass Lake and talk to the folks at the Leech Lake Reservation Department of Motor Vehicles. I was told that since my grandfather was enrolled at Leech Lake but my grandmother was enrolled at White Earth and I lived in Minneapolis, I'd have to register the truck through the state. So I went back to the Cass County offices. Then I went to the bank to see if we could simply transfer the loan over to me rather than refinance. I was told there that I would need a credit report, all my financial information, and a copy of the death certificate. This I had to ask my grandmother for.

They just need proof, I told her. *Just some proof that he's gone.*

She didn't have a copy of the death certificate, but my mother did, so I had to drive back over to my mother's house. Then to the bank.

I walked into First Federal Bank in Bemidji and approached a teller. I told the teller I was taking over payments on my grandfather's truck and I needed to speak to a loan officer. I said my grandfather had died and that the truck was passing to me.

Oh, I'm so sorry, said one of the tellers. Young. Pretty. I was guessing farm-raised. *Who was he?*

Eugene Seelye.

Her hands flew to her face. *Oh! I know him. I'm so sorry. He was so sweet. He was such a sweet guy.*

No, I corrected her. Eugene Seelye.

Yeah, sure. Old. White hair. Kind of like Elvis.

Sweet? I asked.

The final step required that I come in with my grandmother, since she was the beneficiary of his estate. I met her outside the bank with my uncle Davey.

So they need the death certificate? You've got it? asked my grandmother.

I said I did.

Does it— She paused. *It doesn't say what he did, does it? It doesn't say how he died?*

I assured her it didn't. She seemed happy about that.

In the months after he died and I drove the truck around on the rez and off I had a strange feeling. Often as I pulled up in someone's yard or at the bank or the grocery store or a boat landing, people would stop what they were doing. They would stare at the tinted windows. Their hands hung by their sides. Rice knockers would drift down to rest against a leg. Wrenches would miss the nut. At first I thought all this activity stopped because the truck was so nice, or because people couldn't believe my success. But one after another they would say, *I thought you were Gene.* Or, *You scared the shit out of me.* It seemed they hadn't gotten used to the idea that he was dead, either. They expected him to ease his body out of the Silverado and wipe his eyes and say something smart-ass or sweet, depending. They expected him but they got me instead.

It got to be that so many people looked and saw the truck and saw my grandfather in it that I began to see the truck that way, too. I felt there was some overlap. I was driving it but so was he. I was behind the wheel but so was he. It wasn't a matter of succession (him and then

313

me) but of overlap—he and I. Not just that. I was driving and he was driving. I was smoking and he was smoking. I picked my teeth with his toothpicks and he did, too. I drove down the main street of Bena and we were both in the cab and my grandmother was in the back, waving, waving. And my uncle's traps were still there, and the "bat tree" charger. And when my mother took a ride in the truck she rode as "Maximum Margaret" and the "Queen of Bena" and the tough girl she'd been and the tough woman she'd been and the tough mother. And all of us—Indians all, and also writers, and judges, and vets, and criminals, and mothers, sons, grandfathers, and grandsons, and brothers, and sisters, and pagans and lapsed Catholics and unbelievers, and all of us; not succeeding one another and not shedding and donning but taking it all on at once. They say you can't step into the same river twice. But maybe a truer saying is that you can't ever dry off.

Before I got the truck, on the day of his funeral, I delivered the eulogy in the Catholic church in Deer River as my grandmother had asked me to do. Deer River is just over the rez line. The Catholic church in Bena is in disuse and services are no longer held there. The priest wore his vestments and the sash over his shoulders was beaded— some good Ojibwe Catholic must have made it for him. I had never spoken in a church before. I've never been to Mass. I've never been baptized. Christianity seems very strange to me—so ethnic, heavy in its symbolism, with liturgy and different clothes and all the kneeling and standing. My Ojibwe religion, in comparison, feels much more vanilla, much more matter-of-fact. The medicine men I know wear sweatpants and baseball caps more often than not. And there isn't the same kind of respectful heavy silence at the ceremonies. There's a lot of laughter, for one thing, and dirty jokes.

So I read my eulogy and my cousin Dereck read two passages from the Book of Lamentations. At the wake, when Father Paul had asked if one of us could read from the Bible, we'd all looked at one another in a panic. "I can't do that," said my brother Anton tactfully. "But maybe Nate can." Nate suggested Sam. Sam thought perhaps Megan could do it. Everyone was either too shy (never having read aloud in public before) or too pagan (such unbelievers that to read from the Bible would have felt like mocking it and mocking our grandfather, who did believe in it). Finally Dereck said, "Sure, I'll do it. I was an altar boy for Christ's sake."

Dereck usually wore baggy clothes, urban-style: drooping pants and hockey or football jerseys (Raiders). He also usually wore gold chains. His ear was pierced. His black hair was spiked and gelled. But on the day of the funeral he wore a suit. He wore it well. When it was his turn to speak he loped up to the altar confidently and opened the book to where Father Paul had marked it and began reading.

"Now I read to you from the Book of Lamentations. I am the man that hath seen affliction by the rod of his wrath. He hath led me, and brought me into darkness, but not into light. Surely against me is he turned; he turneth his hand against me all the day. My flesh and my skin hath he made old: he hath broken my bones. He hath builded against me, and compassed me with gall and travail. He hath set me in dark places, as they that be dead of old. He hath hedged me about, that I cannot get out: he hath made my chain heavy. Also when I cry and shout, he shutteth out my prayer—"

Father Paul interrupted Dereck impatiently and motioned to me. I rose from where I'd been sitting next to my mother, who was holding my grandmother's hand (I'd never seen them hold hands before). I was nervous, more nervous than I'd ever been before. I'd done hundreds of readings, but this was the first time I was going to read something I'd written for my family. The audience was all family. And the family knew my subject (my grandfather), if not better than I did, then certainly differently. I eulogized him as best I could.

315

The drive from Deer River to the cemetery seemed long, though it's not. It was a beautiful day. As we drove I looked out at the ditches and remembered that for many years, as a member of the U.S. Forest Service, my grandfather had cut that grass and brush and applied Agent Orange to the trees growing under the power lines, dispensing the chemical out of a canister strapped to his back. And the trees, still growing, still going about their single-minded business of up up up, had been logged by my grandfather's grandfather Charles Seelye. I thought of how, down Highway 8, my grandfather had shot a male lynx that was hanging around the dump. How he used to drink at the Bena Bar. How, up the Winnie Dam road, the dam itself had been built with Indian labor from Raven's Point—our ancestral village—brought across the lake on a steam-powered barge and put to work clearing the ground and driving the pilings and installing the sluices and that when it was done the water rose and flooded them out, flooded out the very people who built the dam and that's why the village moved to where Bena is today. Everything had been shaped by us in that place for a couple of hundred years. Everything I saw was saturated with family, with him, with us.

The cemetery was no exception. We gathered near the grave I had not dug because I was busy cleaning up his blood and brains from the floor of his bedroom. It was like the many others I had dug there, the same nice rectangle carved out of the sandy soil, soil that seems made for nothing better, for nothing more, than digging graves. There's hardly room to stand. The ground is filled with the bodies of my family. My aunt and one uncle and dozens of cousins and great-uncles and great-grandparents. I wonder how the ground can hold so many of our bodies. At times like this I think that maybe we won't make it. There are too many of us who are dead for us to make it. Too many of us are getting around to dying too soon. It's a wonder that there is enough Indian land to hold us all, to hold our bodies. And it's hard sometimes not to agree that we're all dead, and rez life isn't so much a life as an excavation: one large empty grave that no one has bothered to fill in or, better, can't fill in because we refuse to climb the crumbling sand.

Lost in these thoughts, I was standing to the side, behind a few rows of mourners. I had been a pallbearer and so I'd had my time with him, had done my duty. My mother, who was yet to break down, leaned over and said, "You're stepping on Stan." So I was. Stan Matthews. He'd been raised in the Cities but reconnected up north. And there was my uncle Boobsy (who had lost three fingers and an eye as a child when some other kids dared him to smoke a blasting cap). And Bumsy—the kindest, gentlest man who ever served thirty to life for holding up a jewelry store. The guy he was with was shot and killed by the owner. Bumsy got thirty. My older brother and I and my cousin Delbert would sit in his tiny tar paper shack on a summer evening and watch him comb his hair back and blot the stains from his Dickies and, when everything was ready, drink a spoonful of melted butter before heading out into the cricket-laden night to get drunk; the same Bumsy who once, while he was out of prison on parole, borrowed a car and got drunk and being lonely drove around Bena asking people if they wanted a ride. He must have been very drunk because everyone declined. Finally, in anger and spite, he picked up every single dog he could coax into the convertible, took down the top, and drove slow circles around the village, singing Johnny Cash so loudly the dogs howled along with him. And Vanessa. She's there, too. Resting in the sand. My cousin, my age. As defiant and tough and sassy an Indian girl as you'd ever meet. She once pushed me off the edge of an embankment into a gravel pit and said, "Take that you son of a bitch." She also said, much later, "Blood is thicker than water," and proved it a week later by driving her car through two yards, up the ditch, and into the path of an oncoming RV. And my uncle Sonny—who hunted deer from his bicycle and when stopped by the warden said there was nothing that said he couldn't hunt deer from a nonmotorized vehicle and the warden had to agree with him; Sonny who could read something once and have it memorized, including the teacher's exam key, which always sat on her desk.

And I began to wonder: maybe the miracle is not that the ground can hold so many Indian bodies. Maybe the miracle is that it is able to hold so much personality, because among the graves of my family and our village are the graves of our friends and neighbors. How on earth is it possible for that little bit of sandy soil on the south shore of Lake Winnibigoshish able to hold all that personality, all that history? And in all of us there is some Scottish blood, and Irish, too. Also French and German. And, going way back, African. There was, during the days of the fur trade, a black slave by the name of Bonga who was manumitted by his British owner at Fort Mitchilimackinac around 1790. He joined the French coureurs de bois, and made the trek from Mackinac Island to Montreal and over to Rainy Lake and back many times before he stopped in what is now Leech Lake and married an Ojibwe woman. There he stayed, as did his descendants, many of whom now have the last name Bonga. We come from them, too. And from Scots and Germans. There's more, I thought, much more. How can it all fit in here, how much more crowded with story and personality and life can the ground get?

The answer: always more. But as I looked around it was easy to see that we're not so short on personality aboveground, either. There's still plenty of that to go around. At Leech Lake and everywhere else, too. None of it is dead. None of the people are dead, none of the sense they made of their lives is dead, and on the reservation at least, none of the whims, acts, and actions of presidents, Indian agents, congressional reformers, tribal leaders, and tribal citizens are dead. Or if any of this is dead, it is certainly not buried: nowhere more than in reservation life can we see, can we feel, the past shaping the present. On the reservation the past is hardly past at all.

The coffin was down. Father Paul did whatever it is that Catholics do. The Leech Lake color guard was there—consisting of veterans from World War II, Korea, Vietnam, the First Gulf War, and Afghanistan. They saluted and fired three volleys, the sounds disappearing over the lake. My cousins and I collected the spent shells and threw them into the grave, and then we bent to work with the shovels and covered up what was left of my grandfather. The funeral was Catholic because he was Catholic. The ground is Indian. And those who dug the grave are Indian. And the lake and the earth that surround it are ours and are Indian, too. The Leech Lake Reservation color guard stood at attention and the American flag flew alongside the Leech Lake Reservation flag. I tried to see which one flew higher but it was impossible to say for sure.

AUTHOR'S NOTE

This book contains no composite characters or pseudonyms. No dialogue appears in quotation marks unless the person being interviewed was recorded on audiotape. Remembered remarks and remarks made that were not recorded do not appear in quotes. This book also does not use the kind of loose historicism that takes the form of "He must have been feeling": unless people said exactly how they felt, to the author or in print, I have refrained from speculating or giving them feelings. Opinions are mentioned as opinions, and facts as facts. When the two get blurred I've tried my best to distinguish between them.

Like reservations themselves, this book is a hybrid. It has elements of journalism, history, and memoir. As such it is meant to be suggestive rather than exhaustive. It is meant to capture some of the history and some of the truth of reservation life—which is not any one thing but many things depending on where you're looking and to whom you're talking. But if readers are interested in further sources, there are many places to begin. David Wilkins has written some of the best stuff on politics, law, and government in *Uneven Ground: Indian Sovereignty and Federal Law, American Indian Politics and the American Political System.* For a history of gaming, *Indian Gaming and Tribal Sovereignty: The Casino Compromise* by Steven Andrew Light and Kathryn R. L. Rand, and *Indian Gaming: Tribal Sovereignty and American Politics,* by W. Dale Mason, are useful. Treaty rights, especially relating to the treaty disputes in Wisconsin, are well documented in *The Walleye War: The Struggle for Ojibwe Spearfishing and Treaty Rights* and *Walleye Warriors,* by Larry Nesper. Melissa Meyer's *The White Earth Tragedy: Ethnicity and Dispossession at a Minnesota Anishinaabe Reservation* is a stunning account of the land grabs during the Allotment Era. And *The State of Native Nations: Conditions under U.S. Policies of Self-Determination,* published by the Harvard Project, contains a wealth of factual information about tribal government and economic conditions. *Education for Extinction: American Indians and the Boarding School Experience 1875–1928,* by David Wallace Adams, is a very good account of Indian boarding schools; and for firsthand accounts and boarding school testimony Brenda Child's *Boarding School Seasons* is a book not to miss.

ACKNOWLEDGMENTS

When you work for five years on something that involves a subject as vast as "reservation life" you are bound to have too many people to thank. But I would like to give special thanks to my family: Robert Treuer; Margaret Seelye Treuer; Eugene Seelye Sr.; Luella Seelye; Lanny and Davey Seelye; Sam Cleveland; Nate, Josh, and Jesse Seelye; and my siblings, Micah, Megan, and Anton. I am proud to call you all family. Also my wife, Gretchen Potter. All of you have been patient and understanding and nonjudgmental as I muddled my way through this. I want to thank Scott Lyons, whose perspective is always a considered one—would that you were chief. Sean Fahrlander, Brooke Ammann, Keller Paap, Shaye Perez, Steve Hagenah, Lisa LaRonge, David and Brian Bisonette, Charley Grolla, and Daniel Jones—you all showed a particular amount of trust. I hope I have earned it. I would also like to thank the very many people I interviewed or talked to, many of whom looked at me as though I had lost my mind when I said things like, "So what is reservation life like?" The answers, as all of you knew better than I, are both obvious and elusive. I hope I've answered them in this book. I relied on many people with different kinds of expertise beyond mine. This book brought me to my knees, but you all helped me up and I thank the Indian people across the country who took time out of their lives to talk to me. Naturally, all mistakes are my own. Problems of perspective are my own, too. For better or worse, this is my take on things, my take on our lives. I have no doubt that faced with the same task, all the people mentioned above and all the people I talked to would have come up with a different vision of reservation life. So it goes. I owe a debt of gratitude to the many writers, academics, historians, activists, and researchers whose work I admire and lean on. Keep it up.

I would also like to thank my agent, Joe Veltre, for believing in this thing; Matt Polly for his strategic advice and open ear and twenty years of friendship; and my editors at Grove; Morgan Entrekin, Brando Skyhorse, and most of all Jamison Stoltz—your vision and input and keen and tireless editorial suggestions saved this book from many a disaster and shaped what it is. I thank you.

NOTES

Introduction

9 William P. Dole, Commissioner of Indian Affairs, to Caleb B. Smith, Secretary of the Interior, November 10, 1862, Office of Indian Affairs Correspondence File, Northern Superintendency, National Archives.

Chapter 1

24 Interview with Charley Grolla, audiotape, May 2010.

24 Interview with Anishinaabe Legal Services attorney Megan Treuer, January 2010.

24 Grolla interview, August 2010; all subsequent direct quotes from Grolla are from this interview.

25 *Princeton Union Eagle,* July 6, 2006.

26 Terry Maddy, interviewed at the Country Kitchen in Bemidji, May 2007. No voice recording.

27 See http://minnesota.publicradio.org/display/web/2006/08/18/waterrights/.

27 Ibid.

28 See http://minnesota.publicradio.org/display/web/2006/10/26/district2b/.

29 Ibid., p. 267.

32 See http://www.oneida-nation.net/brhistory.html. Also in Joseph Glatthaar and James Kirby, *Forgotten Allies* (New York: Hill and Wang, 2007).

35 Peckham, *Indian Uprising,* 226; Anderson, *Crucible of War,* 542, 809n; Grenier, *First Way of War,* 144; Nester, *Haughty Conquerors,* 114–115.

37 C. A. Weslager, *The Delaware Indians: A History* (New Brunswick, NJ, Rutgers University Press:1990) pp. 304–305.

47 See http://www.dnr.state.mn.us/faq/mnfacts/fishing.html.

48 See http://www.kare11.com/news/news_article.aspx?storyid= 72386#readon.

52 See http://news.minnesota.publicradio.org/features/2004/08/09_ robertsont_redlkfish/.

52 See http://news.minnesota.publicradio.org/features/199804/ 15_gundersond_walleye-m/.

54 *Bemidji Pioneer,* August 15, 2006, p. 5.

56 *Bemidji Pioneer,* July 30, 2006; *Minneapolis Star Tribune,* July 30, 2006.

CHAPTER 2

61 All quotes from Sean & Mike Fahrlander recorded April–May 2008.

66 William Warren, *History of the Ojibwe People* (Minnesota Historical Society Press, 1984), pp. 155–156.

67 Ibid., p. 158

70 Treaty of 1837, http://digital.library.okstate.edu/kappler/vol2/treaties/ chi0491.htm.

71 Ibid.

78 *Minneapolis Star,* March 27, 1939, p. 2.

80 *Annual Report of the Secretary of the Interior for the Fiscal Year Ended June 30, 1938* (Washington, DC, 1938), pp. 209–211, http://historymatters. gmu.edu/d/5058.

83 Quoted from David Wilkins's excellent introduction to Felix Cohen, *On the Drafting of Tribal Constitutions* (University of Oklahoma Press, 2009), p. xxi.

84 Ibid.

86 Larry Nesper, *The Walleye War* (University of Nebraska Press, 2002), p. 93.

87 *Milwaukee Journal-Sentinal,* April 4, 1990.

87 Nesper, *The Walleye War*, p. 100.

87 See http://news.google.com/newspapers?nid=1683&dat=19950617&id
    =imsaAAAAIBAJ&sjid=Bi0EAAAAIBAJ&pg=2968,1358204.

94 See http://query.nytimes.com/gst/fullpage.html?res=9B0DE3D9123C
    F932A05750C0A961948260&sec=&spon=&pagewanted=1.

96 Quoted from: http://www.nebraskastudies.org/0700/frameset_reset.
    html?http://www.nebraskastudies.org/0700/stories/0701_0146.html.

96 See http://www.nps.gov/history/history/online_books/5views/5views1e.
    htm.

97 Ibid.

103 See http://www.seattlepi.com/movies/180683_nwbrando03.html.

105 See http://news.minnesota.publicradio.org/features/199903/03_
    engerl_ojibwe-m/?refid=0.

106 See http://community.seattletimes.nwsource.com/archive/?date=
    19980811&slug=2765909.

CHAPTER 3

113 All quotes from Margaret Treuer in this section are from February 2009.

121 Sharon O/Brien, *American Indian Tribal Governments* (University of
    Oklahoma Press, 1993), p. 112.

122 Ibid., p. 206.

122 *New York Times,* August 11, 1881.

124 Wilcomb E. Washburn, *Red Man's Land/White Man's Law: The Past and
    Present Status of the American Indian* (University of Oklahoma Press,
    1995), p. 180.

124 Graves and Abbott, eds., *Indians in Minnesota* (University of Minnesota
    Press, 2007), p. 16.

125 All quotes from Robert Treuer are from August 8, 2009.

128 See http://www.theatlantic.com/national/archive/2010/06/
    a-victory-for-native-americans/57769/.

136 See http://welsa.org/.

144 Information from National Tribal Justice Resource Center, http://www
    .tribal-institute.org/lists/tlpi.htm.

147 See http://www.tribal-institute.org/lists/jurisdiction.htm.

150 David Wilkins, *American Indian Sovereignty and the Supreme Court: The
    Masking of Justice* (University of Texas Press, 1997), pp. 190–191. See
    also, O'Brien, *American Indian Tribal Governments,* p. 208.

151 See http://www.npr.org/templates/story/story.php?storyId=12260610.

151 See http://www.indiancountrytoday.com/national/41568937.html.

152 Cass County Sheriff's Office Arrest Report IC #: 07-015876-CL, October 21, 2007.

152 Ibid.

154 Interview with Steve Hagenah, Bureau of Criminal Apprehension, summer 2007.

156 All quotes from Brian Bisonette are from May 21, 2010.

157 Melissa Myers, *The White Earth Tragedy* (Lincoln: University of Nebraska Press, 1999).

CHAPTER 4

166 Interview with Steve Hagenah, summer, 2007.

167 Interview with Margaret Treuer, November 11, 2009.

168 M. Inez Hilger, *Chippewa Families* (St. Paul: Minnesota Historical Society Press, 1998), p. 38.

169 Andres Duany, *Suburban Nation: The Rise of Sprawl and the Decline of the American Dream* (New York: North Point Press, 2000).

170 See http://seattletimes.nwsource.com/news/local/tribalhousing/partone/undermined.html.

172 Roz Diane Laskner and John Guidry, *Engaging the Community in Decision Making* (Jefferson, NC: , 2009), p. 22.

172 Ibid.

172 Ibid.

173 All quotes from Shalah Tibbetts were recorded in interviews conducted in May 2010.

177 Audio interview with Steve Hagenah recorded on September 17, 2008.

179 From "Tales of the Old Home Town," *Cass Lake Times,* October 19, 1972.

181 See http://www.startribune.com/local/11574686.html.

184 Quoted in *Bena: Celebrating the Centennial History* (Walker, MN: Cass County Historical Society, 2006).

185 See http://www.atg.wa.gov/prescriptiondrug.aspx.

185 Office of Applied Statistics, http://www.oas.samhsa.gov/2k10/182/AmericanIndian.cfm.

188 Stacey Lyon and Keenan Goodfellow, recorded at Cass Lake Boys and Girls club, October 29, 2008.

188 The U.S. Department of Health and Human Services provided these statistics. And for those good at math they offer the following explanation for totals coming to over 100 percent: "Percentages may total more than 100 because Hispanics may be counted by Hispanic ethnicity and race."

189 All of Weise's Internet postings can be found on links at jeffreyweise.com.

190 All quotes from Dustin Burnette were recorded in Cass Lake in May 2010.

194 Frances Densmore, *Chippewa Customs* (Saint Paul, MN: Minnesota Historical Society Press, 1979), p. 48.

194 Ibid.

195 Ibid., p. 59.

197 Warren, *History of the Ojibway People,* pp. 128–129.

198 George Copway, *Life, Letters, Speeches* (Lincoln: University of Nebraska Press, 2006), p. 137.

198 Ibid.

198 Bishop Henry Whipple, reported in Winchell, *The Aborigines of Minnesota* (Minnesota Historical Society, 1911), p. 655. Ashley C. Morrill to Clark W. Thompson, August 18, 1862, in *House Executive Documents,* Vol. 2, *1862–1863,* p. 217.

199 See http://darkwing.uoregon.edu/~adoption/topics/IAP.html.

200 B. J. Jones, *The Indian Child Welfare Act: The Need for a Separate Law* (Chicago, IL: American Bar Association, 1996).

204 See http://darkwing.uoregon.edu/~adoption/archive/ICWAexcerpt.htm.

206 Interviews at Boys & Girls Club in Cass Lake, 2008.

CHAPTER 5

216 *The State of Native Nations* (The Harvard Project on American Indian Economic Development, Oxford Press, USA, 2007), p. 130.

216 Ibid., p. 132.

218 Coachella Valley Water District 2005–2006 Annual Review and Water Quality Report.

218 Ambrose Lane, *Return of the Buffalo* (Westport, CT: Bergen and Garvey, 1995), p. 17.

220 Ibid., p. 20.

228 Interview with Helen (Bryan) Johnson and Bob Johnson conducted at Project 260 offices, Cass Lake, May 2010.

230 Kevin Washburn, "The Legacy of Bryan v. Itasca County: How a $147 County Tax Notice on a Mobile Home Set the Foundation for

$200 Billion in Indian Gaming Revenues," *Minnesota Law Review,* Vol. 92.

230 See http://www.tribal-institute.org/lists/pl_280.htm.

230 Ibid.

231 Washburn, "The Legacy of Bryan v. Itasca County," p. 936.

232 Ibid., p. 942.

234 Ibid., p. 944.

237 Ibid., p. 946.

247 *Minneapolis Star Tribune,* February 1, 2009.

CHAPTER 6

266 Interview with Keller Paap, August 2009, Scattergood Lake.

270 See http://www.nps.gov/archive/alcatraz/tours/hopi/hopi-h1.htm.

270 Ibid.

271 J. Fear-Segal, "Nineteenth-Century Indian Education: Universalism versus Evolutionism," *Journal of American Studies,* Vol. 33, No. 2 (1999), pp. 323–341.

272 Dan Jones interview with author, January 2001.

273 Daniel Jones, Royal Reporting Services, recorded September 24, 2009.

274 Dan Jones interview with author, January 2001.

278 Interview with Brooke Ammann in Milltown, Wisconsin, May 18, 2010.

284 Kevin Diaz, *Minneapolis Star Tribune,* November 10, 2009, http://www.startribune.com/politics/state/69722942.html.

287 See http://www.time.com/time/nation/article/0,8599,1635873,00.html.

292 All quotes from Ryan Haasch are from interviews conducted in May 2009.

297 Olympia Sosangelis, *"Something More Than an Indian": Carlos Montezuma and Wassaja, the Dual Identity of an Assimilationist and Indian Rights Activist,* dissertation (Boston, 2008), p. 49.

298 Interview with David Bisonette at Shue's Pond in Hayward, Wisconsin, May 20, 2010.